American
Independent Film

ROUGH GUIDES

Moline Public Library

MOLINE, ILLINOIS

www.roughguides.com

Credits

The Rough Guide to American Independent Film

Editors: Tracy Hopkins, Alex Ballinger
Layout: Jessica Subramanian
Picture research: Tracy Hopkins
Proofreading: Margaret Doyle, Orla Duane
Indexing: Philippa Hopkins
Production: Katherine Owers, Aimee Hampson

Rough Guides Reference

Series editor: Mark Ellingham
Editors: Peter Buckley, Duncan Clark,
Tracy Hopkins, Sean Mahoney,
Matthew Milton, Joe Staines, Ruth Tidball
Director: Andrew Lockett

Publishing Information

This first edition published September 2006 by
Rough Guides Ltd, 80 Strand, London WC2R 0RL
345 Hudson St, 4th Floor, New York 10014, USA
Email: mail@roughguides.com

Distributed by the Penguin Group:
Penguin Books Ltd, 80 Strand, London WC2R 0RL
Penguin Putnam, Inc., 375 Hudson Street, NY 10014, USA
Penguin Group (Australia), 250 Camberwell Road, Camberwell,
Victoria 3124, Australia
Penguin Books Canada Ltd, 190 Eglinton Avenue East, Toronto,
Ontario, M4P 2YE, Canada
Penguin Group (New Zealand), 67 Apollo Drive, Mairongi Bay,
Auckland 1310, New Zealand

Printed in Italy by LegoPrint S.p.A

Typeset in Bembo and Helvetica Neue to an original design by
Henry Iles

A catalogue record for this book is available from the British
Library

ISBN 13: 978-1-84353-602-4
ISBN 10: 1-84353-602-1

1 3 5 7 9 8 6 4 2

THE ROUGH GUIDE TO

American
Independent Film

by
Jessica Winter

Contents

The Icons:

Conduct Unbecoming:

Money Changes Everything:

The Information:

Introduction

In 1966, the renowned film critic Andrew Sarris wrote, "The Independent Cinema is in many respects a fiction of the journalist's imagination. What makes a film independent? And independent of what? Hollywood? Commercialism? Plot? Production values? Entertainment? In short, how much independence can we bear?"

Some forty years later, all of these questions remain pertinent to an exploration of American independent film, a category that is defined in the eye of the beholder. The dictionary tells us that independent means "free from external control and restraint", but such a designation is virtually impossible to achieve literally in a medium as collaborative and expensive as filmmaking. Does independence denote methods of financing and production? Does it mean that a single, essentially autonomous artist is responsible for the movie's content and style? Is the word a nebulous signifier of an independent vision that doesn't toe the conventional Hollywood line? Is it simply synonymous with the Sundance Film Festival?

The short answer is: any or all of the above. The classification of Amerindie film started getting murky around 1993, when the Disney Corporation purchased the quintessential independent studio of the era, Miramax. In 1994, the year of Quentin Tarantino's quasi-indie blockbuster *Pulp Fiction*, studio-financed films were deemed eligible for the Independent Spirit Awards, an allowance that struck many observers as a contradiction in terms. As conglomeration continued and corporate sponsorship dollars flooded the original indie film festival, Sundance, "independent" increasingly became a label for major studios' boutique divisions, giving rise to derisive nicknames such as "Indiewood" and "dependies".

"Indie" was a brand, an attitude, connoting edge or, when Oscar season came around, prestige. Hence the oxymoronic handle for Warner Independent Pictures, or the self-contradictory statement on the website of another Time Warner unit: "New Line Cinema is the oldest and most successful fully integrated independent film company in the world." By what feat can you be independent and fully integrated at the same time?

The "American" part of the equation is also problematic. International co-productions are the norm across the film world, non-American actors and directors have played key roles in many of the movies discussed in this book and some performers closely identified with Amerindie productions, such as Harvey Keitel and Vincent Gallo, have done some of their best acting abroad. Admittedly, the whole notion is a touch provincial: director Kevin Smith once claimed that he never bothered watching European arthouse cinema because he could get the filtered version through the films of Ohio-born Jim Jarmusch.

Arguably, the easiest means by which to define independence is financing. At the core of this book is the Canon of fifty great American independent films, a list that is weighted slightly towards movies made in the wake of the Sundance/Miramax ascendancy during the 1990s, but that also embraces many older film landmarks. (Of course, there are as many Canons as there are moviegoers.★) With a few significant exceptions, all of the films in the Canon were produced outside of the major studio system, often with scant resources. More than half are first features, which attests to the energy and originality that come a little easier to artists when they're young and hungry, but seems more concretely to be a reflection of financial exigencies, since first-time filmmakers have less access to conventional funding than their more established elders.

Many of the films examined in *The Rough Guide To American Independent Film* were shot very quickly; others were made in several discrete chunks over many months or even years, to allow producers to raise piecemeal funds or to let unpaid cast and crew members return to their day jobs. This was the case with John Cassavetes' *Shadows* (1959), George A. Romero's *Night Of The Living Dead* (1968), David Lynch's *Eraserhead* (1977) and Jim Jarmusch's *Stranger Than Paradise* (1984), to name just a few.

As director John Sayles puts it, "Your budget can become an aesthetic." To see what he means, just watch a lot of low-budget, first-time features in a row – you might notice a consistent reliance on a stationary camera and continuous, wide-angle establishing shots, an approach epitomized

in the low-key *Stranger Than Paradise*. Often, directors on the run simply don't have time for close-ups or more complicated set-ups.

But even if the acting or technical details are ragged, a low-budget film can achieve a sense of intimacy and organic integrity, precisely because it doesn't – or can't – atomize action and conversation through the familiar Hollywood grammar of close-ups and reverse shots. Instead the focus tends to be on performance, dialogue and characterization, on spontaneous and intimate human interaction – qualities native to Amerindie movies as disparate as Sayles' *Return Of The Secaucus 7* (1979), Steven Soderbergh's *sex, lies, and videotape* (1989), Richard Linklater's *Slacker* (1991) and Kimberly Peirce's *Boys Don't Cry* (1999). What's more, the tough economic realities faced by directors outside the movie establishment find an emotional parallel in the prevalent depictions of loners, misfits and margin-dwellers in their films.

All the same, through bold intent or happy accident, it was studio money that backed renegade works like Spike Lee's *Do The Right Thing* (1989) and Spike Jonze's *Being John Malkovich* (1999), and Paul Thomas Anderson, director of *Boogie Nights* (1997) and *Magnolia* (1999), is emblematic of the independent movement despite having never directed a feature outside of the studio system. In the end, what links all of these films is that somehow they were made against the odds.

Jessica Winter, 2006

★ Since the parameters for this book do not cover non-narrative experimental filmmaking, it is also defined by those important independent film artists left out of the discussion. There are too many omissions to list properly, but one could start with Stan Brakhage, Ken Jacobs, James Fotopoulos, Maya Deren, Yvonne Rainer, Jonas Mekas, Bruce Connor, James Benning, Craig Baldwin, Bill Morrison…

Acknowledgements

I am grateful for the warm generosity of Geoff Andrew and Nick Bradshaw, who were kind enough to loan sizable chunks of their video and DVD collections to me during my research, and whose advice and recommendations were a great help to me while mapping out this book. For their smart tips and wise counsel, thanks also to Michael Atkinson, Dave Calhoun, Tom Charity, Gareth Evans, Wally Hammond, Trevor Johnston, Dennis Lim, Mark Peranson, Chris Thomas, Ben Walters and my editors at Rough Guides, Andrew Lockett and Tracy Hopkins. Last but not least, thanks to Adrian Kinloch, for his support, enthusiasm and superheroic patience, not to mention his exegesis of Hal Hartley.

Declarations of Independence:

the American indie story

Ann Savage and Tom Neal in *Detour*, Edgar G.
Ulmer's bleak, no-budget *film noir*

Declarations of Independence:
the American indie story

Independent film is a term that contemporary cinephiles may associate with the relatively recent phenomena of the Sundance Film Festival and Miramax production company, but the concept has existed since the dawn of cinema.

1910–54: the beginnings

Many of the most powerful media conglomerates of the present day began long ago as humble indie outfits. From the silent era onwards, some of the greatest stars and dealmakers of the medium leveraged their success into professional autonomy, while others remained would-be gatecrashers, not by choice but by circumstance. At one extreme of wealth and status, there were the Hollywood luminaries Charles Chaplin, Douglas Fairbanks, Mary Pickford and D.W. Griffith, who together founded **United Artists** as an independent company in 1919 to produce and distribute their movies. At the other extreme, there was African-American film pioneer **Oscar Micheaux** – considered by many to be the first true American independent film-maker – who made and distributed his own films, often with virtually no infrastructure in place to support him. Brothers Roy and **Walt Disney** ran their little animation-focused studio out of the back of a real estate office in the early 1920s, and producing legends David O. Selznick and Samuel Goldwyn both thrived as independent dealmakers.

In 1935, **Republic Pictures** was formed by the merger of several "Poverty Row" studios,

Pilgrim's progress: Oscar Micheaux

One of eleven children born to former slaves in Illinois, **Oscar Micheaux** (1884–1951) proved to be a multiple trailblazer. He forged westward to set up a homestead in South Dakota before becoming the first African-American to make a feature-length film – in both the silent and talkie formats – and eventually completed more than forty films in just thirty years. We might also think of Micheaux as the first American independent filmmaker. He often raised funds door-to-door (just as he had sold his novels to his neighbours in South Dakota) and carried his film cans from theatre to theatre. As Richard Corliss writes, "In the 30-plus years of race cinema, there was only one black man with the drive and doggedness to write, produce, direct, finance and distribute his own films … In so many ways, Micheaux was the **D.W. Griffith** of race cinema. And also its **Edward D. Wood, Jr.**"

Micheaux's films are invaluable historical artefacts – the melodrama *Within Our Gates* (1919), the earliest surviving film by a black American, is a powerful riposte to D.W. Griffith's racist *Birth Of A Nation* (1915). They are also a tribute to an artist's perseverance against all odds, but were often tripped up by a combination of meagre resources, lack of technical know-how and Micheaux's decided indifference to the niceties of film grammar and realistic performance style. A chronic shortage of film stock necessarily meant too many of Micheaux's first takes had to be considered, in Ed Wood's own words, "Perfect!" The wear and tear of time and the scissorings of film censors and exhibitors have also battered his films, sometimes beyond narrative coherence (if they possessed it in the first place).

The archetypal Micheaux film is a roughshod melodrama with Chinese boxfuls of sub-plots. A typical entry is *The Girl From Chicago* (1932), a stilted, gaffe-stacked, yet undeniably intriguing remake of his own silent film *Spider's Web* (1926). Micheaux never had much success attracting the best black talent to his no-budget productions, but the silent 1925 picture *Body And Soul* features the film debut of the magnificent **Paul Robeson**. In dual roles as a womanizing preacher and his saintly brother, Robeson's charisma raises *Body And Soul* above much of Micheaux's other work.

The Girl From Chicago
dir Oscar Micheaux, 1932, 69m, b/w

This compelling but convoluted talkie version of *Spider's Web* stars Micheaux regular Carl Mahon as Alonso White, a Secret Service agent assigned to investigate a crime boss in Mississippi who sweeps a schoolteacher off her feet and carries her away to good-time Harlem. The teacher's landlady follows, plays the numbers, wins big, but gets framed for a murder actually committed by the crime boss's girlfriend, who also happens to be in town…

God's Step Children
dir Oscar Micheaux, 1938, 105m, b/w

The sheer socio-emotional sweep of this melodrama of passing achieves a cumulative poignancy, despite its blunders and convolutions. Lifting much from Fannie Hurst's novel *Imitation Of Life*, this is the story of light-skinned Naomi, who longs to pass in the white world that rejects her. Beyond the ropey staging and technical difficulties, one can glimpse a rich, strange, sad achievement.

so named for the low-budget, B-grade genre pictures cranked out by the independent companies clustered near the intersection of Sunset Boulevard and Gower Street in Los Angeles. (The corner was nicknamed "Gower Gulch" for the prevalence of Western productions in the area.) Another Poverty Row studio, **Monogram**, specialized in Westerns and action-adventure movies; they released the popular *Charlie Chan* series and nurtured John Wayne's early career. Meanwhile, the Producers Releasing Corporation (**PRC**),

under the guidance of production executive **Leon Fromkess**, backed several 1940s films by the outsider director **Edgar G. Ulmer**, including two of his best, *Bluebeard* (1944) and *Detour* (1945).

Fromkess was also a key associate of **Samuel Fuller**, who left a frustrating staff job at Warner Bros to write and direct his own films on the cheap for a new independent called **Lippert Productions**. Lippert backed the World War II combat veteran's typically tough-minded Korean

Salt Of The Earth: fruit of the blacklist

War drama, *The Steel Helmet*, in 1951, which earned $6 million at the box office on a mere $100,000 budget. Following *The Steel Helmet's* success, Fuller alternated between studio and independent ventures for much of the 1950s and early 1960s, and twice set up production companies of his own.

A quintessential maverick, Fuller came of age as a director at the very moment that Hollywood was feeling the sands shift beneath its feet. At the turn of the 1950s, the studios were still reeling from the landmark 1948 decision in *US vs. Paramount* prohibiting the vertically integrated system by which the studios controlled production, distribution and exhibition of their films. No longer did the "Big Five" (Paramount, Warner Bros, 20th Century Fox, RKO and Loews, parent company of MGM) and a few smaller studios have a stranglehold on the marketplace; they had to sell their theatre chains, and filmmaking talent went freelance.

The advent of television and, terribly, of McCarthyism further rattled Hollywood: the small screen lured many talents (not to mention viewers) away from the cinema, while anti-Communist hysteria swept over the industry and cast many a fine career to the wind. The tyranny of the McCarthy era did, however, lead to a most extraordinary one-off, 1954's *Salt Of The Earth*. A polemical drama about a real-life strike by Mexican-American mine workers, *Salt Of The Earth* was written, produced and directed by victims of the Hollywood blacklist who had founded their own production company.

As Hollywood struggled to find its bearings, new approaches to film narrative and technique were stirring far from the studio epicentre. In New York, in particular, young filmmakers embraced low budgets, location shooting and loose-limbed, improvisatory methods. Co-directors Ray Ashley, Morris Engel and Ruth Orkin made the verité-style *Little Fugitive* (1953), which employed handheld cameras and jagged, elliptical editing in its slender tale of a 7-year-old "outlaw" hiding out at Coney Island.

Detour
dir Edgar G. Ulmer, 1945, 68m, b/w

All that hapless nightclub pianist Al (Tom Neal) wants is to get across America to be with his sweetheart in Hollywood. But after he accidentally causes a man's death, he gets entangled with witchy Vera (the fearsome, flinty-voiced Ann Savage), who knows his secret and uses it to blackmail him. Grimy and concise, shot in six days under circumstances as threadbare as those of its hard-bitten characters, this cornerstone of American *noir* is as existentially bleak as Albert Camus's *The Stranger*.

Little Fugitive
dir Ray Ashley, Morris Engel, Ruth Orkin, 1953, 80m, b/w

Under the impression that he's accidentally killed his older brother, 7-year-old Joey (Richie Andrusco) flees for the child's paradise of Coney Island, where he gorges on junk food and finds exhilaration on the carnival rides. Shot and edited with a jaunty free spirit, the movie is a key link between Italian neo-realism and the French New Wave (*Nouvelle Vague*), and it remains a fascinating moving-image archive of early-1950s Brooklyn.

Salt Of The Earth
dir Herbert J. Biberman, 1954, 94m, b/w

In the midst of the McCarthy era, a group of blacklisted film professionals and Mexican-American miners banded together to make this docudrama about a strike at a zinc mine in New Mexico. Largely financed by a miners' union, this legend of leftist filmmaking was denounced in Congress and condemned as a Communist plot in the pages of the *Hollywood Reporter*. Leading lady Rosaura Revueltas was deported to Mexico and never worked in the US again.

Edgar G. Ulmer: the mayor of Poverty Row

Some directors work on a shoestring; the prodigiously talented and resourceful **Edgar G. Ulmer** (1904–72) often had to settle for the lint from the shoestring. Some of Ulmer's films were shot in less than a week for next to nothing (it took four days and $8,000 to produce 1939's *Moon Over Harlem*). Yet rather miraculously, he usually succeeded in putting a personal signature on movies made under extremely cramped conditions, in a startling variety of languages (Ukrainian, Yiddish, Italian) and genres (science fiction, melodrama, historical epic).

Born in what's now the Czech Republic and raised in Vienna, Ulmer was a key player in interwar German cinema, serving as production designer on **F. W. Murnau**'s *The Last Laugh* (1924) and as set designer on Murnau's *Sunrise* (1927) and **Fritz Lang**'s *Metropolis* (1927) and *M* (1931). With his fellow future Hollywood emigrés Robert Siodmak, Billy Wilder and Fred Zinnemann, Ulmer co-directed the buoyant ensemble *People On Sunday* (1930), a portrait of a day by the lake in Berlin.

In America, Ulmer directed the best of Universal's 1930s horror films, *The Black Cat* (1934), a Gothic frightener pairing **Bela Lugosi** and **Boris Karloff**. Shortly thereafter, he was blackballed because of his affair with (and subsequent marriage to) Shirley Kassler, then wed to the nephew of a Universal executive. However, Ulmer never stopped working. After a move to New York, he directed a timeless suite of Yiddish films, including the Lithuanian pastoral *Green Fields* (1937) and the bittersweet *The Light Ahead* (1939), about a star-crossed young *shtetl* couple.

Back on the fringes of Hollywood, Ulmer's work ranged from *Bluebeard* (1944), with **John Carradine** as a nineteenth-century Parisian painter who kills his models, to the *noir*-ish melodrama *The Strange Woman* (1946), made for United Artists, with **Hedy Lamarr** as an unusually complicated and sympathetic femme fatale. (All Day Entertainment's box set *Edgar G. Ulmer: The King Of The Bs* includes 1939's *Moon Over Harlem*, an important artefact of early African-American cinema, as well as *Bluebeard* and *The Strange Woman*.)

Ulmer's most revered work remains the benchmark *noir* film *Detour* (1945). Shot in six days, *Detour* is a no-budget, no-exit four-hander with a world-class case of the cold sweats. "Money – you know what that is, it's the stuff you never have enough of," laments the anti-hero in the hard-boiled voiceover, as if commenting on the film's financial outlay; but like so much of Ulmer's work, *Detour* makes a virtue of necessity.

Smoke signals: Ulmer's existential *Detour*

The 1950s and 60s: do it yourself

The off-the-cuff spontaneity of 1953's *Little Fugitive* – the enlivening sense that its scenes weren't staged so much as happened upon – made a definitive impression on the future filmmakers of the French New Wave (*Nouvelle Vague*). The film also became a hallmark of a New York-based school of independent film-

making that emerged around this time and which *Village Voice* critic **Jonas Mekas**, a film-maker in his own right, dubbed the "New American Cinema". Writer-director **Lionel Rogosin** moulded *On The Bowery* (1956), set among the tramps and addicts of downtown Manhattan, out of a series of improvisations performed by real Bowery denizens, and **John Cassavetes'** *Shadows* (1959), shot in and around Times Square, evolved in a similar manner from Cassavetes' acting workshops.

Coney Island baby: *Little Fugitive* Richie Andrusco

Shadows overturned just about every reigning assumption about how a film should be made. Instead of seeking studio financing, Cassavetes raised much of the tiny $40,000 budget himself, appearing on the radio show *Jean Shepherd's Night People* to urge listeners to send two dollars for an "advance ticket". (According to Ray Carney's indispensable British Film Institute monograph on *Shadows*, contributions topped $2,500 within a week.) The cast was composed of mostly untried young students, and the apartment Cassavetes shared with his wife and future star, **Gena Rowlands**, did triple duty as a home, production office and set. Averse to restrictive blocking and lighting techniques that required an actor to "hit his mark", Cassavetes flooded the set with light (resulting in an image that often appears blown-out) and fitted his performers with battery-operated microphones, leaving them free to move around more spontaneously. New, highly portable cameras also enhanced the flexibility of the guerrilla production – Cassavetes didn't have permits to shoot his iconic New York street scenes, so the cast and small crew often had to be one step ahead of the police.

Cassavetes didn't invent do-it-yourself filmmaking, but for a generation of filmmakers, he transformed a crazy idea into a tantalizing and inspirational possibility: that you could beg or borrow some money, get your friends together and make a movie on your own. You could retain total artistic control over your work, even if the insane pressures of a meagrely budgeted independent production sometimes produced uncontrollable situations.

Alfred Leslie and **Robert Frank**'s half-hour bohemian dinner party *Pull My Daisy* (1959) also exudes an on-the-spot energy, and it's a veritable Beat Generation portrait to boot – **Jack Kerouac** wrote the script, and cast members include Allen Ginsberg and Gregory Corso. (*Pull My Daisy* was screened on a double bill with *Shadows* at Greenwich Village's Cinema 16, the influential film club organized by **Amos Vogel**, who later founded the New York Film Festival.) **Shirley Clarke**'s films *The Connection* (1962) and *The Cool World* (1963), the latter shot entirely on location in Harlem, seemed to efface the boundary between fiction and documentary. By 1962, Jonas Mekas was running the **Film-Makers' Cooperative**, a screening salon and distribution centre for avant-garde filmmakers, out of his Manhattan loft. Anthology Film Archives, another Mekas brainchild, opened to the New York public in 1970.

As the New American Cinema blossomed, Hollywood was becoming increasingly fixated on attracting the purchase power of the teenage demographic. Often, however, the indie companies beat the studios at their own game, reaching the high-school set through inexpensive genre flicks made primarily for the drive-in circuit. Monster movies such as *Beginning Of The End* (1957) and *The Blob* (1958) earned exponential returns on their small budgets. Director **Roger Corman**, "King of the Bs", pumped out scares and titillation at record speeds for drive-in specialists **American-International Pictures** (AIP) (founded in 1954), which catered to the rock'n'roll generation with amusing sci-fi schlock and soapy youth-gone-wild dramas. Corman famously shot the horror comedy *Little Shop Of Horrors* (1960), featuring a young **Jack Nicholson**, in just two days. As the 1960s dawned, indie frighteners were reaching a high-water mark. The timelessly creepy *Carnival Of Souls* (1962) was essentially an out-of-hours project by the employees of an educational and industrial-movie firm, while **Herschell Gordon Lewis** became known as the "godfather of gore" for grisly drive-in shockers such as *Blood Feast* (1963) and *Two Thousand Maniacs!* (1964).

Standards of "decency" in independent fare loosened rapidly during the 1960s, reflecting convulsions in the culture at large. **George A. Romero**'s *Night Of The Living Dead* (1968) stunned audiences with its visceral horrors, though shock value wasn't measured solely by the volumes of blood and guts spilling from drive-in screens. Samuel Fuller alienated critics with his scalding allegories of American social chaos and hypocrisy, *Shock Corridor* (1963) and *The Naked Kiss* (1964). **Russ Meyer**, who learned his trade as a cameraman with the US Army Signal Corps in World War II alongside fellow future director Morris Engel, concocted gleeful extravaganzas of big boobs, fast cars, brassy quips and grim violence. **Andy Warhol**'s blasé real-time documents of sex and drug use caused a sensation and, in the cases of *Lonesome Cowboys* (1967) and *Blue Movie* (aka *Fuck*, 1968), ran into trouble for breaching obscenity laws.

Exciting movements in documentary filmmaking were also a legacy of the 1960s. Filmmakers such as **D.A. Pennebaker**, Frederick Wiseman and the Maysles brothers, with the help of new, relatively lightweight camera and sound equipment, developed the "direct cinema" or *cinéma vérité* style of fly-on-the-wall non-fiction filmmaking. Direct cinema avoided explanatory voiceover as much as possible; the documentary filmmaker became a silent, invisible observer to scenes that unfold organically before the camera.

John Cassavetes: indie godfather

There's an old line about the Velvet Underground that says only 1,000 people bought their debut album when it first came out, but every one of them started a band. The legacy of filmmaker **John Cassavetes** (1929–89) might be considered in similar terms. The global reach of his influence, the sheer range of filmmakers and film movements that show traces of his forms and methods, is significantly disproportionate to the degree of commercial and critical success he enjoyed in his lifetime. Just consider that the foundation stone of the American independent movement, 1959's *Shadows*, couldn't find an American distributor (**British Lion** released the film in the States).

A family portrait and an interracial love story, *Shadows* could today be considered Cassavetes' "calling-card", since it led to two studio projects: *Too Late Blues* (1961), with Bobby Darin as a jazz musician, and *A Child Is Waiting* (1963), with Judy Garland and Burt Lancaster as teachers of mentally disabled children.

On The Bowery
dir Lionel Rogosin, 1956, 65m, b/w

Loosely structured around a new arrival to Manhattan who loses his suitcase and his bearings, this portrait of a boozy life on skid row is, while not strictly non-fictional, an ethnographic film. Rogosin melds documentary with scripted scenes that cling closely to the realities of day-to-day life on the Bowery. His innovative methods were widely influential, and a notable inspiration to John Cassavetes.

Carnival Of Souls
dir Herk Hervey, 1962, 83m, b/w

The sole survivor (Candace Hilligoss) of a disastrous drag race arrives in a new town, where she's followed by a bizarre, zombie-like figure and oddly ignored by everyone else. Industrial filmmaker Hervey claimed Bergman and Cocteau as his inspirations for this rough-hewn horror landmark (shot on a shoestring in Kansas),

which has proved to be hugely influential in its own right – providing a 37-year-old template for the blockbuster *The Sixth Sense*.

The 1970s: New Hollywood and beyond

Increasingly, the young directors recruited to infuse new blood into the ageing studio system were able to sneak daring material under the radar. Leftist cinematographer **Haskell Wexler**'s *Medium Cool* (1969), which brandished startling footage of police brutality against protesters at the 1968 Democratic Convention, originally earned

Cassavetes and Hollywood found the relationship mutually unsatisfactory (producer **Stanley Kramer** re-edited *A Child Is Waiting* without the director's consent) and Cassavetes took on well-paid acting jobs in films such as *The Killers* (1964) and *The Dirty Dozen* (1967) to fund his own projects. He put much of his earnings from *Rosemary's Baby* (1968) towards post-production costs on *Faces* (1968), an unflinching chronicle of marital meltdown. The fearless cast included Cassavetes' wife and frequent leading lady, **Gena Rowlands**, and the inimitable **Seymour Cassel**, who co-starred with Rowlands in the madcap *Minnie And Moskowitz* (1971).

Cassavetes found his groove with *Faces*, which typifies the director's explosive, actor-driven portraits of personal and domestic crisis. The film also set a pattern whereby he and Rowlands would take acting jobs, borrow money from friends (**Peter Falk**, another member of his informal repertory company, put up half the money for 1974's *A Woman Under The Influence*) or even remortgage their house to fund the next movie. Cassavetes had to self-distribute *A Woman Under The Influence*, starring

Rowlands as a loving but disturbed wife and mother, which went on to earn $16 million and Oscar nominations for Rowlands and Cassavetes, but his other efforts didn't fare as well. Reviewing the studio-backed *Gloria* in 1980, **Roger Ebert** went so far as to say that the fascinating genre riff *The Killing Of A Chinese Bookie* (1976) had "become an unseen, lost film", and at the time he might have said the same thing about the barely released *Opening Night* (1977), which starred Rowlands as an ageing, unravelling stage actress.

The raw spontaneity and emotional volatility of his best work, the dialogue that so convincingly reproduces the erratic rhythms and jagged imperfections of real speech, the willingness to let a scene thrash itself out long after most directors would have moved on – none of these qualities recommended the filmmaker as a commercial prospect. Long before the advent of digital video and iMovie software, Cassavetes proved that, by sheer ingenuity and force of will, anyone could make a movie. In re-imagining the possibilities of film performance, narrative, pacing and *mise en scéne*, he made it new.

an X rating for a frank bedroom scene, though Wexler and company suspected the branding was politically motivated. Discussing his irreverent satire *M*A*S*H* (1970), set during the Korean War but intended as a statement on American involvement in Vietnam, **Robert Altman** joked that Fox didn't release the film so much as it "escaped". One might say much the same of Altman's subsequent, stubbornly independent-minded films, including *McCabe & Mrs. Miller* (1971), *The Long Goodbye* (1973) and *Nashville* (1975), in which he developed his singular roving camera style and trademark overlapping dialogue – and all with studio funds.

The decisive cultural event that heralded the "New Hollywood" era, *Easy Rider* appeared the same year as *Medium Cool*, and also ended with a fatal road accident that stood for all the crushed and mangled promise of the 1960s. The film's co-writer and co-star, **Peter Fonda**, had previously starred in two of Roger Corman's movies for AIP, the violent Hell's Angels flick *The Wild Angels* (1966) and the druggy fantasy *The Trip* (1967) (which was written by *Easy Rider* co-star and Corman regular Jack Nicholson). **Bert Schneider**, who had made his name and money producing *The Monkees* television show, took a leap of faith in backing

Son of *Easy Rider*: Warren Oates in *Two-Lane Blacktop*

Easy Rider, a film about a pair of biker drop-outs (played by Fonda and director **Dennis Hopper**) who score a massive cocaine deal and then set out cross-country towards an oasis of retirement in Florida. Amazingly, the movie made nearly $20 million on roughly a $500,000 budget.

Schneider's **BBS Productions** became one of the key players in the New Hollywood movement, producing **Bob Rafelson**'s *Five Easy Pieces* (1970) and *The King Of Marvin Gardens* (1972), Jack Nicholson's *Drive, He Said* (1971) and **Peter Bogdanovich**'s *The Last Picture Show* (1971). Schneider also produced **Peter Davis**'s documentary on the Vietnam War, *Hearts And Minds* (1974), a powerful example of unapologetic leftist filmmaking that can be placed alongside Barbara Kopple's *Harlan County, USA* (1976).

The cost-efficient success of *Easy Rider*, meanwhile, sent the major studios clamouring for the next low-budget hit by a hot young director, though mostly in vain. Set up in 1969, **Universal**'s youth unit released, in 1971 alone, Hopper's disastrous *The Last Movie*, Fonda's underrated *The Hired Hand* and the stripped-to-the-bone road trip *Two-Lane Blacktop*. Each made for less than $1 million, none came close to replicating the impact of *Easy Rider*, though *Blacktop*, directed by *Wild Angels*' editor **Monte Hellman**, became a cult classic.

Hellman and the *Easy Rider* staff weren't the only New Hollywood talents to get their start with Corman. Peter Bogdanovich worked on the script for *The Wild Angels* and served as Corman's assistant director. **Francis Ford Coppola** met Corman at UCLA film school, worked variously as his assistant, sound man and associate producer, and directed his Corman-produced first feature, the murder mystery *Dementia 13* (1963),

on a set in Ireland that Corman was using for another film. Coppola founded the short-lived first incarnation of his own production company, **American Zoetrope**, in 1969, and put up $20,000 of his own money to fund his breakthrough, *The Rain People*, that same year. He then went on to make *The Godfather* films and *The Conversation* (1974) for Paramount during the halcyon reign of **Robert Evans**.

Yet another Corman apprentice, **Martin Scorsese**, won entry into the Directors Guild via the AIP production *Boxcar Bertha* (1972), but he faced the disapproval of John Cassavetes. "You just spent a year of your life making a piece of shit," he told Scorsese, who had worked for the elder filmmaker as a sound editor on the screwball comedy *Minnie And Moskowitz* (1971), which had emerged more or less out of Universal's youth-oriented division. The verdict was especially significant given that Cassavetes was an enthusiastic fan of Scorsese's rough-hewn but powerful first feature, *Who's That Knocking At My Door?* (1969). Taking his friend and mentor's assessment to heart, Scorsese proceeded to make the seminal, independently financed *Mean Streets* (1973), his breakthrough film. Cassavetes, however, had trouble getting a foothold even in the "New" Hollywood, and continued to take on well-paid acting roles to subsidize his directorial work.

Although he was the perennial underdog, Cassavetes possessed, like Corman, a great eye for young talent, including Scorsese and **Steven Spielberg**, who worked as a production assistant on Cassavetes' *Faces* (1968). Another member of the "movie brat" generation of the 1970s, **Brian De Palma**, went so far as to make an Oedipal spectacle out of the indie godfather by making Cassavetes literally explode at the end of his 1978 film, *The Fury*.

De Palma found his feet in the late 1960s and early 1970s with a string of independently financed movies, and he introduced a young actor named **Robert De Niro** to a small audience in oddball, experimental comedies such as *Greetings* (1968), *The Wedding Party* (1969), and *Hi, Mom!* (1970). (All three films subsisted on very low budgets; most of the five-figure cost of *Greetings*, for example, came courtesy of the producer's friends and family.) Owning a virtual trademark on split screens, meta-movie tricks and postmodern femmes fatales, De Palma is foremost an **Alfred Hitchcock** acolyte. For his boldly derivative breakthrough film, 1973's *Sisters*, De Palma even recruited the great composer **Bernard Herrmann** to self-plagiarize the soundtracks he composed for the Master of Suspense.

For *Sisters*, De Palma was lucky to hook up with **Edward R. Pressman** – a producer extraordinaire in the making – who that same year produced **Terrence Malick**'s incandescent debut, *Badlands*, a fictionalized recounting of a 1950s murder spree in the heartland of America. In a prodigious career that alternated between mainstream fare and challenging indie work, Pressman went on to produce De Palma's *Phantom Of The Paradise* (1974), Charles Burnett's *To Sleep With Anger* (1990) and Abel Ferrara's *Bad Lieutenant* (1992). Heir to a toy-company fortune, Pressman also backed several films by his childhood friend **James Toback**, whose debut feature, 1978's *Fingers*, starred *Mean Streets* lead **Harvey Keitel** as a conflicted young man leading a bizarrely bipolar existence as both a classical-piano prodigy and heavy for his loan-shark father.

Though cinephiles regard the American cinema of the 1970s with awe and reverence – as a prelapsarian moment before the coming of the blockbuster age – there are more than a few films and filmmakers of the era that have not received their due. A striking descendant of the New York school of filmmaking, **Robert Kramer**'s *Ice* (1969) adapted a *verité* style to imagine a dystopic future in which a guerrilla group mobilizes against a fascist American regime. **John Avildsen**'s *Joe* (1970) detailed the unlikely friendship between a blue-collar guy and a white-collar adman, the latter racked with guilt over the accidental killing of his daughter's boyfriend. The movie is a coarse but effective measure of the Vietnam-era generation gap, boasting **Susan Sarandon** in her first film role and a magnificent turn by **Peter Boyle** as the title character.

In 1974 *Claudine* marked director **John Berry**'s return to the American film fold after many years of blacklist-enforced exile; starring Diahann Carroll as a mother bringing up six children in Harlem, the movie mixed comedy, drama and romance to endearing effect. Carroll won an Oscar nomination for *Claudine* during an exciting decade for fledgling black film talent in both the indie and studio sectors. **Melvin Van Peebles**' *Sweet Sweetback's Baadasssss Song* (1971) was the first in a string of blaxploitation flicks that catered to an underrepresented African-American audience. Liberally dosed with sex, drugs, crime, violence and killer soundtracks, the sensational blaxploitation genre overshadowed the lower-key black films that emerged a little later, such as **Charles Burnett**'s quietly observed *Killer Of Sheep* (1977).

The Rain People
dir Francis Ford Coppola, 1969, 101m

The female flip side of *Easy Rider*, Coppola's road movie trails an unhappily married pregnant woman (Shirley Knight) who embarks on an impulsive cross-country trip and encounters a brain-damaged hitchhiker (James Caan) and a troubled cop (Robert Duvall) along the way. A promising breakthrough for the young auteur, the movie boasts beautiful cinematography and a trio of superb performances from Knight and future *Godfather* stars Caan and Duvall.

Hi, Mom!
dir Brian De Palma, 1970, 87m

De Palma's career-long examination of voyeurism gets a workout in this early curio. A Vietnam vet (Robert De Niro) tries to invent a new genre of surveillance pornography by setting up a camera in his apartment to film his neighbours'

sex lives. When that endeavour fails, he turns to another form of performance art – occasioning the movie's anarchic *coup de grâce*, an extended "interactive theatre" piece in which Black Power pranksters terrorize their hilariously complicit white liberal patrons.

Two-Lane Blacktop
dir Monte Hellman, 1971, 102m

Following in the wake of *Easy Rider*, Hellman's road movie was a flop on its release but has since earned a devoted following. The primal minimalism of its approach is indicated in the characters' elementary names: the Driver (folk-rock star James Taylor) and the Mechanic (Dennis Wilson of the

Beyond blaxploitation: the LA School

Many filmgoers associate black independent filmmaking primarily with the flashy blaxploitation movies of the 1970s – the sibilant string of *Shaft*, *Superfly*, *Sweet Sweetback* and other flicks that celebrated black rebellion, sexual prowess and criminal acumen. But these movies weren't the only cinematic voice of black Americans, just the loudest. "A lot of us were angry at those films because they became the only representation of our experience in the movies," writer-director **Charles Burnett** told *Senses Of Cinema*. "We needed the spectrum, the full range of the black experience."

This wider picture could be gleaned in an informal movement of young black filmmakers – sometimes known as the "LA School" – who trained at UCLA in the late 1970s and early 1980s and included Burnett, **Julie Dash**, **Billy Woodberry** and the Ethiopian-born **Haile Gerima**. Reviewers compared Burnett's black-and-white 16mm debut, *Killer Of Sheep* (1977), with films by John Cassavetes and the second-wave Italian neo-realist Ermanno Olmi. The film detailed the grim day-to-day drudgery and petty cruelty of its disenfranchised South Central LA milieu, while also letting in narrow shafts of radiant humour and gentleness.

Drawing directly upon **Roberto Rossellini**'s war film *Paisan* (1946) for inspiration, Burnett sought the tone

and rhythm of a documentary for *Killer Of Sheep*, as did Gerima for the rough-and-ready *Bush Mama* (1979), also set in the Watts area of LA, which plumbed everyday life and explosive violence in the ghetto. Julie Dash, the youngest member of the group, forged her own course for the unclassifiable *Daughters Of The Dust* (1991), a mysterious, exposition-free tale of black women living on an island off the southeastern coast of America.

Burnett wrote the screenplay and was the cinematographer for Woodberry's *Bless Their Little Hearts* (1984), about a man struggling to find and keep work in the ghetto. The movie revisited the grim terrain of *Killer Of Sheep*, but without the earlier film's moments of hope and optimism, perhaps in anticipation of the drug epidemic and gang violence about to convulse South Central. Burnett later filmed the critically acclaimed *To Sleep With Anger* (1991), winner of four Independent Spirit Awards and his second film to be selected to the National Film Registry of works recognized as "culturally, historically or aesthetically significant and worthy of preservation". The first was *Killer Of Sheep*, which is still widely considered Burnett's best film. Despite the official accolades, however, the movie remains unavailable on video or DVD and is rarely screened – a sad fate for a milestone.

Beach Boys), accompanied by the Girl (Laurie Bird), accept a challenge to a cross-country race from a middle-aged Pontiac GTO owner of ill repute, GTO (Warren Oates).

Harlan County, USA
dir Barbara Kopple, 1976, 103m

In recording a bitter, frequently violent 1973 coal miners' strike in Kentucky, Kopple's Oscar-winning documentary achieves a visceral immediacy and, at the same time, provides a cogent historical context for the battle between a corporate Goliath and the David of organized labour.

The Killing Of A Chinese Bookie
dir John Cassavetes, 1976, 135m

When nightclub owner Cosmo Vitelli (Cassavetes mainstay Ben Gazzara) lets his gambling arrears get out of control, his loansharks force him to repay his debt by carrying out the titular crime. While unmistakeably a Cassavetes affair, this film represents the director's most overt engagement with genre, as he internalizes the nocturnal fatalism and underworld grime of classic *film noir*.

Opening Night
dir John Cassavetes, 1977, 144m

In one of her greatest performances, Gena Rowlands plays Myrtle, an addled, alcoholic actress who resents being cast as a menopausal woman in her latest role. After the death of a young female fan seeking her autograph, she starts to unravel completely: she sees the girl's ghost, hits the bottle harder than ever and goes wildly off-script both onstage and backstage. Hilarious, scary and courageously over-the-top, this movie demands to know: what is acting, what is "real life" and when, if ever, can the two be separated?

Into the 1980s: good business on a small scale

As the 1970s waned, a domino row of blazing young talent, most of whom had begun as scrappy indie tyros, crashed and burned with over-budget,

underwhelming flops. The bloom was coming off the rose of New Hollywood, and it wilted altogether when erstwhile hotshot **Michael Cimino** delivered *Heaven's Gate* in 1981. The turgid epic became one of the biggest box-office disasters of all time and contributed to the bankruptcy of its studio, United Artists.

But even as New Hollywood lurched beneath the burdens of megalomania and mountains of cocaine (a downfall detailed in Peter Biskind's compulsively readable history of the era, *Easy Riders, Raging Bulls*, 1999), a new indie renaissance was already taking shape. The **Utah/US Film Festival**, later to take the name of Robert Redford's Sundance Institute, began in 1978, and brothers Bob and Harvey Weinstein founded **Miramax Films** the following year. Also in 1979, producer **Sandra Schulberg** founded the **Independent Feature Project** (IFP), a non-profit organization devoted to aiding, developing and promoting indie film talent.

As usual, New York City remained the epicentre of the darkest and weirdest strains of no-budget filmmaking. For the invaluable artefact *The Blank Generation* (1976), **Amos Poe** recorded the vanguard of NYC punk and New Wave bands playing live at the legendary downtown performance venue CBGB. (In 1981, **Penelope Spheeris** provided the West Coast flip side to *Blank Generation* with her punk documentary *The Decline Of Western Civilization*.) For *Subway Riders* (1981), Poe cast John Lurie, a downtown musician and future star of **Jim Jarmusch**'s early films, as a saxophone-playing serial killer. (Lurie disappeared partway through filming and Poe himself replaced the actor.)

Bronx-born director **Abel Ferrara**, having shot the porn flick *Nine Lives Of A Wet Pussy* (1976) under an assumed name, made his debut proper with *The Driller Killer* (1979), about a starving-artist Gothamite whose seething frustration explodes in a fury of power-drill murders. In the intriguing *Liquid Sky* (1982), a low-budget one-off by Russian émigré **Slava Tsukerman**, aliens arrive in New York to feed off its downtown heroin addicts.

The Chelsea neighbourhood of Manhattan was the home of the Elgin Theater, where **Ben Barenholtz** originated the notion of the strange and seedy "midnight movie". The epitome of the midnight movie, the scandalous cult classic *Pink Flamingos* (1972) was directed by giddy trash provocateur **John Waters**, who'd been making bargain-basement scatological comedies in his hometown of Baltimore since the 1960s. *Pink Flamingos* proved to be the first breakout success for **New Line Pictures**, which **Bob Shaye** founded in 1968 from his fifth-floor walk-up apartment in Manhattan.

In 1975, Barenholtz started **Libra Films**, which released two independent landmarks: *Eraserhead* (1977) and *Return Of The Secaucus 7* (1979). Five years in the making, *Eraserhead* was an unnerving experiment in domestic horror by Philadelphia-based director **David Lynch**. For his debut feature, *Secaucus 7*, director **John Sayles** took a page from the Cassavetes handbook and self-financed his semi-autobiographical tale of leftist college friends reuniting for an eventful weekend. Another Barenholtz entity, Circle Films,

distributed the Texas neo-*noir Blood Simple* (1984), the first film by **Joel and Ethan Coen**, and Barenholtz subsequently served as a producer on several movies by the Minnesota brothers.

Joel Coen was among an all-star group of young filmmakers, including **Susan Seidelman**,

Blood Simple's M. Emmet Walsh phones it in

Spike Lee and Jim Jarmusch, who attended New York University's film program in the early 1980s. For her $100,000 debut, *Smithereens* (1982), Seidelman recruited her cast and crew from among her friends and classmates at NYU, and the film won the distinction of being the first American independent film to compete for the Palme d'Or at the **Cannes Film Festival**. Lee, who counted Martin Scorsese as one of his instructors at NYU, became a local celebrity following the release of his frank and raunchy sex comedy *She's Gotta Have It* (1986). The film was mounted on a budget cobbled together from arts-council grants, handouts from friends and $10,000 in completion funds from producers' representative **Jon Pierson**, who later became a key associate of directors Michael Moore (*Roger & Me*), Kevin Smith (*Clerks*) and Rose Troche (*Go Fish*). Jarmusch's *Stranger Than Paradise* (1984) stands as what Pierson calls an "I-can-do-that" film: the spartan production values, stationary camera setups and taciturn dialogue suited Jarmusch's tale of anomie and dislocation on a bleak stretch of the Lower East Side, and rendered filmmaking a practical possibility for intimidated would-be directors.

More than ever, indie directors in the 1980s had to prove themselves masters of stretching a dollar to untold limits. **Lizzie Borden** toiled for five years with a mere $40,000 to complete *Born In Flames* (1983), a black-and-white science-fiction parable of a fiercely Marxist and feminist persuasion. **Wayne Wang**, who was based in San Francisco, produced, directed, edited and co-wrote his debut feature, *Chan Is Missing* (1982), for a preposterous initial budget of $22,000, gathered through grants from the American Film Institute (also a source of support for *Eraserhead*) and the National Endowment for the Arts (NEA).

Though some of these productions were labours of love, many of them reaped real material benefits, making exponential returns on their tiny outlays. *Stranger Than Paradise* earned $2.5 million, its release overseen by the Samuel Goldwyn Company's **Jeff Lipsky**, who got his start helping John Cassavetes to distribute *A Woman Under the Influence* and later founded the late, great October Films with **Bingham Ray**, the future United Artists honcho. Circle Films' *Blood Simple* pulled in $2.1 million, and *She's Gotta Have It*, distributed by the indie outfit Island, earned a dazzling $7 million-plus.

Another new production and distribution company, **Cinecom**, was launched in 1982 and went on to release economical money-makers such as **Jonathan Demme**'s Talking Heads concert picture *Stop Making Sense* (1984) and John Sayles' *The Brother from Another Planet* (1984), which grossed $3.7 million on a $400,000 budget. Cinecom also distributed some of the finest British imports of the era, especially in the fantastic year of 1986: Alex Cox's *Sid And Nancy*, Stephen Frears' *My Beautiful Laundrette,* Neil Jordan's *Mona Lisa* and the Merchant Ivory art-house blockbuster *A Room With A View*, which raked in some $23 million.

During the 1980s, creative control in Hollywood had been wrested from auteurs and back into the hands of the studio heads, who kept their eye on the top stars and the bottom line. These developments had an immediate negative impact on American filmmaking – in terms of quality, mainstream cinema hit an unmatched nadir during the 1980s – but they also opened a void in the marketplace for smart, offbeat movies that privileged a filmmaker's vision and fed an audience left unsatisfied by Hollywood's glut of action-schlock sequels.

More to the point, indie films were simply good business. In her memoir *Shooting To Kill* (1998), ace independent producer **Christine Vachon** cites *Stranger Than Paradise*, *My Beautiful Laundrette* and **Bill Sherwood**'s AIDS drama *Parting Glances* (1986) as signs of "a new kind of moviemaking ... Here were movies that didn't need to gross fifty or a hundred million dollars to justify the leading actor's salary or the studio's massive overhead. Here were movies that could find a small sliver of an audience and still manage to earn their money back, launch careers and – oh yes – enrich the culture."

Like Cinecom, Miramax built up their portfolio by distributing UK hits, scoring their first significant success with the English concert film *The Secret Policeman's Other Ball* (1982). In addition to homegrown sleeper hits such as *Working Girls* (1986) and *The Thin Blue Line* (1988), Miramax hit critical and commercial paydirt with the imports *Scandal*, *My Left Foot* and *The Cook, The Thief, His Wife And Her Lover*, which all appeared in 1989. That same year, Miramax also had the honour of releasing two auspicious American feature debuts: one, **Hal Hartley**'s *The Unbelievable Truth*, all but sank without a trace; the other, **Steven Soderbergh**'s *sex, lies, and videotape*, became a cultural milestone.

The Decline Of Western Civilization
dir Penelope Spheeris, 1981, 100m, b/w and colour

Featuring interviews and performances with the avatars of the late-1970s/early-1980s LA hardcore scene (including Black Flag, the Circle Jerks, the Germs and X), Spheeris's documentary contextualizes the movement as cause and effect of socio-political upheaval. Its sequel, 1988's *Part II: The Metal Years*, is a deadpan joke on big hair and rocker hubris, while *Part III* (1998) marks punk as a refuge from a city that's only become more economically bipolar.

Smithereens
dir Susan Seidelman, 1982, 89m

Wren (Susan Berman) is an obnoxious New Jersey transplant who tries to break into the New York post-punk scene by latching onto an unreliable hipster played by downtown icon Richard Hell. Seidelman's first feature boasts a terrific soundtrack by alternative rock band The Feelies and fascinating location footage that captures the ravaged, almost unrecognizable East Village of the early 1980s.

Chan Is Missing
dir Wayne Wang, 1982, 80m, b/w

A pair of Chinese-American taxi drivers in San Francisco's Chinatown search out the titular Chan, who has disappeared with $4,000 of their money, in Wang's debut as a solo director. Shot for a mere $22,000, this movie gracefully entwines issues of assimilation and cultural identity with a satisfying mystery yarn.

Born In Flames
dir Lizzie Borden, 1983, 90m

A decade after a bloodless revolution installs a socialist government in the US, rumblings of dissatisfaction stir among the Women's Army and radical pirate radio stations. After one of their leaders dies in prison, the disparate groups come together in an organized rebellion that puts the media foremost in the firing line. Borden's rough-hewn feminist treatise is pointedly strident; its renegade energies and idealism belong to another era.

The 1990s: the Amerindie explosion

An unknown 26-year-old based in Baton Rouge, Louisiana, **Steven Soderbergh** premiered *sex, lies, and videotape* at the Utah/US Film Festival. He eventually won the Palme d'Or at Cannes and an enthusiastic Miramax promotional campaign for his cool yet intimate four-hander, which came to represent the twin ascendancies of Miramax and **Sundance** (as the Utah/US Film Festival renamed itself in 1991). Once alternatives to Hollywood bluster and glitz, both Miramax and Sundance would shortly become mainstream powerhouses in their own right, for better and worse. (Sundance, Miramax and their major- and indie-studio rivals are discussed in greater depth in "Money Changes Everything: the Hollywood connection", see pp.225–244.)

Following on from strong showings by **Gus Van Sant** (*Drugstore Cowboy*, 1989) and Spike Lee (*Do The Right Thing*, 1989), American film-making seemed to be turning a bright new leaf at the beginning of the 1990s. Scores of promising directors and striking new films emerged over the next few years: **Richard Linklater** with *Slacker* (1991), Allison Anders with *Gas, Food Lodging* (1992), **Quentin Tarantino** with *Reservoir Dogs* (1992), Scott McGehee and David Siegel with *Suture* (1993), **Lodge Kerrigan** with *Clean, Shaven* (1994) and many more.

In 1991 and 1992, the Sundance Film Festival served as a launch pad for several superb gay-themed films that were given the umbrella moniker "New Queer Cinema" in a widely read *Village Voice* article by B. Ruby Rich. One of the short-lived movement's signature films, **Gregg Araki**'s nihilistic road movie *The Living End* (1992), was the first acquisition by Jeff Lipsky and Bingham Ray's newly formed **October Films**, which quickly proved itself as a distributor to be reckoned with. Among October's early releases were the buzz-worthy documentary *The War Room* (1993), John Dahl's delectably nasty *noir* film *The Last Seduction* (1994) and two updates of the vampire myth, **Michael Almereyda**'s *Nadja* (1994) and Abel Ferrara's *The Addiction* (1995).

In its fleeting but amazingly fertile moment, New Queer Cinema highlighted the arrival

of two producers who were already becoming crucial players on the Amerindie scene: Christine Vachon and **James Schamus**, both of whom served as producers on **Tom Kalin**'s *Swoon* (1992) and **Todd Haynes**'s *Poison* (1991) and *Dottie Gets Spanked* (1993). Vachon's company, **Killer Films**, remains a vital driving force in thought-provoking, even disobedient cinema, and Schamus, who founded **Good Machine** with **Ted Hope** in 1990 and is lately the head of Focus Features, is best-known as the writing and producing collaborator of director **Ang Lee**. The Schamus-Lee partnership dates back to Lee's first films, *Pushing Hands* (1992) and the gay-oriented *The Wedding Banquet* (1993), which boasted the highest budget-to-earnings profit of any film in its year of release: it earned an astonishing 4,000 percent on its investment.

Vachon and Schamus started out in a film-producing culture that could still rely on modest wellsprings of public funding from the NEA, state arts councils, the Public Broadcasting System (PBS) and the PBS offshoot **American Playhouse**, which had a remit to present original American drama. Lee's *She's Gotta Have It* and Haynes' *Superstar: The Karen Carpenter Story* (1987) both received funding from the New York State Council on the Arts (NYSCA). **Ross McElwee**'s comic documentary *Sherman's March* (1986) was made with the support of NEA, Guggenheim and American Film Institute grants. American Playhouse's stellar list of credits include Gregory Nava's *El Norte* (1983), Julie Dash's *Daughters Of The Dust* (1991), Kalin's *Swoon*, Haynes' *Safe* (1995) and multiple films by **Hal Hartley** and **Errol Morris**.

Poison and another film associated with New Queer Cinema, **Marlon Riggs**' hour-long *Tongues Untied* (1990), both received NEA grants. And they both became flashpoints of controversy about the public funding of allegedly obscene art, a charge led by the Rev. Donald Wildmon, the unabashedly homophobic founder of a right-wing activist group, the American Family Association. Previously, NEA chairman **John Frohnmayer** had tried to alleviate conservative pressures by rejecting four potentially controversial grant applications (leading to the infamous "NEA Four" case, which was decided in favour of the artist-plaintiffs). To his credit, Frohnmayer staunchly defended *Poison* on artistic grounds, but PBS stations in twenty states refused to air *Tongues Untied*, an impressionist portrait of the lives of gay black men. The first President Bush fired Frohnmayer in 1992, and Congress slashed the NEA's already humble budget by a crippling $9 million in 1994.

Individual NEA grants to artists were almost completely eliminated in 1996; the few exceptions to the new rule did not include filmmakers.

PBS was also strapped for cash due to funding cuts in the early 1990s, leaving American Playhouse in jeopardy. In 1994, producers briefly sought private funds for a new for-profit entity, Playhouse Pictures, which would distribute films through the Samuel Goldwyn Company. Sadly, Goldwyn's own financial woes scared off potential investors and sealed Playhouse's doom; the organization began a terminal downsizing in 1995.

Although the first half of the 1990s seemed to serve up an out-of-nowhere success story every year, financial support tended to come from tapped-out friends and maxed-out credit

Cross currents: Amerindie cinema and the French New Wave

No national cinema is an island, and American independent cinema is not strictly American but flavoured with countless world influences – its longest-lasting love affair has been with the extraordinary movies of the French New Wave.

As in so many areas of world cinema, filmmaker **Jean-Luc Godard** looms largest. In *Pulp Fiction* (1994), Uma Thurman's dark bob and cat-eyed allure acknowledges Godard's former wife and leading lady, **Anna Karina**. For *Schizopolis* (1996), Steven Soderbergh borrowed a page from the doomed Godard-Karina union by casting his soon-to-be ex-wife in a film that acts out the painful demise of their marriage. Hal Hartley's movies also take a cue from Godard in their postmodern flourishes, self-aware performance styles and daring mix of arch, breezy comedy and jarring violence.

Of course, other New Wave personnel get their due. Jim Jarmusch paid homage to **Robert Bresson**'s *Un Condamné a mort s'est échappé* (*A Man Escaped*) in

Down By Law (1986), and dedicated 2005's *Broken Flowers* to **Jean Eustache**, director of *La Maman et la Putain* (*The Mother And The Whore*). The appeal of filmmaker **François Truffaut**'s cockeyed humanism can be detected in Wes Anderson's films, as well as in Noah Baumbach's *The Squid And The Whale* (2005).

Although the French New Wave can be found in many an Amerindie film's DNA, Truffaut acknowledged an American film from 1953 as planting the seeds of the movement: "Without *Little Fugitive*, the French New Wave could not have happened." Truffaut adapted *Little Fugitive*'s ostensibly casual, *vérité* style for his first feature, 1959's *Les quatre cents coups* (*The 400 Blows*). A devoted student of alternative American cinema, Godard dedicated *A bout de souffle* (1960) to the Poverty Row studio Monogram. In 1965, he gave Samuel Fuller an iconic cameo in *Pierrot le fou* in which the maverick director delivers a credo worthy of engraving: "A film is like a battleground. It's love, hate, action, violence, death – in a word, emotion."

cards, as was the case with **Robert Rodriguez**'s *El Mariachi* (1992), Eric Schaeffer's *My Life's In Turnaround* (1993) and **Kevin Smith**'s *Clerks* (1994). What usually went politely unmentioned, of course, was that the means of production in each case were far more interesting than the

ends. Rather than celebrating the movie, critics and audiences celebrated the fact that it existed at all, and the extravagant – not to mention condescending – praise poured on these films seemed to make it more likely that their director would suffer from arrested-development

Uma Thurma's *Pulp Fiction* look paid homage to French New Wave star Anna Karina

syndrome. Perhaps in part because the arts grants and non-profit foundations had largely fallen out of the equation, leaving only the business component, in the 1990s the indie world increasingly attracted filmmakers who approached their first effort as a calling card – an investment in their future Hollywood career.

Writing in the *Dallas Observer* in 1993, Matt Zoller Seitz pinpointed this trend by refracting it through what he called "the recent rise of the twentysomething gangster film", a glut that included *Boyz N The Hood*, *Menace II Society*, *My New Gun*, *Laws Of Gravity*, *Reservoir Dogs* and many more. "Maybe the real problem … is that, with few exceptions, the independent film industry in this country isn't independent anymore, either in financing or in choice of subject matter," Zoller Seitz continued. "Count the number of times you've heard supposed indie filmmakers eagerly confess to interviewers that they made their first film to 'get a foot in the door' in Hollywood, and you'll be counting all day. Rather than nurturing the next John Cassavetes or Melvin Van Peebles or **Stan Brakhage** – iconoclasts whose determination to experiment drove them to independent filmmaking because it was the only option they could live with – the industry has become a farm team for Hollywood."

As wellsprings of public funding dried up, the coffers at Miramax overflowed with infusions of cash from new corporate owner Disney, and, for the first time, the studio broke the magic $100 million barrier with Tarantino's *Pulp Fiction* (1994) – yet another gangster film, but also a lurid, kinetic thrill. For several years, Miramax enjoyed a barely broken run of critical and commercial successes, an excellent record at the Oscars and a cash cow in the form of its genre division, **Dimension Films**. Hoping to emulate the triumph of *Pulp Fiction*, each of the major

studios eventually established their own "specialty film divisions", geared towards producing relatively inexpensive films for the arthouse and awards circuits.

Although the studio boutiques increasingly dominated the competition, they have never been the only names in the game. The **Independent Film Channel** (IFC) launched in the autumn of *Pulp Fiction* as the first television network devoted to screening indie movies 24 hours a day, but the company soon diversified. They started a film production wing in 1997, which backed sterling efforts including **Kimberly Peirce**'s *Boys Don't Cry* (1999), **Jim McKay**'s *Our Song* (2000) and films by Richard Linklater, Steven Soderbergh and Michael Almereyda.

Another relative newcomer, **Lions Gate**, sprung from the Canadian company Cinepix, the distributor of mid-1990s indie highlights such as Hal Hartley's *Flirt* (1995), James Mangold's *Heavy* (1995) and Richard Kwietniowski's *Love And Death On Long Island* (1997). Lions Gate distributed the fine documentary *Sick: The Life And Death Of Bob Flanagan, Supermasochist* (1997) and enjoyed a good night at the Oscars with *Gods And Monsters* and *Affliction* (both 1998). The company also took Kevin Smith's Catholic satire *Dogma* (1999) off Miramax's hands when the heat of controversy proved too much for the Disney subsidiary.

When **Newmarket**, the independent production group that backed *Memento* (2000), couldn't find a distributor for Christopher Nolan's audacious *noir*-in-reverse, they decided to release it themselves. They mounted a superb campaign headed up by **Bob Berney**, who had previously co-ordinated publicity opportunities for another tough sell, Todd Solondz's inflammatory *Happiness* (1998). Newmarket later distributed **Richard Kelly**'s wondrous debut *Donnie Darko* (2001); Patty Jenkins' true-crime drama *Monster* (2003); and **Mel Gibson's** divisive, essentially self-financed *The Passion Of The Christ* (2004).

Another relative newcomer, **Artisan**, made an impact in the late 1990s with **Darren Aronofsky's** jittery black-and-white thriller *Pi* (1998), but they truly arrived courtesy of a little horror movie that could: *The Blair Witch Project* (1999). A cheap and terrifyingly efficient horror movie, *Blair Witch* was partly shot on

digital video, the sole format used on another of Artisan's Sundance acquisitions, *Chuck & Buck* (2000).

Paris Is Burning
dir Jennie Livingston, 1990, 71m

In the late 1980s, underground costume balls provided a social nucleus for black and Hispanic gay men in Harlem, who strut their stuff in school uniforms, military attire and business-executive duds in Livingston's documentary. In capturing the parties and interviewing the participants,

Point and shoot: Diane Lane in *My New Gun*

the movie pinpoints the scene as a collection of intriguing paradoxes – of rebellion and longing, harsh reality and thrilling fantasy, impeccable passing and uncompromised individuality – where the men find both a sense of family and a fierce, exhilarating battleground.

Daughters Of The Dust
dir Julie Dash, 1991, 112m

Unique in both form and content, Dash's engrossing film takes place at the turn of the twentieth century on Gullah island off the coast of Georgia, among a group of African-American women whose language and culture marks a point midway between their West African ancestors and their mainland American neighbours. Dash's impressionist style eschews linear storytelling in favour of mood, landscape and characterization: some of the women hang on to their memories while others look impatiently outward for a glimpse of their future.

The Hours And Times
dir Christopher Münch, 1992, 60m, b/w

Münch's debut feature is a wistful, romantically fraught speculation on the holiday that John Lennon (Ian Hart) and Brian Epstein (David Angus) took together in Spain in 1963, during the first stirrings of Beatlemania. Rather heroically, Münch shot the self-financed film with a single crewman in just six frenetic days – only appropriate for a two-character study that transpires over a pivotal weekend.

Pushing Hands
dir Ang Lee, 1992, 105m

Alongside his longtime filmmaking partner James Schamus, Ang Lee evinces a particular interest in cultural and generational conflicts as they play out within and between individuals, beginning with his first, low-budget feature, *Pushing Hands*, in which an ageing Chinese Tai Chi master relocates to upstate New York to live with his son's family.

My New Gun
dir Stacy Cochran, 1992, 99m

Vividly drawn characters and light-fingered suburban satire characterize *My New Gun*, wherein a New Jersey couple (Diane Lane and Stephen Collins) acquire a pistol

and nothing is ever the same – not after the weapon falls into the hands of boyish Skippy (James Le Gros), their enigmatic neighbour.

Suture
dir Scott McGehee and David Siegel, 1993, 96m, b/w

Seemingly everyone in this playful, philosophical *noir* comments on the striking resemblance between half-brothers Vincent (Michael Harris) and Clay (Dennis Haysbert), though to the naked eye they look nothing alike. Rich and ruthless Vincent thinks the likeness so uncanny that he tries to stage his own suicide using Clay as his stunt double, but when Clay survives, though badly burnt and suffering from amnesia, he must rebuild his own identity – or is it someone else's? McGehee and Siegel's first feature is consistently surprising and delightfully droll.

Clean, Shaven
dir Lodge Kerrigan, 1994, 79m

A mentally disturbed man (Peter Greene) tries to get his daughter back from her adoptive family, while at the same time a serial killer preys on local children in Kerrigan's unnerving debut feature. Like his later, superficially similar film *Keane* (2004), Kerrigan and his lead actor create a visceral sense of the troubled protagonist's fear, alienation and humanity, while never whitewashing the uglier consequences of his condition.

The Last Seduction
dir John Dahl, 1994, 110m

Sexy beast Bridget (Linda Fiorentino) is "a total fucking bitch" by her own reckoning, and by all appearances: she sets up her husband (Bill Pullman) and absconds with his cash to a small town where she swiftly identifies and grooms her next victim (Peter Berg). Dahl's neo-*noir* is disfigured by some ridiculous plot turns, but it's good nasty fun, and Fiorentino's fearsome Bridget could give any of the original femmes fatales a run for their stolen money.

Heavy
dir James Mangold, 1995, 105m

Obese and painfully shy, Victor (Pruitt Taylor Vince) makes pizzas in the greasy spoon run by his widowed, domineering mother (Shelley Winters) and fixates on beautiful new waitress Callie (Liv Tyler), whose arrival disrupts the sleepy rhythms of the restaurant. Suffused with regret and loneliness, Mangold's first feature is measured in pace and slender of plot, ceding centre stage to the fine performances and characterizations.

Sick: The Life And Death Of Bob Flanagan, Supermasochist
dir Kirby Dick, 1997, 89 mins

Debilitated by cystic fibrosis, performance artist Bob Flanagan used self-inflicted pain to protest and counteract his own body's betrayals. Enormously moving, this amazing documentary neither flinches from Flanagan's voluntary self-tortures (he hammers his penis to a board and then extracts the nail, all in extreme close-up), nor turns politely away when the disease finally takes the upper hand.

Pi
dir Darren Aronofsky, 1998, 84m, b/w

Mathematical genius Max Cohen (Sean Gullette) is reclusive, paranoid and plagued by horrendous migraines – and no wonder, since a shadowy consortium is hounding him for the numerical key to the stock market and a group of Orthodox Jews seem convinced that he can reveal the name of God. Shot guerrilla-style in New York for an initial budget of $60,000, Aronofsky's flashy debut blurs hallucination and exterior reality to trace the contours of its anti-hero's addled mind.

The new millennium: digital streams

As the century flipped, digital video (DV) had arrived, inspiring scores of optimistic think pieces about the democratization of filmmaking as well as many a mournful essay on the imminent "death of film". Erstwhile *enfant terrible* **Harmony Korine**, screenwriter of the teenage wasteland *Kids* (1995), made *Julien Donkey-Boy* (1999) on DV according to the spartan dictates

What are we talking about, anyway?

"What does it really mean to be independent? Independent from what? There is no independent cinema, with the exception of the home movie made for the family album."

Werner Herzog, director

"Independent films stand the test of time. They are not reliant on the latest fad, trend or special effect. Instead they are provocative, challenging and enlightening – representing a point of view, the personal vision of the filmmaker. This vision remains valid, the stories remain relevant, and the emotional connection is still as real years later as it was the day the film was released."

from the Independent Film Channel website

"I define independent film as the product of a singular vision. I'm in the financing business, and financing can come from a million different places. To define it by financing is completely irrelevant, especially as financing evolves. To me, independent films are not the product of a committee but the product of a person … We're talking about auteurism; otherwise it's a slippery slope."

John Sloss, executive producer of films by Richard Linklater, Errol Morris and John Sayles

"The 'independent' should be taken out of 'independent cinema'; commerce and capitalism have pretty much taken over."

Tom Bernard, co-president of Sony Pictures Classics

"I'm so sick of that word. I reach for my revolver when I hear the word 'quirky'. Or 'edgy'. Those words are now becoming labels that are slapped on products to sell them. Anyone who makes a film that is the film they want to make, and it is not defined by marketing analysis or a commercial enterprise, is independent."

Jim Jarmusch, director

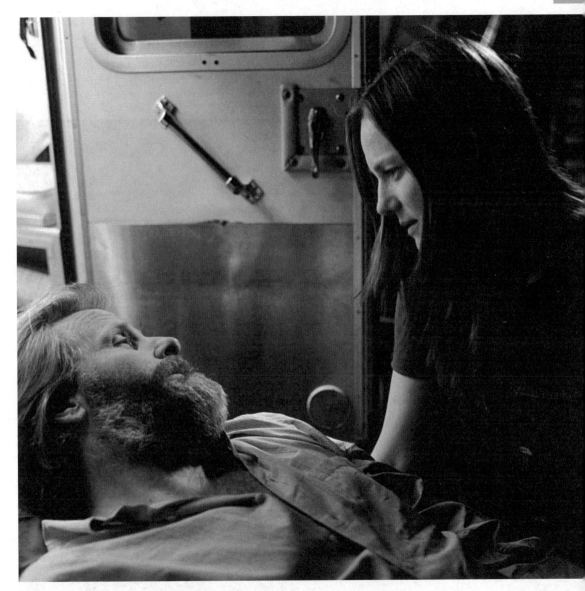

Divorce, American style: *The Squid And The Whale*

of the **Dogme 95 Collective**. This influential group of Danish filmmakers composed a manifesto-cum-instruction manual known as the "Vow of Chastity", which required signatories to shoot only on location with a handheld camera; they were furthermore barred from using special lighting, soundtrack music or props not found on location. The cheap-and-dirty doctrines of Dogme cohered with millennial Amerindie trends. Steven Soderbergh came up with his

Battle royale: indie filmmaker vs. Big Mac in *Super Size Me*

own spin on Dogme for *Full Frontal* (2002): members of the starry cast were responsible for their own wardrobe and styling, had no drivers, trailers or craft services, and were encouraged to improvise.

The digital-video enterprise Independent Digital Entertainment, known as **InDigEnt**, began in 1999, and a distribution wing followed in 2000. Their releases have included Richard Linklater's minimalist three-hander *Tape* (2001), Gary Winick's May–December romantic comedy *Tadpole* (2002), the sleeper sensation *My Big Fat Greek Wedding* (2002) and **Miranda July**'s charming first feature, *Me And You And Everyone We Know* (2005). At Sundance, the InDigEnt-affiliated triptych *Personal Velocity* (2002) by **Rebecca Miller** won the cinematography award – a sign that DV was becoming not just a means to an end, but also an aesthetic in its own right.

Inexpensive digital-video technology has made a major contribution to the documentary renaissance of recent years, which witnessed a marvellous streak of critically and commercially successful non-fiction films by the likes of **Michael Moore**, Errol Morris, **Morgan Spurlock**, Jeff Feuerzeig and brothers Andrew and Eugene Jarecki. (For more on indie documentaries, see p.126.) And as the technology rapidly improves, DV has become increasingly indistinguishable from celluloid to many a layman's eye.

In recent years, **Noah Baumbach**'s bittersweet, autobiographical film *The Squid And The Whale* (2005) is notable as a rare low-budget project to hang onto the celluloid aesthetic – Baumbach shot the movie in a mere 23 days for $1 million, on 16mm film. Perhaps it's no coincidence that Baumbach came of age as a moviegoer during the 1980s, when the film is

set, drinking in the low-budget celluloid work of Jim Jarmusch and Spike Lee (who ventured into DV for the first time in 2000 with *Bamboozled*).

The 16mm format was also the medium of choice for first-timers **Andrew Bujalski** and **Shane Carruth**. Bujalski made *Funny Ha Ha* (2002), a drolly hilarious *vérité* slice of post-collegiate bewilderment, with amateur-actor friends and an elastic script, and Carruth's *Primer* (2004), shot on an initial budget of just $7,000, is an enigmatic, brain-bending sci-fi thriller. Both *Funny Ha Ha* and *Primer* are genuinely independent films in both practical and aesthetic terms – and nowadays, that makes them an exotic species indeed.

Tadpole
dir Gary Winick, 2002, 77m

Home from boarding school for Thanksgiving, 15-year-old Oscar (Aaron Stanford) moons after his stepmother (Sigourney Weaver), and quite literally stumbles into a one-night stand with her best friend (Bebe Neuwirth). This modest, light-hearted coming-of-age tale gets a whiff of danger from Oscar's jailbait status; it's as sweet and unassuming a comedy as they come, though the grimy DV imagery detracts from its appeal.

Super Size Me
dir Morgan Spurlock, 2004, 100m

One-upping Michael Moore for performative-documentary antics, Morgan Spurlock undertakes a tough, possibly deadly mission: subsisting on nothing but McDonald's fast food for thirty days, at tremendous hazard to his liver, cholesterol levels, waistline and sex life (his girlfriend is, of all things, a vegan chef). As a polemic, the movie worked wonders: after its Sundance premiere, the Golden Arches ever so coincidentally announced the phasing out of its "Super Size" meal option at their restaurants.

Primer
dir Shane Carruth, 2004, 77m

First-time writer-director Carruth won the Grand Jury Prize at Sundance 2004 for his first feature, shot on 16mm film with an initial budget of just $7,000 in his hometown of Dallas. A densely plotted mind-twister about a pair of corporate-tech friends who invent a mysterious device that becomes a Pandora's box of paranoia and betrayal, Carruth's brain-teaser poses the tough, even frightening questions of speculative fiction at its best.

The Squid And The Whale
dir Noah Baumbach, 2005, 88m

Based on memories of his parents' divorce, Baumbach's fourth feature casts Jeff Daniels and Laura Linney as Park Slope literati whose angry split leaves their precocious sons (Jesse Eisenberg and Owen Kline) ricocheting between houses and allegiances, increasingly bewildered by their parents' sexual indiscretions and festering resentments. Plangent and wry, the film showcases Baumbach's spry verbal wit and offers a startlingly frank view of parent-child relations and teen sexuality.

Opposite: Ann (Andie MacDowell) turns the camera on fetishist videographer Graham (James Spader) in Steven Soderbergh's cultural milestone, *sex, lies, and videotape*

The Canon: 50 essential indie films

The Top Ten indie films

1 A Woman Under The Influence
1974; see p.136

The ultimate declaration of independence: self-financed, self-distributed and utterly singular filmmaking from indie godfather Cassavetes.

2 Mean Streets
1973; see p.77

Scorsese's powerful semi-autobiographical tale of friendship and loyalty marked his career breakthrough and spawned countless imitators.

3 Pulp Fiction
1994; see p.98

This exhilarating multi-strand gangster comedy made a superstar out of director Tarantino and turned Miramax into "the house that Quentin built".

4 Safe
1995; see p.104

At once cerebral and heartbreaking, Haynes's portrait of a woman allergic to her surroundings lends itself to a rich array of metaphorical readings.

5 Do The Right Thing
1989; see p.53

Lee's incendiary tale of racial conflict in Brooklyn roused fierce controversy and reminded audiences of cinema's power to stir debate.

6 The Thin Blue Line
1988; see p.128

Stylish, innovative and hugely influential, Morris's true-crime documentary also just happened to get a wrongly convicted man off Death Row.

7 Eraserhead
1977; see p.60

Weird, entrancing, utterly unique, Lynch's avant-garde nightmare was the awakening of a superlative career.

8 Before Sunrise
1995; see p.35

Dense and dizzy with walking and talking, this brief encounter is possibly the sexiest of American independent films.

9 Bad Lieutenant
1992; see p.33

A harrowing descent into hell with a spiritually debased New York cop becomes the most unlikely of redemption stories.

10 sex, lies, and videotape
1989; see p.108

Soderbergh's pensive four-hander was the film that signalled the Sundance-Miramax indie renaissance in the early 1990s.

The Canon:
50 essential
indie films

Bad Lieutenant

dir Abel Ferrara, 1992, 96m

cast Harvey Keitel, Frankie Thorn, Victor Argo, Zoe Lund

cin Ken Kelsch *scr* Zoe Lund, Abel Ferrara

In 1991, batsman Darryl Strawberry was still a contender for the Baseball Hall of Fame, despite the alcoholism and domestic-violence charges that had begun to tarnish his superstar façade. However, Strawberry subsequently began a decade-long descent into a haze of substance abuse and a string of criminal charges. Of course, when **Abel Ferrara** and **Zoe Lund** wrote *Bad Lieutenant*'s screenplay – in which **Harvey Keitel**'s titular protagonist places increasingly desperate bets on Strawberry's hapless team in a (fictitious) Mets-Dodgers playoff series – they could not possibly have foreseen Strawberry's downward spiral. But this historical irony adds a retrospective dollop of tragic inevitability to the movie: the New York cop keeps redoubling his bets on the hapless team, convinced that his man Strawberry will finally come through at the plate. If there was ever

The sacred and the profane: Abel Ferrara's *Bad Lieutenant*

a shred of doubt that the Lieutenant is a lost soul, wagering his life on Darryl Strawberry clinches the matter.

The Lieutenant may be in denial about the bookies breathing down his neck, but he is anguished by the quiet fortitude of a nun (**Frankie Thorn**) who refuses to name the two young men who raped and tortured her on a church altar. She calls them "good boys", and points out mildly that Jesus also loved those who hated him. Her beatific piety is as extreme as both the rapists' unspeakable brutality and the Lieutenant's physical and spiritual abjection. As the Lieutenant's debt mounts, he slides lower and lower. He shakes down hoodlums for their stolen cash and, in one excruciating eight-minute-long sequence, terrorizes a pair of harmless Jersey girls who've pilfered Daddy's car. This drug-gobbling menace to society is unworthy even of a name (he's identified only as "LT" in the closing credits).

A last-minute replacement for **Christopher Walken**, Keitel was roiling in the aftermath of his ugly split with **Lorraine Bracco** (of *Goodfellas* and, later, *The Sopranos*) when he took the role. "That was the most traumatic breakup in the history of the world," Ferrara later said. "And you see it in the movie. Originally, *Bad Lieutenant* wasn't written to be quite as nightmarish and hellish." According to the director, Keitel improvised the infamous scene in which he forces a girl to simulate fellatio as he masturbates by the side of her car. Ferrara cedes the screen to Keitel's naked performance (quite literally in one scene), a keening howl at an indifferent God. "Is there somethin' you wanna say to me, you fuck? You rat fucker, you rat fuck!" the Lieutenant screams at a vision of Christ (actually a *deus ex machina* in the form of a grandmotherly churchgoer).

"Vampires are lucky; they can feed on others. We gotta eat away at ourselves," observes the junkie played by the film's late co-writer Zoe Lund (who, as Zoë Tamerlis, became a cult heroine as star of Ferrara's 1981 rape-revenge fantasy *Ms. 45* (aka *Angel Of Vengeance*)). In this respect, the Lieutenant is ravenous; his appetites are nearly all we know of him. Self-forgetting and mortification of the flesh are constants of both religious ecstasy and all-consuming addiction, and *Bad Lieutenant* deploys Catholic iconography to link the cop's suffering to the sister's martyrdom: the nun's rape is cross-cut with Christ's dying agonies, and the Lieutenant's heroin reverie is juxtaposed with his vision of Jesus dead on the cross. The film suggests the possibility of transcendence through degradation. The nun finds it, and so does the Lieutenant, in a final act that seals his doom, but which also lets in a slender beam of redemptive light.

Before Sunrise

dir Richard Linklater, 1995, 97m

cast Ethan Hawke, Julie Delpy *cin* Lee Daniel *scr* Richard Linklater, Kim Krizan

As morning breaks over Vienna in **Richard Linklater's** *Before Sunrise*, the American wayfarer Jesse (**Ethan Hawke**) recites a fragment of a W.H. Auden poem to Céline (**Julie Delpy**), the French student he met the day before: "But all the clocks in the city / Began to whirr and chime: / 'O let not Time deceive you, / You cannot conquer Time … In headaches and in worry / Vaguely life leaks away, / And Time will have his fancy / To-morrow or to-day.' "

Time is of the essence in *Before Sunrise*. Jesse and Céline click instantly when they meet on a Eurorail train, and decide to spend the rest of the afternoon and night walking around Vienna together, encountering a pair of avant-garde stage actors, a mysterious fortune teller and a waterfront poet. As the night wanes and the pair's intellectual and sexual chemistry grows more intense, every passing moment gains in urgency.

Julie Delpy and Ethan Hawke advance French–American relations in *Before Sunrise*

Linklater's films are typically verbose, and *Before Sunrise* unspools reams and ribbons of get-to-know-you chat, theory-spinning, flirtatious repartee and confessional exchange. The heady buzz of this meeting of minds is matched in Jesse and Céline's physical magnetism. A thrillingly awkward interlude in a cramped record-shop listening booth (scored to Kath Bloom's imploring ballad "Come Here") leads to a first kiss at sunset atop Vienna's famed *Reisenrad* Ferris wheel (previously seen in 1949's *The Third Man*), a roll in the park by moonlight and a heart-stopping last clinch on a train platform. American indie cinema is hardly renowned for its erotic charge, but *Before Sunrise* is one of the sexiest movies of the 1990s.

Despite their youthful energy, their seize-the-moment spontaneity, Jesse and Céline also seem ruefully self-conscious. They stand at a slight remove from their lives; they mythologize, look for portents, impose a narrative. Céline imagines that her whole life is but the deathbed reminiscences of an old woman; Jesse says he feels like a boy taking notes in preparation for the start of his adult life. Even the terms of their final parting suggest they're conscious of their assigned roles in a movie-size romance. They promise to rendezvous in six months, not exchanging so much as a phone number, thus leaving *Before Sunrise* with a wide-open ending, both bittersweet and hopeful. Jesse and Céline go their separate ways come morning, but by then the blinding flash of infatuation – or maybe even love – has cast their whole world and future in a new light.

Before Sunset

dir Richard Linklater, 2004, 77m

cast Ethan Hawke, Julie Delpy *cin* Lee Daniel *scr* Richard Linklater, Julie Delpy, Ethan Hawke

The final scene of **Richard Linklater**'s *Before Sunrise* left one burning question: did Jesse and Céline, young lovers from different continents who met and parted in Vienna one summer, ever meet again? How you answer that question, Jesse tells a bookstore audience at the beginning of the wondrous sequel *Before Sunset*, depends on whether you're a romantic or a cynic; part two has it both ways.

(The couple did show up in bed together in Linklater's 2001 film *Waking Life*, which would have settled the issue had not the film been someone else's dream.)

Before Sunset picks up the story nine years later in Paris, where Céline lives and where Jesse, now a bestselling novelist, is promoting *This Time*, a thinly veiled account of their Viennese brief encounter. In the hour or so before he's scheduled to leave for the airport, Jesse and Céline walk around the Left Bank, reacquaint, banter and flirt. As their defences swiftly fall away, they reveal how that magical night long ago has both haunted and sustained them through the drudgery and disappointment of their subsequent relationships.

In *Before Sunrise*, Jesse and Céline tried to articulate their shared sense of detachment from the slightly unreal events of their own lives. By now, the dream life is over, and this ambling trip down memory lane transforms inexorably into a piercing recognition of lost years and missed chances. Less than eighty minutes long, the movie virtually unfolds in real time, intensifying the undercurrents of existential panic – the queasying intuition that the sands of the hourglass are running out on your life. Vaguely life leaks away.

Much like its predecessor, *Before Sunset* is a metaphysical chase movie, pitting Jesse and Céline against the hairy-knuckled hands of time. The ticking clock pursues their boat trip down the Seine like a seething leviathan. In the cab to Céline's apartment, it rattles like a time bomb in the trunk. But it finally gets winded on the stairs to her flat, and once she starts singing her waltz ("out of nowhere, out of my thoughts"), the enemy slinks away sheepishly, soundly defeated. As **Nina Simone** sings on the stereo, the lovers run out of time, into another realm entirely.

Being John Malkovich

dir Spike Jonze, 1999, 112m
cast John Cusack, Cameron Diaz, Catherine Keener, John Malkovich *cin* Lance Acord *scr* Charlie Kaufman

Being John Malkovich is the exhilarating mindfuck to end all exhilarating mindfucks, in which its impeccably controlled lunacy comprises a slapstick comedy, a transsexual love story and a serious philosophical investigation. Yet it's all presented so matter-of-factly that the confusion and pain of the characters is never in doubt or belittled, even at the hysterical peak of the film's gleefully contorted metaphysics.

Craig Schwartz (**John Cusack**) is a sad-sack puppeteer who lives in a cramped New York apartment with his frazzled wife, Lotte (**Cameron Diaz**), and her roving menagerie of rescued pets. To pay the bills, Craig takes a menial filing job on the seventh-and-a-half floor of an office building. Here, the stooped employees seem to embody his stunted growth as an artist, and though he lusts for his acid-tongued colleague Maxine (**Catherine Keener**), her rejection further emasculates him. The drudgery of Craig's existence is turned upside-down when he discovers a tunnel behind some cabinets that leads straight into the mind of one John Malkovich (**John Malkovich**)…

How in the world did this film get made? As Sharon Waxman has it in her book *Rebels On The Backlot* (2005), this extraordinary collaboration between the music-video dynamo **Spike Jonze** and the brilliant TV-sitcom veteran **Charlie Kaufman** coalesced during a volatile period of studio reshufflings and personnel changes (its production company, Gramercy, folded into the short-lived USA Films during filming). Waxman writes, "Amid the mergings, firings, transfers and deal-making, everyone forgot about an odd little movie being made on the back streets of downtown Los Angeles called *Being John Malkovich*." Shot for a budget in the low teens, the movie became an independent film by default – you might say it thrived on neglect.

Fearlessly cerebral, *Being John Malkovich* ponders celebrity worship, gender confusion, the wages of ambition and envy, and the mutability of identity, among other things. This is a movie that sets a chase scene inside a film star's subconscious and stages a *ménage à trois* in two bodies; a movie in which Malkovich enters the portal into his own head and finds himself in a room crowded with Malkoviches eerily intoning "Malkovich"; a movie in which a frustrated artist can have his professional jealousy piqued by the sight of a sixty-foot **Emily Dickinson** puppet on television. Indeed, so dense is it with ideas and drolly outlandish incident that one hardly notices that Malkovich takes over the role of Craig from John Cusack two-thirds through the film. (Only ostensibly playing himself, the eponymous actor fully embraces his greatest role.)

Although it's one of the most stunning comedies that an American studio has produced, the laughter provoked by *Being John Malkovich* is only a permeable line of defence against the sad, frightening questions it asks about love, aspiration and personality, all posed against the rich backdrop of **Carter Burwell**'s shivery orchestral score. In their lyrical, subliminally tragic last scene, Jonze and Kaufman nod to the amphibious, in-utero nature of identity, creating one of the most haunting finales in cinema.

The Blair Witch Project

dir Daniel Myrick & Eduardo Sanchez, 1999, 86m
cast Heather Donahue, Joshua Leonard, Michael Williams
cin Neal Fredericks *scr* Daniel Myrick, Eduardo Sanchez

Countless movies have practised the art of the slow reveal, but *The Blair Witch Project* is singular in its deployment of the no-reveal. Deep in an accursed forest peopled by three members of a film crew, the movie works its voodoo through intimation: the rustle of leaves underfoot, shivers of wind through the trees, snatches of voices in the distance, the discovery of crude occult icons fashioned from twigs. Sometimes a wild-eyed phantom figure will rear into the frame, but it's one of the doomed filmmakers, caught by another's camera. Creating and sustaining an almost unbearable tension from the terror of anticipation, *Blair Witch* concentrates all the dread and panic inherent in the words, *Did you just hear that?*

The Blair Witch Project is presented as fact from its terse opening titles: "In October of 1994, three student filmmakers disappeared in the woods near Burkittsville, Maryland while shooting a documentary. A year later their footage was found." The documentary's voluble director, Heather (**Heather Donahue**), and fellow crew members, Josh (**Joshua Leonard**) and Mike (**Michael Williams**), are introduced while interviewing Burkittsville residents about the eighteenth-century curse of the Blair Witch. They then hike into the Black Hills, where they lose their bearings and seem to be pursued by unknown,

Faces of death: *Blair Witch* crewman Josh documents his own demise

increasingly aggressive beings or spectres. As relations between the trio splinter and unravel and one member disappears, Heather maintains her dedication – even compulsion – to record every possible moment of their ordeal. "It's all I have left," she cries at a low point.

An instant media phenomenon that eventually grossed roughly 6,000 times what it cost to make, *The Blair Witch Project* was the brainchild of **Haxan**, a creative think-tank made up of five graduates of the film school at the University of Central Florida. Contrary to the brilliant marketing campaign by distributor Artisan, first-time filmmakers **Daniel Myrick** and **Eduardo Sanchez** never implied that the footage was real, but the documentary elements of the production helped conjure the film's raw immediacy. It wasn't just great PR that left audiences thinking they were seeing a bona fide, paranormally provoked meltdown in triplicate, captured live by the subjects themselves.

Season of the *Witch*

The Blair Witch Project created a sensation from the moment of its midnight premiere at **Sundance** in 1999. Made for a mere $40,000, the movie made the covers of *Time* and *Newsweek* simultaneously and eventually grossed nearly $250 million worldwide, setting a box-office record for the highest budget-to-earnings ratio of all time.

Vigorous debate on the Internet centred on the film's veracity, and its distributor, **Artisan**, fully exploited the "controversy" with its promos and inspired website, which filled in more fictitious back story and provided supplementary artefacts and evidence. (The unnervingly straight-faced site, blairwitch.com, is still in operation.) The Internet Movie Database (IMDB) even listed the principal actors, each of whom shared a name with his or her character, as "deceased". Lead actress **Heather Donahue** told interviewers at the time of the film's release that people would approach her expressing relief that she was alive – a measure of how *Blair Witch*'s hyper-real aesthetic shook millennial audiences to the core.

The directors did not direct conventionally, but trailed their cast with handheld tracking devices after giving them a filmmaking crash course and providing them with 16mm and Hi-8 video cameras. (The film's rough-hewn imagery, which trembles along with the frightened characters or becomes a frantic smear when the camera operator sprints away from imminent danger, left many a viewer with motion sickness.) Donahue, Leonard and Williams did not work from a standard script, but improvised from sets of directing notes that the directors left at various checkpoints with food and equipment. The movie was shot sequentially and the actors were never sure of what would befall their characters.

Thus Heather Donahue and her filmmaking counterpart may not be the same person, but they share much in common. They're both pulling double duty as performer and filmmaker, and they're both cold, exhausted, living in the woods, overburdened with gear and hungry (by the end of the shoot, a day's ration was a Power Bar and a banana). As Sanchez told the *World of Fandom* website, "We knew that if we got them out there for six days in the woods, something would come out on film that hadn't been seen before." But as *The Blair Witch Project* proves, what you don't see can be the scariest vision of all.

Blood Simple

dir Joel Coen, 1984, 95m

cast Frances McDormand, John Getz, Dan Hedaya, M. Emmet Walsh, Samm-Art Williams, Deborah Neumann
cin Barry Sonnenfeld *scr* Joel Coen, Ethan Coen

The imprecisely defined term "neo-*noir*" has been affixed to many key American independent films of the last two decades. Released in US theatres at the start of 1985, **Joel and Ethan Coen**'s first feature, *Blood Simple*, was the first of a wave that comprised films as diverse as *The Grifters* (1990), *One False Move* (1992), *The Last Seduction* (1994), *Hard Eight* (1996) and *Memento* (2000), not to mention much of the Coen brothers' subsequent output.

The movie assembles the tropes and archetypes of hard-boiled writers such as Dashiell Hammett, Raymond Chandler and especially **James M. Cain** – whose novel *The Postman Always Rings Twice* (1934) is perhaps *Blood Simple*'s most overt pulp antecedent – and relocates them to the dirt-and-asphalt landscape of hottest Texas. As they later acknowledged, the Coens were inspired by Cain's intersections of domestic strife and criminal acts, his workaday realms where people of ordinary intelligence with ordinary jobs commit extraordinary acts of betrayal and brutality. The title derives from a line in Hammett's detective fiction *Red Harvest* (1929), in which the investigator worries that he's "going blood simple", or acquiring a mindless mania for violence.

At its outset, *Blood Simple*'s plot lines are smooth and classical. An unhappy wife, Abby (**Frances McDormand** in her first movie role), begins an affair with her husband's employee, Ray (**John Getz**). Her cuckolded husband, Marty (**Dan Hedaya**), owner of a sleazy bar, hires a sleazier private eye (**M. Emmet Walsh**) to run surveillance on the adulterous couple and, later, to kill them both. This appointment with murder is made but not kept – at least not in the expected manner. It's from this point onwards that *Blood Simple* begins tying itself into elaborate knots, as the characters make pre-emptive moves and inaccurate assumptions at wild cross-purposes. The savvy audience member, meanwhile, may know enough not to jump to conclusions when the movie offers every indication that all three members of the love triangle are dead before the 45-minute mark.

Sweaty and nocturnal, laconic and sometimes languid, *Blood Simple* has a vicious side. Joel Coen cut his film-crew teeth as assistant editor on **Sam Raimi**'s splatter classic *The Evil Dead* (1981), and his own directing debut spills its share of gore, occasionally shading towards horror: in a sequence at once ghastly and farcical, a man is buried alive; another character's hand is impaled on a windowsill, the camera lingering over the grisly sight. (The cinematography is by **Barry Sonnenfeld**, who would go on to direct the *Addams Family* films and *Men In Black* movies in the 1990s.)

Blood Simple reaches a black-comic apex when one of the principals methodically implicates himself in a murder he didn't commit. The Coens delight in tormenting their wretched characters, not least by denying their downfalls any overlay of romance. Intrigues play out on the monotonous highway or in grimy rented rooms, and the only infusion of grandeur comes from repeat plays of the propulsive **Holland-Dozier-Holland** classic "It's The Same Old Song", performed by the Four Tops. Still, the Coens embed a modicum of justice in the cruel world of *Blood Simple*. Given her *noir* context, Abby should shape up as a femme fatale, but mostly she's just femme, and largely free of guilt. She's relatively unscathed by the film's end – *relatively* being the operative word, given the state the men are in.

Boys Don't Cry

dir Kimberly Peirce, 1999, 118m
cast Hilary Swank, Chloë Sevigny, Peter Sarsgaard, Brendan Sexton III *cin* Jim Denault *scr* Kimberly Peirce, Andy Bienen

The seeds of *Boys Don't Cry* were planted in 1994, when fledgling director **Kimberly Peirce** read a cover story in *The Village Voice* about Brandon Teena (born Teena Brandon), an anatomical female who had passed as a man – and quite a ladies' man at that – in the small town of Falls City, Nebraska. Brandon was dating local beauty Lana Tisdel and when his biological identity was revealed, he was raped and badly beaten, and later murdered by two men he had befriended in Falls City, John Lotter and Marvin "Tom" Nissen. Brandon had just turned 21.

Though the sensational aspects of Brandon's life and death were obvious (he was also an unsuccessful petty criminal with convictions for grand theft auto and passing bad cheques), Peirce viewed his story as a classical all-American tale of self-invention, about the ecstatic release and frightening hazards of being true to oneself. "This was a trailer-park girl who didn't have role models or economic means, but created a fantastic vision of herself," said Peirce in 1999. The filmmaker travelled to Nebraska to attend Lotter and Nissen's murder trial (Lotter was sentenced to death; Nissen received consecutive life sentences) and to interview the surviving principals of Brandon's last days alive, including Lana Tisdel. Casting Brandon took three years; Peirce saw hundreds of actresses and transgender

Dangerous love: Chloë Sevigny and Hilary Swank in *Boys Don't Cry*

non-professionals before settling on former *Beverly Hills, 90210* star **Hilary Swank**, who later won an Oscar for her winning, wounded and uncanny performance (one that netted her the princely sum of $75 a day).

To the men of Falls City, Swank's Brandon is one of the guys, even if he's the runt of the bunch; to the women, he's the perfect boyfriend: courtly, adoring, a fabulous kisser, a magician in the sack. Shot in and around Dallas, *Boys Don't Cry* is mostly nocturnal, its nightscapes given an effulgent eeriness by cinematographer **Jim Denault**. The cover of darkness is apt for a film of stolen kisses and terrifying violence, and for a protagonist who lives a secret life in public, who must at once conceal and craft his true identity.

The wee-hours visuals also capture what Peirce describes as "a whole Qwik Stop culture of narcotized kids that sleep all day and hang out all night". Friendly and eager, instantly loveable with a dazzling smile, Brandon's arrival oxygenates the stultifying prison of Falls City, where teenagers cope with perpetual tedium via binge drinking, graffiti, arson and self-harm. Not long before she and Brandon share their first kiss, Lana (**Chloë Sevigny**), the karaoke-singing town goddess, laments being "stuck in a town where there's nothing to do but go bumper-skiing and chase bats every night of your evil fuckin' life". (Peirce and **Andy Bienen**'s script, and Sevigny's lovely performance, adroitly handle the unanswerable question of what Lana knew, when she knew it and how she processed it.)

As its intimations of a dreadful inevitability mount, the movie shows how endemic boredom in a conservative, dead-end environment can incubate rage and brutality. Tom (**Brendan Sexton III**) shows Brandon the knife scars he gave himself in prison, and Brandon's entire social circle seems to live in an abusive relationship with John (**Peter Sarsgaard**), a mercurial ex-con lacking "impulse control". From its very first scenes, in which Brandon makes his debut as a man at a roller rink (Peirce borrowed setups for this sequence from *The Wizard Of Oz*), a mixed sense of danger and elation thrums through *Boys Don't Cry*, as Brandon repeatedly bounds into harm's way.

Brandon Teena was undoubtedly a sexual transgressor, and in death became a martyr and rallying point for the worldwide transgender community. But even taking his rap sheet into account, there's little that's defiant or rebellious about him in *Boys Don't Cry*. He's just being himself, which is still enough to get you killed in America.

Buffalo '66

dir Vincent Gallo, 1998, 110m

cast Vincent Gallo, Christina Ricci, Anjelica Huston, Ben Gazzara, Rosanna Arquette, Mickey Rourke *cin* Lance Acord *scr* Vincent Gallo, Alison Bagnall

The last word on New York State's second most populous city might have been provided in *A Chorus Line*, which includes the maxim, "To commit suicide in Buffalo is redundant." Buffalo's bleak reputation is not altogether deserved, but it's certainly a town that can't catch a break, as the entire nation witnessed during the early 1990s when the Buffalo Bills lost four consecutive Super Bowls. Their most memorable loss was in 1991, when place-kicker Scott Norwood flubbed a potentially game-winning field goal. In *Buffalo '66*, writer-director-star **Vincent Gallo** takes this defining trauma to the municipal psyche and claims it as his own. As far as the hilariously wretched protagonist Billy Brown is concerned, his life ended the moment that infamous kick veered wide right of the goal.

Already badly damaged by a loveless upbringing, Billy (played by Gallo, who was born and raised in Buffalo) reaches a point of no return when he bets $10,000 that he doesn't have on the Bills and, to escape the wrath of his bookie

Alley cat Vincent Gallo

Home economics

Much more than their far-flung and well-financed studio counterparts, indie directors stay close to home – and often shoot their movies there too. Edward Burns, **Vincent Gallo** and **Nicole Holofcener** are just a few of the indie talents who have kept costs down by using their parents' homes as readymade sets. **Todd Haynes** also turned to family members to create Carol White's antiseptic environs in *Safe* (1995), borrowing his grandparents' kitchen and his uncle Ronnie's living room. **John Waters'** filmmaking career began on the roof of his parents' house, and **Greg Mottola** was able to keep his initial budget for *The Daytrippers* (1996) at a bargain-basement $60,000, in part because he shot much of it in his folks' home and his own apartment.

Of course, commandeering your mum and dad's house isn't the only form of home economics perfected by the cash-strapped indie director. You can also go ahead and cast your family (a tradition stretching from **John Cassavetes** to **Andrew Wagner**, director of 2005's *The Talent Given Us*), sell your parents' house to fund your movie (Paul Bartel did just that for 1982's *Eating Raoul*) or remortgage your house whenever funding is short (Cassavetes again). But what is the ultimate home movie? **Jonathan Caouette**'s *Tarnation* (2003): his entire life has been a movie in the making, and everywhere he's ever lived has been his set.

(**Mickey Rourke**), he takes the rap for a crime committed by one of the fearsome man's "associates". Sprung from jail, Billy kidnaps a buxom dance student, Layla (**Christina Ricci**), informs her that this evening she'll be playing the part of his wife, Wendy Balsam, and drags her home to his frightful parents, Jan (**Anjelica Huston**) and Jimmy (**Ben Gazzara**). He also plans to avenge his nemesis, football player Scott Wood, who now runs a seedy strip joint.

Billy begs the selfless Layla to hold him and, as soon as she comes near, yelps "Don't touch me!" He desperately wants to impress his parents, yet he detests them. Jan is a Bills freak, Jimmy is a hot-tempered letch, and both regard Billy from a bemused, hostile distance. The film occasionally flashes back to Billy's miserable childhood, using 16mm reversal-film stock for a grainy, 70s vintage effect. In a typical snatch of dinner-table chatter, Jan tells Layla that she missed the only championship victory in the Buffalo Bills' history because she was giving birth to her son, and thus wishes he were never born. (Viewers need not speculate on Billy's namesake.)

"Those characters are not exaggerations of my parents," Gallo told the *San Francisco Chronicle* in 1998. "My parents are exaggerations of those characters." *Buffalo '66* was a painfully personal effort: the Brown family scenes were shot in the last house that Gallo shared with his parents before he lit out for New York City as a teenager, and Gazzara lip-synchs to a recording of Vincent Gallo Sr. crooning "Fools Rush In". After leaving the Browns' residence, Billy's mood hardly improves, especially during a humiliating encounter with his great unrequited love, who happens to be named Wendy Balsam (**Rosanna Arquette**). "I'm Wendy Balsam, too," says Layla, unperturbed. Indeed, Layla never breaks character: she's equal parts Method actress and angel of mercy. No matter how much Billy berates or ignores her, she sticks adoringly by his side. "You are so nice," she tells him, with all evidence to the contrary. And, as it turns out, Layla is something of a miracle worker, her steadfastness transforming a caustic tale of how you can't go home again into a cockeyed, weirdly convincing love story.

Citizen Ruth

dir Alexander Payne, 1996, 105m
cast Laura Dern, Swoosie Kurtz, Kurtwood Smith, Mary Kay Place *cin* James Glennon *scr* Alexander Payne, Jim Taylor

In the past, controversy has been Miramax's bread and butter. So *Citizen Ruth*, the rare film to take on the irreconcilable American abortion wars (and a comedy, to boot) may have seemed tailor-made for the studio. **The Weinsteins** acquired **Alexander Payne**'s debut film even before its Sundance premiere, but its rabble-rousing potential proved to be a bane. Presumably weary from battles with parent company Disney over *Kids* (which shared *Citizen Ruth*'s producer, **Cary Woods**) and the gay-themed *Priest* (1994), Miramax did little to hype the movie.

Unlike *Kids*, *Priest* or earlier Miramax sensations such as *The Crying Game* (1992) and *Pulp Fiction* (1994), *Citizen Ruth* could

Under the influence: Laura Dern (centre) as *Citizen Ruth*

promise little in the way of sex, violence, shock value or other marketable titillations. The eponymous heroine, Ruth Stoops (**Laura Dern**), is a hard-drinking, glue-huffing indigent who is forever in and out of jail and rehab. Pregnant for the fifth time (none of her four children are in her custody), Ruth is arrested for "criminal endangerment" of her foetus. A well-meaning judge privately suggests that she might win a reduced sentence if she obtains an abortion, but when Ruth shares a cell with members of an anti-abortion protest group called the Baby Savers, the wheels of a media sensation roll into motion. Ruth is first taken under the wing of a pro-life married couple (**Kurtwood Smith** and **Mary Kay Place**), who urge her to complete the pregnancy. Then she's co-opted by a pro-choice double agent (**Swoosie Kurtz**) and her girlfriend (**Kelly Preston**), who arrange an abortion for Ruth. As TV crews come sniffing and the upper echelons of both camps become involved, Ruth's pregnancy sets off a bidding war and she becomes the befuddled centre of a political storm. To both the pro-choicers and the Baby Savers, Ruth is the embodiment of their beloved cause, and thus they have trouble processing the awkward details of Ruth in body and soul.

Citizen Ruth is fastidiously even-handed for a social satire. Payne and screenwriting partner **Jim Taylor** are careful to etch both sides of the abortion debate as self-righteous, self-deluded and hypocritical, and Payne signals much of his critique through snarky set and costume design. When the storyline arranges a perfectly timed miscarriage for Ruth – a very likely scenario, given her substance intake and stress levels – the film is excused from having to confront the consequences and visceral reality of an abortion or birth.

The movie's boldest gambit isn't its snide politics of disengagement, but Ruth herself: rarely has a comedy's nominal heroine been so frequently appalling. Ruth is a hopeless recidivist, an outrageously flawed child-woman consumed by her addictions; she lies, steals and uncomprehendingly parrots the views of whichever camp happens to be feeding her. Dern's all-out performance is a constant reminder of the human being at the core of the slogan-chanting and broadcast clamour. The lyrical last shot persuasively implies that, however messed-up she is, the only person qualified to make decisions for Ruth is Ruth, even if her final victory also serves to reinforce the film's everyone-for-herself cynicism. Unsympathetic though she might be, Ruth is the only flesh-and-blood person among characters cut from cardboard placards and banner cloth.

Crumb

dir Terry Zwigoff, 1994, 119m

with Robert Crumb, Aline Kominsky, Charles Crumb,
Maxon Crumb, Robert Hughes *cin* Maryse Alberti

Terry Zwigoff's portrait of **Robert Crumb** is breathtakingly blunt in its approach to the renowned comic-book artist's tormented family background and gnarled psychosexual profile. Frankness is perhaps to be expected from Crumb, a wry, stubbornly anti-commercial maverick who prides himself on his impeccable bullshit detector, and whose often autobiographical work thrives on the fuel of his misanthropy, fetishes and sexual hang-ups. The intimacy achieved in *Crumb*, which is as much a family album as it is an artist's profile, attests to the affinities between the filmmaker and his subject. Friends since 1970, Crumb and Zwigoff both grew up behind the picture-perfect façade of 1950s America, and share a passion for old Blues 78s and a contempt for their native country's mainstream culture. They had previously collaborated on a couple of unproduced screenplays before Zwigoff began shooting a documentary about the Zap Comix creator, whose bawdy drawings became defining images of the late-1960s counterculture.

Famous for his representations of strapping women – instantly recognizable by their Olympic-sprinter's thighs and solid, shelf-like asses – Crumb speaks amiably on camera about his early sexual attractions to **Bugs Bunny**, his aunt's boots and the 1950s television character Sheena, Queen of the Jungle. Such disclosures, alongside interviews with art critic **Robert Hughes** and the various women in Crumb's life (including his current wife, **Aline**), contribute to the depiction of Crumb's career as a particularly fertile case study of arrested development. His images of monster-headed or decapitated Amazons evince a mixed fascination and revulsion towards the female of the species ("I have these hostilities toward women, I admit it," Crumb says), while his bizarre representations of black characters can be viewed as either a critique of racism or the thing itself.

Zwigoff convincingly proposes that a miserable but artistically active childhood is ground zero for Crumb's oeuvre. Son of an amphetamine-addicted mother and an abusive father, the future comix legend and his siblings immersed themselves in drawing and play-acting, but only Robert forged the semblance of a functional adulthood. His brothers, **Charles** and **Maxon**, also showed abundant artistic talent, but by the time we meet them in *Crumb*, Charles is a heavily medicated recluse still living with their addled mother (he committed suicide before the film was released) and Maxon is a panhandler with a record for sexual molestation. (Their two sisters declined to appear in the film.) "What kept him mentally healthy – as opposed to his brothers – is that people have seen his work and responded to it," Zwigoff told the *Houston Chronicle* at the time of *Crumb's* theatrical release in 1995. "It's meant money, women, fame. Without that recognition, Robert might be very much like Charles or Maxon."

Nine years in the making, *Crumb* was completed when **David Lynch** stepped in as a producer. The film earned more than $3 million at the US box office, which was a huge payday for a documentary. The movie's star, however, was shaken by the film's visibility and success; having already emigrated to the South of France with Aline and their daughter, Crumb grew a beard and let his hair grow long to escape public notice. It may seem odd that an artist who shows such naked abandon in his work and remarkable candour in front of the camera would shrink from public recognition, but his reaction only underlines the sense of a private, personal space that Crumb creates in his art and that Zwigoff creates in *Crumb*.

Do The Right Thing

dir Spike Lee, 1989, 120m

cast Danny Aiello, Ossie Davis, Ruby Dee, Giancarlo Esposito, Spike Lee, Bill Nunn, John Turturro, Richard Edson, Rosie Perez, Samuel L. Jackson *cin* Ernest Dickerson *scr* Spike Lee

---

Racial tensions in a Brooklyn neighbourhood combust on a sweltering summer's day in *Do The Right Thing*, which dominated the national cultural conversation on its release in June 1989. From *Newsweek* to *Oprah*, pundits debated the film in generally Manichean terms. Was **Spike Lee**'s movie an artistic and moral triumph, a clarion call for America to open its eyes to the sorry state of its race relations? Or was it a form of what *New York* magazine's Joe Klein called "dangerous stupidity", an endorsement or even an encouragement of vigilante justice? Part of the genius of *Do The Right Thing* was in getting its audiences as hot and bothered – as voluble and apparently irreconcilable – as the film's fictional characters.

True colours: Spike Lee and Danny Aiello in *Do The Right Thing*

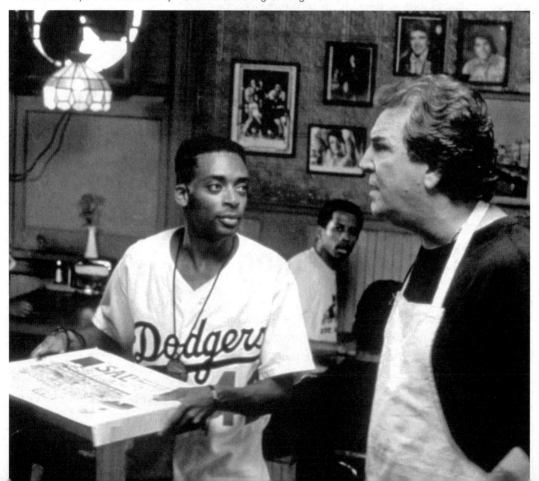

Do The Right Thing is inspired by events in Howard Beach, Queens in 1986, when three young black men from Brooklyn leaving a pizzeria were attacked by a white mob wielding baseball bats; 23-year-old Michael Griffith was chased into traffic and killed by an oncoming car, and thereafter "Howard Beach" became nationally synonymous with homicidal racism. "We kept three things from the actual incident: the bat, the pizzeria and a conflict between blacks and Italian Americans where a black man gets killed," Lee explained to *The Guardian* newspaper. The writer-director set his expressionist polemic in a fictional block of Bedford-Stuyvesant, populated for the most part by purposefully flat characters – drawn in broad, bold strokes to represent particular points of view.

Lee plays Mookie, recently hired as deliveryman at Sal's Famous Pizzeria, an institution in Mookie's poor, predominantly black neighbourhood. Decent but short of fuse, Sal (**Danny Aiello**) runs his place with his two sons, affable Vito (**Richard Edson**) and openly racist Pino (**John Turturro**). Mookie plays de facto mediator in the tense relations between his white employers and his black pals, including Radio Raheem (**Bill Nunn**), who infuriates Sal when he blasts Public Enemy's "Fight The Power" from his boom box, and the aptly named Buggin' Out (**Giancarlo Esposito**), who's incensed that Sal only hangs photographs of famous Italians, not blacks, on the walls of his restaurant. As Mookie tries and fails both to placate Buggin' Out and talk some sense into Pino, he neglects his Hispanic girlfriend (**Rosie Perez**) and their toddler son. (As the henpecking harpy with a gratuitous nude scene, Perez has a thankless part, although her shadow-boxing dance routine to "Fight The Power" makes for a thrilling, kinetic opening-credits sequence.)

Painted in rippling crimson shades by cinematographer (and future director) **Ernest Dickerson** and scored by Lee's father, **Bill**, *Do The Right Thing* captures the lazy, hazy and crazy of a New York summer scorcher, as the entire block rumbles like a volcano ready to erupt. Buggin' Out and Radio Raheem stage a protest at Sal's, triggering an eruption of violent chaos; by night's end, Raheem is dead by a white cop's hand. (Lee dedicates the film to several victims of police brutality.) Mookie, previously the stoic local diplomat, throws a trash can through the pizzeria window, sparking a riot – a pathetic spectacle born of rage, grief and anguished futility – that leaves Sal's in smoking ruins.

Do The Right Thing is a powerful tragedy about a community caught in the throes of a centuries-old cultural sickness; the film is diagnosis, reportage and prophecy. Before the summer was out, another young black man, teenager Yusuf Hawkins, was killed by a white mob, this time in Bensonhurst. In the film's final scene, local DJ Mr. Señor Love Daddy (**Samuel L. Jackson**) encourages his listeners to register to vote; the following November, New York elected **David Dinkins**, the city's first African-American mayor.

Drugstore Cowboy

dir Gus Van Sant, 1989, 100m
cast Matt Dillon, Kelly Lynch, James Le Gros, Heather Graham, James Remar, William S. Burroughs, Max Perlich *cin* Robert Yeoman *scr* Gus Van Sant, Daniel Yost, from the novel by James Fogle

The poster image of *Drugstore Cowboy* radiates a defiant allure, capturing stars **Matt Dillon** and **Kelly Lynch** in a loving embrace, all black leather and sultry solidarity. However, **Gus Van Sant**'s second feature doesn't romanticize young marrieds Bob (Dillon) and Diane (Lynch), junkie thieves who knock off pharmacies in early-1970s Portland, Oregon. Sure, they can afford a nice house with room for their baby-faced apprentices Rick and Nadine (**James Le Gros** and **Heather Graham**) but Bob and Diane exist on a quivering knife's edge of criminal compulsion, always just one step ahead of the law – or less. Hours after Diane has safely buried their most recent haul, a narcotics squad rips that nice house to shreds in search of incriminating evidence, and Diane herself piquantly sums up the general drudgery of the outlaw lifestyle when she complains to her husband, "You won't fuck me and I always have to drive."

Bob isn't impotent, like the male half in *Bonnie And Clyde*; rather, he's always so amped up by the tantalizing prospect of his next job or befogged by his latest fix that he can't spare a moment for his lithe bride's advances. Perhaps his depressed libido is simply a side effect of opiate dependency, but it's also part and parcel of Bob's ascetic sensibilities. As Van Sant winkingly indicates with an early close-up on a Virgin Mary figurine, Bob approaches addiction as a quasi-religious vocation with its own litany of superstitions and portents – a hat on a bed, to take the most extreme example, begets a fifteen-year hex. Nadine's fatal overdose isn't merely a tragedy but a sign that Bob must lead a "virtuous life". The link between dependence and devotion becomes most explicit in the casting of **William S. Burroughs**, patron saint of junkie literature (a category that includes **James Fogle**'s autobiographical novel on which the film is based), as Father Tom Murphy, an opiate-addicted Catholic priest from Bob's boyhood.

Shot on location in Van Sant's adopted Portland, *Drugstore Cowboy* took top honours (best film and best director) from the National Society of Film Critics in a banner year for American cinema, during which **Spike Lee**'s controversial *Do The Right Thing* and **Steven Soderbergh**'s Palme d'Or-winning *sex, lies, and videotape* also debuted. The film's mainline success may have been due to – or in spite of – its refreshingly matter-of-fact approach to its subject matter. Van Sant, who co-adapted the screenplay with **Daniel Yost**, doesn't glamorize a drug-driven subculture and doesn't ensure a tidy redemption for Bob once he resolves

The needle and the damage done

American indie film has a special place in its heart for misfits, outsiders and fuck-ups of all stripes, many of whom seem hopelessly drawn to the hardest of hard drugs: heroin. Scag addicts come across as insufferable gabbers in early entries such as **Andy Warhol**'s *Chelsea Girls* (1966) and **Shirley Clarke**'s *The Connection* (1962). The drug trade is a perilous, even lethal alleyway in many blaxploitation films, and also in **Joshua Marston**'s *Maria Full Of Grace*, which was a hit at Sundance 2004. In 2000's *Requiem For A Dream*, heroin addiction is a one-way ticket to a tortuous living death; in *Drugstore Cowboy*, it's a figurative prison sentence – and the junkie doesn't get paroled once he kicks the habit, as **Matt Dillon**'s

hapless protagonist discovers. (*Drugstore Cowboy* director **Gus Van Sant** later helmed 2005's *Last Days*, a film that seems to internalize and mimic the heroin experience like no other.) It's not all cautionary tales and stairways to hell, however. Despite the prevailing angst and depravity in *Bad Lieutenant* (1992), the overwhelming bliss that washes over the title character as the drug enters his veins certainly speaks of its appeal. And in *Pulp Fiction* (1994), Vincent Vega's opiate fix is cross-cut with a dreamy nocturnal driving sequence that makes a heroin habit look positively groovy – that is, until his boss's wife mistakes the smack for nose candy, with infamous onscreen results.

to get clean; instead, his recovery is a form of penance. He takes a monotonous job working a drill press, rents a dreary bedsit and loses Diane to his protégé, Rick. When Diane gives her ex a pharmaceutical grab-bag, the gift occasions Bob's own Gethsemane moment – he neither ingests nor sells the drugs, but gives them to the delighted Father Tom, who promises Bob that such an act of kindness will earn him an indulgence. Bob's martyrdom is complete when he takes a beating and a bullet from David (**Max Perlich**), the same snivelling hood whom Bob could eat for breakfast back in his high cowboy era. Bruised and bleeding, Bob hits rock bottom, where he finds the serenity of the flagellants and saints; his stations of the cross are complete and so is the movie. As Bob puts it, "There's nothing more life-affirming than getting the shit kicked out of you."

Easy Rider

dir Dennis Hopper, 1969, 94m
cast Peter Fonda, Dennis Hopper, Jack Nicholson, Luke Askew *cin* Laszlo Kovacs *scr* Peter Fonda, Dennis Hopper, Terry Southern

"They're not scared of you," **Jack Nicholson** tells **Dennis Hopper**'s hairy, wild-eyed biker in *Easy Rider*. "They're scared of what you represent to 'em." Its symbolism as thick as its cannabis vapours, Hopper's epochal road trip achieved a monumental stature in the pop-cultural imagination. Long of hair and THC-enhanced, scorned and ultimately destroyed by the America that created them, travel buddies Billy (Hopper) and Wyatt, aka Captain America (**Peter Fonda**), epitomized the druggy rebellion of the 1960s drop-out generation. With their Wild West monikers and symbolic costumes – Wyatt, as in Earp, wraps himself in the Stars and Stripes, while Billy, as in the Kid, dons a mix of cowboy and Indian garb – the duo also epitomized a timeless Americana of frontier wanderlust and staunch individualism.

Despite its singular fame, *Easy Rider* was no one-off, but rather a confluence of already established trends and professional associations. Fonda, the film's producer and co-writer (with Hopper and *Dr.*

Billy and Captain America take the world in a love embrace

Strangelove scribe **Terry Southern**), starred in **Roger Corman**'s *The Wild Angels* (1966), which kick-started a trend for low-budget biker movies designed for the drive-in circuit. Hopper and Nicholson also had biker flicks under their belts: Hopper acted in *The Glory Stompers* (1967), also made by Corman's American-International Pictures (AIP), and Nicholson co-starred in *Hell's Angels On Wheels* (1967), which featured cinematography by future *Easy Rider* lensman **Laszlo Kovacs**. In *Hell's Angels,* Nicholson provided a kind of audience surrogate, a disgruntled emissary from the straight world who hitches a ride with the road warrior – a role that presaged his Oscar-nominated turn as the soused ACLU lawyer George Hanson in *Easy Rider.*

The first film to deploy a rock'n'roll soundtrack in lieu of a traditional score, *Easy Rider* also became the first independently financed film to be distributed by a major studio (Columbia), although the very possibility that a movie might emerge from the chaotic shoot was in doubt from the start. Hopper's drug-addled paranoia and occasional violence were serious liabilities, and reached an early nadir with a disastrous attempt to shoot footage in New Orleans during Mardi Gras. However, the director showed excellent instincts in casting non-professionals in small but crucial parts, especially the small-town Louisianans who serve as the lynch-mob chorus in the film's supremely uncomfortable diner scene. (Sample ad-lib: "You name it, I'll throw rocks at it, Sheriff.") Hopper also unleashed his impressive powers of persuasion while filming the psychedelic, warped cemetery sequence, when he convinced a reluctant Fonda to enact his real-life childhood grief over his mother's suicide while embracing a statue. Overall the acting in *Easy Rider* is surprisingly good – perhaps partly because of the cast's Method approach to their characters' pot consumption – and Kovacs' camerawork, sensitively attuned to the musical rhythms of the highway, lends a subliminal lyricism to a rough-and-tumble affair.

As Wyatt and Billy drift from desert commune to redneck hell, from whorehouse to graveyard, the movie celebrates its trio of transgressors, while at the same time lining up a violent end for each of them. Playing catch-up with a scene in time to announce its premature death, *Easy Rider* was at once a beginning and an ending: just as it heralded the counterculture's arrival in the mainstream and effectively launched the New Hollywood of the 1970s, the movie also bid a bitter farewell to an era, or maybe to a boyhood ideal, of America the Beautiful. As Fonda's disillusioned wanderer so famously puts it, "We blew it." Depending on the eye of the beholder, it either enhances *Easy Rider*'s dippy pathos or reinforces the film's sentimental nihilism that Captain America is rueing the loss of something that never existed.

Eraserhead

dir **David Lynch, 1977, 89m, b/w**
cast **John Nance, Charlotte Stewart, Judith Anna Roberts, Laurel Near** *cin* **Frederick Elmes, Herbert Cardwell** *scr* **David Lynch**

According to **David Lynch**, "*Eraserhead* is an American film, but it's a little bit in an in-between place. It's like a dirty, little, forgotten, hidden corner. And I love those areas. You can discover secrets."

A surreal chronicle of the tribulations of Henry Spencer (**John Nance**), a man bewildered by his strange circumstances on the industrial fringes of an unnamed city, *Eraserhead* transpires within an eerie, hermetic interworld, riddled with dirty secrets and uncanny phenomena. A smash hit on the midnight-movie circuit of the late 1970s, this black-and-white film masterfully sustains an unnerving nocturnal ambience over its ninety-minute running time. It was quite a feat, given that Lynch shot his first feature over four and a half years, filming only at night on a tiny, piecemeal budget cobbled together in part from American Film Institute funds (at one point, Lynch took on a paper round to make ends meet). As the director told Chris Rodley in *Lynch On Lynch* (1997), "There was one shot where Henry walks down the hallway, turns the doorknob and a year and a half later he comes through the door!"

A hunched, puzzled-looking fellow with an eraser-like flat top haircut, Henry works as a printer at a factory that dominates the film's grey, depopulated landscape, forever humming, clanking and hissing with mechanized noise. Summoned for a hellish dinner at the home of his girlfriend's parents, Henry receives the news that he's a father. But of what? "They're still not sure it is a baby!" cries Henry's horrified bride-to-be, Mary (**Charlotte Stewart**), of the slimy, goat-like thing they've conceived. Henry installs his instant family under the roof of his spartan apartment, but soon the kid's incessant cries drive Mary back to her parents. Left alone with the baby, Henry fantasizes about the beautiful woman across the hall and sees or imagines a pustule-ravaged lady who lives inside his radiator. As she shuffles around crooning an inane ditty ("In heaven, everything is fine…"), tiny foetus heads and umbilical cords rain down around her and somehow end up in Henry's bed – an unnerving sign of the permeable barrier between Henry's waking life and fantasy world.

Haunted by a constant, engine-like drone, *Eraserhead* inhabits an "in-between place": the setting is neither urban nor exactly remote, the mood implacably dream-like, while the ghastly baby epitomizes a Gothic *unheimlich*. Influenced by **Kafka**, one of Lynch's favourite writers, the movie expresses a studious disgust towards the human body and its processes, notably eating and reproduction; at the home of Mary's parents, whimpering puppies scrabble at their mother's teats and the roast-chicken dinner twitches and bleeds on the plate.

"I felt *Eraserhead*, I didn't think it," Lynch has claimed. Capable of nurturing many a psychoanalytic interpretation, the movie can be viewed as a portrait of the artist as a young man whose creative urges – his dream life, perhaps – collide with his familial duties. The theme may have had autobiographical resonances: the aspiring painter and filmmaker had to support a wife and baby by age 22 (Lynch's marriage broke up about a year into the movie's production). Although *Eraserhead* was shot in Los Angeles, **Jack Fisk**'s production design took its cue from Lynch's spell living with his spouse and infant daughter in a bleak, crime-ridden Philadelphia neighbourhood – indeed, Lynch has wryly called *Eraserhead* "my *Philadelphia Story*". The anxiety that the artist's imagination can be colonized by domestic drudgery is most viscerally imparted when Henry's head flies off his body (spirited away by a child to provide raw material for erasers) and the wailing baby's head pops up in its place. Incidentally, just how Lynch and his crew made the creature remains one of the best-kept secrets in American cinema, and the director insists he will never reveal the mechanics behind it – a refusal that only enhances the nightmarish mysteries of *Eraserhead*.

The Evil Dead

dir Sam Raimi, 1981, 85m

cast Bruce Campbell, Ellen Sandweiss, Hal Delrich, Betsy Baker, Sarah York *cin* Tim Philo *scr* Sam Raimi

"We were making what we thought was the quintessential drive-in movie," producer **Robert Tapert** has said of *The Evil Dead*, directed by his college buddy **Sam Raimi**. Stranding five friends in a remote cabin, where they discover a "Book of the Dead" and swiftly incur the wrath of the haunted woods surrounding them, Raimi's first feature was a rough-and-ready synthesis of horror conventions and iconography as they stood circa 1980. In addition to its echoes of *The Night Of The Living Dead* and **Herschell Gordon Lewis**'s drive-in gorefests, the movie explicitly aspired to the lineage established by **Tobe Hooper**'s landmark *Texas Chainsaw Massacre* (1974) and **Wes**

The cold hand of death: *The Evil Dead*

Craven's early screamers. Caked in blood and guts (and deploying splatter ingredients as exotic as semi-skimmed milk and creamed corn), *Evil Dead* also launched its own influential trilogy and pre-saged the mix of horror and comedy that Craven would master in his *Nightmare On Elm Street* and *Scream* series.

Raimi was barely 20 years old when shooting began in late 1979. But he had already helmed several Super 8 shorts with his high-school friends **Bruce Campbell**, *The Evil Dead*'s square-jawed star and co-executive producer, and **Ellen Sandweiss**, the brave soul whose character, Cheryl, is sexually violated by a swarm of vines and branches in the movie's most infamous sequence. Although it takes place during a single gruesome night, *Evil Dead* came together over the course of several years and locations – the piecemeal shoot would break up when money ran out and resume when new funds were found. Under these circumstances, the filmmakers were fortunate in one significant respect: once the extended overture was established – friends arrive at cabin, summon malevolent spirits, transform into the titular demons – they could recruit anyone available to play the fiends, given the identity-concealing make-up and negligible acting ability involved.

That's not to say that the birth of *The Evil Dead* was easy. Much of the movie was shot in an actual abandoned cottage in Tennessee with no running water (filming later shifted to Raimi's garage in Michigan); the production had zero money to spare for wardrobe designers, make-up artists, continuity staff or stuntmen; and most of the cast and crew absconded by Christmas 1979 with plenty yet to shoot. The scrappy let's-make-a-movie quality of *The Evil Dead* is part and parcel of its charm, and although some of its laughs are derived from the primitive means of production, Raimi and company intended a genre parody. In the early stages of the zombie mayhem, Campbell is an amusingly ineffectual hero – sitting uselessly on the couch or standing frozen with an axe as ghouls run riot around him – and characters go hilariously out of their way to leave themselves vulnerable. The botanical assault on Cheryl commences after she's strayed far from the cabin, alone in a skimpy nightgown, whimpering, "I know someone's out there!"

The Evil Dead routinely transcends its budget. One of the movie's signature devices, the sprinting point-of-view shot that the filmmakers dubbed "The Force", was achieved with nothing more elaborate than a camera bolted to a two-by-four. And the climactic sequence, in which the demons wither and disintegrate via stop-motion animation, looks all the more impressive in the post-CGI era for its painstaking, artisanal panache. The scene builds to a lunatic crescendo of accelerated putrefaction and exploding organs – a satisfying money shot, got on the cheap.

Faster, Pussycat! Kill! Kill!

dir **Russ Meyer, 1966, 83m, b/w**
cast **Tura Satana, Haji, Lori Williams, Susan Bernard, Stuart Lancaster, Paul Trinka** *cin* **Walter Schenk** *scr* **Jack Moran**

How to begin? "Ladies and gentlemen, welcome to violence: the word and the act. While violence cloaks itself in a plethora of disguises, its favourite mantle still remains – *sex*." A sober disclaimer from a deep voice of authority, intoned as the striations of the optical soundtrack quiver across the screen. CUT! A frenzied montage of go-go dancers, shot from low angles for maximized jiggle, their male audience crazed with desire, virtually electrocuted with lust for those bobbing breasts, those swivelling hips. CUT! A vampy girl in an open-top sports car cackles with malevolent glee as she roars through the California desert accompanied by urgent, sax-driven jazz.

Welcome to *Faster, Pussycat! Kill! Kill!* Exploitation-film pioneer **Russ Meyer** concisely described his lust-in-the-dust spectacle as "three tough girls who go out on a spree of kicking the crap out of people". Not to mention each other, since the movie's first skirmish is an undermotivated catfight between huge-eyed minx Rosie (**Haji**) and corn-fed blond Billie (**Lori Williams**). However, it's alpha broad Varla (**Tura Satana**) who is violence incarnate in *Faster, Pussycat*. She breaks a guy's neck (the queasying sound effect was achieved by cracking a walnut), instigates the kidnapping of the dead man's childish girlfriend (**Susan Bernard**) and sets her sights on relieving a wealthy desert misanthrope of his life and cash.

Jack Moran's script, from a story by Meyer, spills over with one-liners ("Would you like to look under my hood?" Billie purrs), and *Faster, Pussycat* adheres to a tightly packed schedule of car chases, cleavage shots, sand-swept tussles and yet more cleavage shots, climaxing with multiple deaths by car or blade. Consistently sensational, *Faster, Pussycat* is also incongruously beautiful. **Walter Schenk**'s

Tura Santana, woman on top

black-and-white cinematography is impeccably sharp and detailed, especially given the movie's softcore-trash market and the difficult shooting conditions presented by the Death Valley locations. Just as improbably, Meyer's scantily clad anti-heroines are complicated: they're the American male's wildest fantasy and his biggest nightmare. Meyer couldn't be mistaken for a feminist, yet his vision of an autonomous universe ruled by ample, horny, tough-talking women still carries a subversive kick.

Maybe *Faster, Pussycat* was ahead of its time. Despite the come-on of sex and boundary-pushing violence ("For the first time on screen we will see a woman kill a man with her bare hands," Meyer promised), it was one of the rare Meyer efforts to fail at the box office. Today, it's generally considered one of the twin peaks of his canon, alongside *Beyond The Valley Of The Dolls* (1970). Meyer-devotee **John Waters** led the campaign to enshrine *Faster, Pussycat* in his 1981 book *Shock Value*, declaring it "beyond a doubt, the best movie ever made". After the rockabilly-punk band the Cramps covered the theme song in 1983, *Faster, Pussycat* got a new lease of life: it provided a namesake for a 1980s metal band and exerted influence on **Quentin Tarantino** in *Kill Bill* (2003) (his fearsome DiVA squad descends directly from the Pussycats) and on Waters' trash oeuvre in its entirety, gaining a theatrical re-release in 1995.

Though Tura Satana is indisputably the karate-chopping queen of this jungle, it's Haji who gets the line that sums up the Pussycats in all their unhinged allure and iron-fisted will. Offered a soft drink, Rosie sneers in her inimitable south-of-the-border drawl, "We don't like nothing soft. Everything we touch is *hard*."

Gas, Food Lodging

dir **Allison Anders**, 1992, 98m
cast **Fairuza Balk, Ione Skye, Brooke Adams** *cin* **Dean Lent** *scr* **Allison Anders**

Allison Anders was the sole female member in the informal "Class of '92" of breakthrough independent directors, which included Quentin Tarantino (*Reservoir Dogs*), **Alexandre Rockwell** (*In The Soup*) and **Robert Rodriguez** (*El Mariachi*). (The four directors all collaborated in 1995 on the slapdash omnibus *Four Rooms*.) Among her contemporaries, Anders relied the least on established genre templates and seemed the most attuned to the mundane realities of working life, focusing attention on a family of female characters in *Gas, Food Lodging*.

Nora (**Brooke Adams**) is raising two teenage daughters in a trailer on a waitress' salary in Laramie, New Mexico, a tumbleweed town just off the highway. Trudi (**Ione Skye**) skips school and stays out late with boys, much to her angry mother's distress. Younger sister Shade (**Fairuza Balk**), who delivers the movie's voiceover, is more introverted; she whiles away afternoons at the local cinema watching Mexican melodramas starring the (fictional) diva Elvia Rivero (named after Anders' landlord). Various boys and men drift in and out of the family's day-to-day routines. Nora is trying to wrap up a dalliance with a married man, while Trudi meets a young English geologist and enjoys her first fulfilling sexual experience with him in a cave. Shade tries to seduce a friend, but has better luck with a young Mexican-American projectionist. She also longs for a father figure ("I knew what was missing from my life – a man!") and an intact family, a prospect that seems even more unlikely when pregnant Trudi moves out of the trailer. Shade makes brief, melancholy contact with her biological dad, but is also drawn to her mother's new boyfriend.

Anders loosely based *Gas, Food Lodging* on the novel *Don't Look And It Won't Hurt* (1973) by **Richard Peck**, but also infused the movie with her own autobiography. Like Trudi and Shade, she grew up the daughter of a single mother from a "trailer-trash" background. Like Trudi, she was gang-raped at an early age and became pregnant in her teens by a visiting student from England, and like Nora, Anders raised two daughters on her own. The future filmmaker was a single mother on welfare when she enrolled in the film program at UCLA, and a fan letter to **Wim Wenders** led to a correspondence and a job as a production assistant on Wenders' *Paris, Texas* (1984).

Gas, Food Lodging has its share of flaws – the dialogue and acting are broad, the camera setups and blocking inelegant, the ending abrupt – but it is refreshing in its heartfelt understatement and lack of sentimentality. *Gas, Food Lodging* wisely avoids striking any triumphal notes in compiling its characters' little victories and quietly absorbed disappointments. Dreams don't come true so much as they come just a little closer.

Go Fish

dir Rose Troche, 1994, 84m, b/w

cast Guinevere Turner, V.S. Brodie, T. Wendy McMillan, Anastasia Sharp *cin* Ann T. Rossetti *scr* Rose Troche, Guinevere Turner

Rose Troche's debut feature, *Go Fish*, is about the halting birth of a new relationship, but the film was almost derailed by a messy break-up. Troche co-wrote the script with her lover and lead actress, **Guinevere Turner**, but the Chicago production ground to a halt midway through filming after the pair's acrimonious split in late

1992. Shooting didn't resume again until the following spring, after consummate independent producer **Christine Vachon** and *Swoon* director **Tom Kalin** – both key figures in the New Queer Cinema movement – had come aboard as executive producers.

The New Queer Cinema was predominantly a male phenomenon with a pronounced outlaw sensibility (witness the hustlers, thieves and murderers who populate *Swoon*, Todd Haynes' *Poison* and Gregg Araki's *The Living End*); Troche's distaff contribution captured a lighter mood that hardly compromised its political motivations. "Lesbian lives and lesbian relationships barely exist on paper ... We begin to want to change history," says mother-hen intellectual Kia (**T. Wendy McMillan**) at the film's outset. *Go Fish* seeks to correct the historical record by inscribing Sapphic ardour into classical Hollywood romantic comedy. Shot on black-and-white 16mm film for next to nothing and performed with cheerful brio by non-professional actors (mostly friends of Troche and Turner), the movie sparked a Sundance bidding war – the first of its kind – and eventually grossed an impressive $2.4 million at the American box office.

Tomboyish Max (Turner) hasn't had a date in ten months, which she regards as a minor tragedy; she's set up with shy Ely (**V. S. Brodie**), but Ely is a bit "crunchy" for Max's tastes, and it turns out she's got a long-distance girlfriend. The rest of *Go Fish* delays the inevitable gratification of this girl-meets-girl scenario while dropping in on other members of Max and Ely's tight circle. Max's roommate, Kia, revels in an idyllic relationship with her girlfriend, Evy (**Migdalia Melendez**), but Evy is badly shaken when her ex-boyfriend outs her to her horrified mother. Ely's housemate, the sensuous Daria (**Anastasia Sharp**), sleeps with a guy and, in one of the film's several expressionist sequences, meets an imaginary mob of her angry fellow lesbians who believe that this one-night stand throws her sexual identity into serious doubt.

Notwithstanding the odd macho incursion (at one point, an unseen male voice bellows an epithet, swiftly met with Kia's authoritative "Fuck you!"), *Go Fish* illustrates both the comforts and constrictions of an essentially enclosed, self-sufficient world at odds with the tired norms of the dominant society but saddled with its own stereotypes and taboos. Creating a perfect negative image of a silver-screen history of love that has edited out queer desire, the movie also interrogates its own point of view.

On their first date, Max and Ely politely argue about the gay-themed movie they've just seen: Max feels that queer filmmakers have a responsibility to screen positive representations of gay and lesbian life, but Ely disagrees, arguing that it's more important for an artist to be true to his or her own experiences. Troche manages to do both, both satirizing and affirming lesbian culture, but also simply affirming its rights to visibility. Her erotic closing montage of kisses and caresses is a political statement in itself.

Kids

dir Larry Clark, 1995, 91m

cast Leo Fitzpatrick, Chloë Sevigny, Justin Pierce, Rosario Dawson *cin* Eric Edwards *scr* Harmony Korine

Strange though it may seem, **Larry Clark** intended *Kids* – his pseudo-*vérité* look at hormone-crazed, drug-addled teenagers wandering New York City in an aggressive, nihilistic daze – as family entertainment: "It's definitely a movie kids should be able to see with parents," he told the *St. Paul Pioneer Press*. The photographer-turned-director hoped that his first film would spark much-needed domestic discussion about what teenagers get up to when grown-ups aren't around. It would have appeared fortuitous, then, that *Kids*' intended distributor, Miramax, was a subsidiary of family-focused Disney, except for the Mouse House's policy against releasing NC-17 rated films; Miramax chairmen **Bob and Harvey Weinstein** had to set up an ad-hoc entity, Shining Excalibur, to release *Kids* unrated.

Released in US theatres at the same time as Calvin Klein's infamous "kiddie porn" TV commercials (featuring scantily clad, seemingly underage models), *Kids* was the most controversial movie of 1995, its jailbait jolts eliciting binary reactions. Rita Kempley in the *Washington Post* deemed the film "virtually child pornography disguised as a cautionary documentary" and an "irresponsible Little Bo Peep show", while, in contrast, the *New York Times*'s Janet Maslin hailed it as "a wake-up call to the world".

A day in the life of a loose-knit clan of wayward Manhattanites, the movie unravels as a floating conversation – adolescents at their leisure, talking trash about fucking and each other, while the escalating storyline is punctuated by the occasional sex (or rape) scene. The kids inhabit a world unto themselves and pointedly, the sole parental appearance is by a woman who smokes while breast-feeding. The film's slender narrative through-line is provided by Jennie (**Chloë Sevigny**), whose air of level-headed calm sets her apart from her braying, sex-obsessed peers. She's perhaps unique among her friends for only having had intercourse once, with Telly (**Leo Fitzpatrick**), the self-proclaimed "virgin surgeon" whose idea of safe sex is to limit his partners to first-timers. After Jennie discovers she is HIV-positive, and as day stretches into night, she combs New York City looking for Telly before he plucks his next candidate, or victim.

We're the kids in America

Both positive and negative reviews of *Kids* tended to refer to its *"vérité"* aspirations, and Clark encouraged the movie's reception as virtual reportage on troubled urban youth. "This film was written from the inside by a young man," Clark said, referring to **Harmony Korine** (now a director in his own right), who was still in his teens when he began writing the *Kids* script; the pair met in Washington Square Park where Clark was photographing young skateboarders, many of whom appeared in the film. However inadvertently, *Kids* is an expressionist work, and not just for its characters' libidinous monomania. A park scene in which a man gets beaten to pulp by a mob in broad daylight (with skateboards, no less) is boldly ridiculous, as is the notion that a leering, swollen-tongued kicker of cats like Telly could seduce so many willing young ladies.

Kids' most notable achievement might have been the casting of Sevigny, soon to be an indie-film axiom, in her first screen role. Heart-bruised and watchful, Sevigny's Jennie hovers ethereally above the movie's moist, smutty fray – until, that is, she's subjected to the film's crowning indignity. When Telly's pal Casper (**Justin Pierce**) blinks into the light of the morning after and slurs out the film's last line, "Jesus Christ, what happened?", chances are that the viewer feels as burnt-out and befogged as he does.

The Living End

dir Gregg Araki, 1992, 84m
cast Mike Dytri, Craig Gilmore, Darcy Marta *cin, scr*
Gregg Araki

Like a couple of its colleagues in the early-1990s onrush of provocative gay American cinema, *The Living End* hones in on the warped, violent bond between a pair of criminal lovers who are at turns glamorous and repellent. But while **Todd Haynes** in *Poison* (1991) and **Tom Kalin** in *Swoon* (1992) observed their outlaw outsiders through the intellectual prisms of semiotics, psychoanalysis and queer theory, *The Living End* is a rough-hewn road movie running on the pungent fumes of hormonal fury, further intensified by the ravages of the AIDS crisis. Declaring itself in the opening credits as "an irresponsible movie

by **Gregg Araki**", the film brandishes its adolescent nihilism like a
badge of honour – a stance that could be gleaned from its working
title, *Fuck The World*. Eager to bite the hand that feeds, Araki even
plants a red flag in front of any film journalists in the audience when
his co-lead character, Jon (**Craig Gilmore**), himself a movie critic,
declares, "Those who can't do, teach; those who can't teach, get paid
25 cents a word to rip other people's work to shreds."

   As *The Living End* begins, Jon has just tested positive for HIV, still a
virtual death sentence in 1992. He hasn't yet met Luke (**Mike Dytri**),
a hustler-drifter who's also HIV-positive and also having a hell of a
week. After narrowly escaping death at the hands of a nasty lesbian
couple, Luke avails himself of their car and gun, hooks up with a
married man soon to be stabbed to death by his jealous wife and shoots

Love and other catastrophes: Mike Dytri (top) and Craig Gilmore in *The Living End*

dead a few gay-bashers (one wears a *Drugstore Cowboy* T-shirt, another wears a *sex, lies, and videotape* top). He thinks he might have killed a cop, too. Luke also finds time to sleep with the mild-mannered Jon, who, for reasons he can't articulate, drops everything and hits the highway with this scary slice of beefcake, heading in the general direction of San Francisco. Their only contact with the outside world is Jon's occasional collect calls to a concerned friend, Darcy (**Darcy Marta**).

"I have this vision of you as this vampire – you're sucking the life force out of me," Jon tells Luke during one of their many vicious spats. The duo's love-hate relationship often seems simply hate-hate, but the sex is pretty good, and Jon's anger and despair find a channel through Luke's nothing-to-lose madness (Luke suggests at one point that they detour to Washington and "blow Bush's brains out"). Meanwhile, Luke's murderous impulses reveal themselves as a death wish projected outwards; he becomes increasingly obsessed with suicide and asks Jon more than once to kill him.

Written, directed, shot and edited by Araki with all the subtlety and finesse of a claw hammer, the movie revels in its dirty-mouthed incorrectness; from its early roll call of penis slang – "pussy plunger", "baloney pony, smiling meat puppet…" – to its climactic, abortive collision of Eros and Thanatos. Although it's tame compared with the various outrages perpetrated in Araki's subsequent teen trilogy, *Totally Fucked Up* (1993), *The Doom Generation* (1995) and *Nowhere* (1997), *The Living End* embodies a no-exit vision of gay-punk youth rebellion, writ with blood and larger than life. Jon's voiceover couldn't have put it better: "Live fast, die young, leave a beautiful corpse – yeah right. Death is weird."

El Mariachi

dir Robert Rodriguez, 1992, 81m

cast Carlos Gallardo, Consuelo Gómez, Peter Marquardt, Reinol Martinez *cin, scr* Robert Rodriguez

El Mariachi will forever be "The $7,000 Movie". Some films camouflage or overcome their budgets, but in no other instance in Hollywood history has the price tag of a studio-distributed product

One of *El Mariachi*'s two thousand-plus shots

dictated both its aesthetic and its marketing hook. The fruits of **Robert Rodriguez**'s frugal labours exert a certain primal force and infectious energy, but cheapness is its *raison d'être*. More than a movie, *El Mariachi* is a proof and a case study: it is theoretically possible to direct a feature for seven grand, and here's how you do it. At this juncture, sceptics will quite empirically point out that Columbia Pictures came up with some $200,000 in post-production costs, plus untold publicity campaign funds, on behalf of *El Mariachi*, which nonetheless remains in perpetuity "The $7,000 Movie".

The dedicated Rodriguez raised a chunk of the film's budget while acting as a medical-research subject at an Austin hospital, where he recruited fellow patient **Peter Marquardt** to play the movie's drug lord, Moco, despite the fact that Marquardt didn't

The lowest of the low: bottom-dollar budgets

Tight, scarce or non-existent finances are part and parcel of American independent cinema, but only from the 1990s could a laughably low budget become a movie's selling point. The $7,000 price tag for *El Mariachi* is to Amerindie film what Roger Bannister's four-minute mile is to track and field, and many a cineaste has sought in vain to match or underbid **Robert Rodriguez**'s feat. The writer **Joe Queenan** tried, failed and wrote a book instead, called *The Unkindest Cut: How A Hatchet-Man Critic Made His Own $7,000 Movie And Put It All On His Credit Card*. **Kevin Smith** made *Clerks* (1994) for an initial budget of about $27,000 and **Edward Burns** came in at $23,800 for *The Brothers McMullen* (1995), which he shot at weekends over a period of eight months. **Shane Carruth** matched Rodriguez at $7,000 for *Primer* (2004) (and that's without adjusting for inflation) and **Jonathan Caouette** set a new benchmark with his three-figure budget for *Tarnation* (2003).

Of course, these fantastical numbers don't tell the whole story, as **Christine Vachon** points out in *Shooting To Kill* (1998): "Bogus low figures are widely circulated as macho badges of indie honor, and then used to make everyone else feel as if they're not resourceful enough." A suspiciously low figure doesn't factor in post-production costs like a 35mm blow-up, soundtrack rights, ADR (additional dialogue recording) and other necessities that, in the case of *Clerks*, swelled the total budget by some $200,000. And, of course, a studio might spend additional millions on a publicity campaign – the kind that will get everyone buzzing about that terrific little movie that only cost a few grand.

speak a word of Spanish. Rodriguez cast his friend and co-producer **Carlos Gallardo** as the titular musician, who arrives in the little town of Jimenez, Mexico looking for an honest day's work, but is mistaken by Moco for the killer Azul (**Reinol Martinez**, then a medical student), who carries his weapons in a guitar case. The guileless strummer spends the rest of the film on the run from various heavies without actually leaving town, and in the meantime takes an interest in sultry barkeep Domino (**Consuelo Gómez**).

The fast, resourceful director built no sets and paid no actors. He shot the film alone (his book about the making of *El Mariachi* is called *Rebel Without A Crew*); the dialogue was recorded after filming because he had to do without sound recording, his lighting scheme consisted of a few 250-watt bulbs and the performers wore the same clothes from scene to scene to pre-empt any continuity problems. A dolly shot consisted of Rodriguez holding the camera and being pushed in a wheelchair borrowed from the local hospital; a crane shot was achieved with nothing more elaborate than a ladder. Rodriguez had to make do with an undersized camera stand – a contraption he grew to like, because the resulting low-angle shots made the bad guys appear larger and more menacing. Similarly, the limited means of production enforced the movie's signature trait: a blistering pace, with more than 2,000 cuts in just eighty minutes. The cuts largely served to disguise mistakes, to hide the many occasions when the dialogue falls out of sync with the image and to keep the film racing along so quickly that the eye will overlook a mismatched axis or a backfired squib.

The director assumed his movie was heading straight for the Spanish-language home video market, but then *El Mariachi* won the Columbia distribution deal as well as the Audience Award at Sundance in 1992. Rodriguez is now firmly ensconced in the big-budget Hollywood ranks, but *El Mariachi* continues to be a creative and financial wellspring: *Desperado* (1995) was essentially a big-budget remake of *El Mariachi*, and *Once Upon A Time In Mexico* (2003) was a semi-sequel to *Desperado*. That fabled seven grand may be posting returns for many years to come.

Mean Streets

dir Martin Scorsese, 1973, 110m
cast Harvey Keitel, Robert De Niro, David Proval, Richard Romanus, Amy Robinson, Cesare Danova *cin* Kent Wakeford *scr* Martin Scorsese, Mardik Martin

In the opening-credit sequence of *Mean Streets*, weathered home movies flicker onscreen to the lovelorn thump of the Ronettes' "Be My Baby", and then the projector turns to cast its light straight into the shot. It's clear from the start of **Martin Scorsese**'s propulsive third feature that he's also making a home movie of sorts, training his camera on himself and his circle. As he put it years later, "In my

Car, trouble: Harvey Keitel in *Mean Streets*

mind, it's not really a film, it's a declaration of who I am and how I was living."

Scorsese's alter ego in *Mean Streets* is Charlie (**Harvey Keitel**), a young man still living at home in New York's Little Italy (where Scorsese grew up from the age of 7). Charlie's religious devotion and introspection set him slightly apart from his pals Tony (**David Proval**), who runs a bar, Michael (**Richard Romanus**), a loanshark, and Johnny Boy (**Robert De Niro**), a walking powder keg who's introduced blowing up a mailbox. Johnny has a big mouth and owes money all over town, and Charlie's always making excuses for him, buying him time. Acting as his protector is a means of atonement for Charlie, whose conscience speaks in Scorsese's own voice: "You don't make up for your sins in church – you do it in the streets."

Here, the streets are paved and policed by organized crime. Charlie's uncle Giovanni (**Cesare Danova**), the local mob boss, is grooming his eager nephew to take over a restaurant, but warns him away from Johnny as well as Johnny's cousin, Teresa (**Amy Robinson**), with whom Charlie is having a clandestine affair. (Teresa has epilepsy, but in Giovanni's cruelly inaccurate estimation she is "sick in the head".) Since Charlie's professional future hinges on casting aside the two people he's closest to, he would seem to be lamentably well-acquainted – as are many of Scorsese's characters – with Catholicism's toxic twins, Guilt and Shame. The religious imperative behind *Mean Streets* is further bolstered for taking place during the Feast of San Gennaro, an annual event that, as Scorsese has noted, creates an "intense carnival atmosphere" in which "emotions get heightened". (Though the film epitomizes the grit and hustle of 1970s Little Italy, Scorsese only shot in New York for six days; most of the interiors were filmed in Los Angeles.) The wages of sin are frighteningly real to Charlie, who often holds his fingers to a flame, trying to imagine "the pain of hell". (His Gethsemane scene comes when he and Johnny take brief refuge in the cemetery of Old St. Patrick's Cathedral.)

Scorsese's mode is breathless and kinetic, whether the camera is chasing Johnny down the street or strapped to Keitel and undercranked to mimic his drunken character's disoriented stumbling. Largely episodic, the movie conjures the mood and texture of Charlie's shapeless days and antic nights, the ribbing and joshing among friends (Abbott and Costello are clearly the forefathers of Charlie and Johnny's ping-pong comic rapport), the boozy time-killing and unwarned punctuations of brawls or gunfire. The undercurrent of narrative momentum, and of seeping dread, derives from Johnny's seemingly suicidal insolence as he sinks deeper and deeper into debt and then spits in the face of his angry creditors, while the loyal Charlie stands helplessly by. The film implicitly begs an urgent, and perhaps impossible, question: how do you define a moral code and adhere to it amid the corruption and brutality of your environment? "St. Francis of Assisi had it all down," Charlie explains – and so does Scorsese in *Mean Streets*, an act of catharsis for a filmmaker only just beginning an astonishing career.

Medium Cool

dir Haskell Wexler, 1969, 110m

cast Robert Forster, Verna Bloom, Peter Bonerz, Harold Blankenship *cin, scr* Haskell Wexler

In 1968, embarking on his first full-length feature as director, the cinematographer **Haskell Wexler** began to build a film around the footage he might capture at the upcoming Democratic National Convention in his hometown of Chicago. Wexler had an informed hunch that havoc lay in store, and his prediction proved to be horribly accurate. Brutal police tactics condoned by **Mayor Richard Daley** provoked a riot in which cops clubbed and tear-gassed antiwar protesters. Inside the Chicago International Amphitheatre, the head of the Colorado delegation demanded, "Is there any rule under which Mayor Daley can be compelled to suspend the police-state terror being perpetrated at this minute on kids in front of the Conrad Hilton?"

Resonant moments such as this abound in *Medium Cool*, Wexler's innovative, often elliptical hybrid of activist reportage, *cinéma vérité* and fiction. The movie's name refers to media theorist Marshall McLuhan's designation of television as a "cool medium", meaning one that requires viewers to apply their own knowledge and interpretive skills to the broadcast image. (For instance, Wexler presents, without commentary or context, startling footage of the Illinois National Guard in the midst of a "war game" or a staged demonstration in which soldiers rehearse how to handle unruly protesters.) But the titular phrase could also pertain to protagonist John Cassellis (**Robert Forster**, in a role originally intended for John Cassavetes), a TV cameraman who approaches his craft with practised detachment. In the film's opening minutes, he shoots the scene of a car accident and, task completed, strides away untroubled. In another early sequence, a soundman half-jokingly describes himself as "an elongation of a tape recorder", suggesting that a certain mechanized estrangement between one's work and one's emotions might be a professional necessity for the TV-news crewman, especially in such a convulsive year as 1968. (Democratic presidential candidate **Robert F. Kennedy** was assassinated during pre-production, and Wexler incorporates the death of both Kennedy and the recently slain **Martin Luther King, Jr.** into the movie.)

Over the course of *Medium Cool*, John's icy demeanour starts to thaw – foremost because of his deepening relationship with Eileen (**Verna Bloom**), a single mother transplanted from Appalachia to the Chicago slums with her young son, Harold (**Harold Blankenship**), but also due to a series of events that force John to confront his professional ethics. A tense encounter with some black activists moves John to consider the taint of exploitation on his lens, and he's enraged to discover that his television station has been sharing their footage with the police and FBI.

Wexler pitched *Medium Cool* on the fertile middle ground between fiction and documentary. He would often let his actors talk in their own words, preserving all the imperfect phrasings, rhythms and cross-talk of real, spontaneous speech. Most audaciously, in the film's celebrated last half-hour, Wexler injects a fictional character into a tumultuous historical episode *as it is happening*, when Eileen goes in search of her missing son only to become enmeshed in the bloody convention riots. It's in this final movement that Wexler most overtly acknowledges the influence of **Jean-Luc Godard**: the fatal auto accident that brings *Medium Cool* full-circle echoes the tragic finale of 1963's *Contempt*, and when Eileen walks past a seemingly endless line of military jeeps, armoured personnel carriers and National Guardsmen, it conjures up the famous traffic-jam scene in 1967's *Weekend*. Here and elsewhere in *Medium Cool*, Wexler, his actors and their characters take on the traits of fearless combat correspondents, reporting from the front lines of an occupied city in a nation at war with itself.

Memento

dir Christopher Nolan, 2000, 113m, b/w and colour
cast Guy Pearce, Carrie-Anne Moss, Joe Pantoliano, Mark Boone Junior, Stephen Tobolowsky *cin* Wally Pfister
scr Christopher Nolan

A backward-spooling *noir* about grief, revenge and short-term memory loss, *Memento* was perhaps the most heartening independent-film success story of 2001. After every studio and independent distributor rejected **Christopher Nolan**'s second feature, the Newmarket Capital Group – which had provided funding for the production – decided to self-distribute the movie with a masterful slow-build campaign. *Memento* eventually became an art-house smash, earning some of the year's most ecstatic reviews, a Sundance screenwriting prize and the admiration of one **Steven Soderbergh** (who executive-produced Nolan's next film, *Insomnia*, in 2002).

"When we were trying to put *Memento* out there," the British-born Nolan told this writer in 2002, "all of the things that made the film distinctive, and that eventually made it very successful, were the things that the independent distributors were afraid of, which was pathetic – I mean, that's what they're *there* for." *Memento*'s most distinguishing characteristic, shared with **Harold Pinter**'s play *Betrayal* (1978), is its reverse chronology. The film also weaves in monochrome expositional sequences that move forward but

Leonard Shelby (Guy Pearce) reviews his notes in *Memento*

The quiet man: Bob Berney

Bob Berney has been the chief operator behind an array of significant Amerindie films of the 1990s and 2000s, while maintaining an endearingly low-key profile. A *Variety* portrait called him "soft-spoken, relaxed and more than a little disarming" – not the adjectives usually used to describe movie executives, especially if they're involved in controversy-courting productions such as *Happiness* (1998) and *The Passion Of The Christ* (2004). Berney got his start as an art-house programmer and cinema owner in Texas. His career breakthrough came when he was chosen to head the marketing and distribution campaign for **Todd Solondz**'s *Happiness*; he was then recruited into a similar role by Newmarket for the release of **Christopher Nolan**'s *Memento*.

The next year, IFC lured Berney away to head their new theatrical division, where he released the smash hit *My Big Fat Greek Wedding* (2002) as well as several foreign-language hits. Back at Newmarket, the fearless Berney backed a series of sensation-seekers, including **Mel Gibson**'s contentious blockbuster *The Passion Of The Christ*, *The Woodsman* (2004), starring **Kevin Bacon** as a convicted paedophile trying to readjust to the outside world after serving his prison term, and *Monster* (2003), the serial-killer melodrama that won leading lady **Charlize Theron** an Oscar and a Golden Globe – the actress praised Berney as a "genius" from the Golden Globes stage. Berney is, at the time of writing, head of Picturehouse, the Time Warner indie division that essentially replaced Fine Line in 2005.

transpire in the past (and come replete with flashbacks), so that the backward-moving colour sequences eventually catch up with the black-and-white scenes.

Shot in 25 days and based on a short story, "Memento Mori", written by the director's brother, Jonathan Nolan, the film opens with what would be the climax of a conventionally structured film: Leonard Shelby (**Guy Pearce**), seeking vengeance against the man who raped and murdered his wife, kills his suspiciously altruistic right-hand man, Teddy (**Joe Pantoliano**). Brain-damaged in the same attack that left his wife dead, Leonard cannot make new memories, and keeps tabs on his ongoing amateur murder investigation – not to mention his moment-to-moment circumstances – with snapshots and constant jottings; he's even innovated the permanent tattoo as Post-It note. As the narrative regresses, Leonard also encounters Natalie (**Carrie-Anne Moss**), a sad-eyed helpmate turned femme fatale.

Although *Memento*'s reverse configuration provided a ready-made marketing hook, it's no mere gimmick. The movie may confuse on first viewing, but the net effect is empathic: the viewer plunges into Leonard's befogged perspective and sinks or swims along with him. Like many of the best *noirs*, *Memento* is an existential investigation:

the monomaniacal protagonist inhabits a world without time where character and audience alike are left to helplessly contemplate what has already happened. Leonard's constant mental backtracking also provides for plenty of droll humour, as when he suddenly finds himself running at full tilt and muses in voiceover, "So what am I doing? I'm chasing this guy. No, he's chasing me."

His "condition", as Leonard calls it, is also a piercing metaphor for the deranging properties of grief. Like any sorrowful lover, Leonard is overwhelmingly defined by a past event that froze his life and mind in one awful moment. Yet he's also a blank slate, and the seedy denizens of his LA circuit of dive bars and discount motels are all too happy to write all over him for their own purposes. Leonard can't trust anyone or anything – not even himself or his own "evidence" – and neither can we.

However, there's one quibble about this ingeniously conceived film (raised by *Salon*'s Charles Taylor among others): if Leonard can remember nothing that's happened since his attack, how does he remember that he has a "condition"? The question rankles a bit, but it only spoils *Memento*'s manifold pleasures and puzzles if you assume that this definitively unreliable narrator doesn't have a few gaps in his story himself.

Metropolitan

dir **Whit Stillman, 1990, 98m**

cast **Edward Clements, Chris Eigeman, Carolyn Farina, Taylor Nichols, Elizabeth Thompson** *cin* **John Thomas**
scr **Whit Stillman**

For his movie debut, like many a first-timer, **Whit Stillman** wrote what he knew. *Metropolitan* whiles away the short days and long nights of one Christmas vacation "not so long ago" with the university-age scions of the Upper East Side aristocracy, home for a few weeks of debutante balls and "after-parties". Direct descendent of William the Conqueror, great-grandson of the first president of Citibank and son of an aide to Franklin Roosevelt, Stillman was heir to the kind of plush WASP demi-monde depicted in *Metropolitan* until the age of 14, when his mother and father divorced. In the movie, Stillman's alter ego is Tom Townsend (**Edward Clements**), whose parents have split and whose trust fund has evaporated. One winter's evening, quite by happenstance, Tom gains entry into the Park Avenue deb circuit as an "escort".

To most viewers, this will be exotic terrain – old-money thorough-breds in their natural habitat – and it's Tom who locates our point of view: he provides an insider's knowledge but with the critical stance of the outsider, which in his case is complicated by a sense of disenfran-chisement. Stillman affably ribs his wealthy characters for their assorted vanities and juvenile myopia, but never belittles them for their profit-able accident of birth. (This clique is surprising for their genteel con-sistency: in one pleasingly dry joke, an inter-title announces the start of "Orgy Week", which the kids kick off with a game of bridge.)

Stillman casts the sharpest eye on his less privileged stand-in, who's marked out by his red hair, socialist politics, use of public transportation and his raincoat in winter ("It has a lining," Tom points out more than once). He is a benign hypocrite, declaring his opposition to debutante parties "in principle", while attending those selfsame debutante parties as escort to sweet, pretty Audrey (**Carolyn Farina**). He's demonstrably silly ("You don't have to have read a book to have an opinion on it," he explains). He's also emotion-ally nearsighted, unaware that his hopeless infatuation with Serena Slocum (**Elizabeth Thompson**) is an embarrassment to both himself and to Audrey, who's nursing a crush on him.

It's a credit to Whitman's gifts of characterization that Tom is as infuriating and as loveable as any smart, decent kid in the throes of late adolescence. So is Nick (**Chris Eigeman**), who possesses light-ning wit, bad judgment and endless snap opinions ("The Surrealists were all a bunch of social climbers"). And so is Charlie (**Taylor Nichols**), who fancies Audrey and frets without end about the "downward mobility" of "the whole preppie class" – what he prefers to call the UHB, or Urban Haute Bourgeoisie. Ostensibly, Charlie suffers from a case of morbid entitlement, but his affliction is far more youth-universal: in a brilliantly scripted conversation with a slightly older WASP, Charlie gives strong hints that he prefers a safely predetermined guarantee of failure than the daunting uncertainty of adult choices and responsibilities.

Christmas break can't last forever. Tom and Charlie find them-selves cut adrift from the "rat pack" even before year's end. After

Tom finally sees the light about Audrey, they cast themselves as knights errant on a mission to the Hamptons to track the damsel down. None of the three quite fit their prescribed social context, and the movie's exhilarated final movement cuts them loose from the stifling UHB salon; the hopeful last shot of *Metropolitan* suggests that they're closing a circle all their own.

Near Dark

dir **Kathryn Bigelow, 1987, 95m**
cast **Adrian Pasdar, Jenny Wright, Bill Paxton, Lance Henriksen, Tim Thomerson, Jenette Goldstein** *cin* **Adam Greenberg** *scr* **Eric Red, Kathryn Bigelow**

One of the most endearing aspects of *Near Dark*, which relocates the vampire myth to the American southwest, is how it internalizes the hormonally exaggerated drama of teenage romance. This is a milieu where making out, making curfew and making a good impression on your girlfriend's clique are life-altering propositions. Caleb (**Adrian Pasdar**) is a bored boy from the sticks who, one empty evening, lays eyes upon Mae (**Jenny Wright**), a luscious blond licking an ice-cream cone. "You've never met a girl like me," she tells him repeatedly, but is it an invitation or a warning? He takes the bait, gets the kiss of undeath and is suddenly conscripted into a posse of vampires, who roar around the dusty hinterlands killing for food and kicks, and starting the odd fire or fistfight. Meanwhile, Caleb's father (**Tim Thomerson**), who proves to be crucially handy with emergency transfusions, hunts down the gang with Caleb's little sister in tow.

Co-written by director **Kathryn Bigelow** and **Eric Red**, the movie melds familiar genres to produce an original alchemy, mixing *Nosferatu* (1922) and *Mad Max* with elements of the Western: Caleb is introduced in a cowboy hat and, in a beautifully cornball moment, rides backlit on horseback through a mist of dry ice. *Near Dark* becomes an all-out horror movie during a lengthy, brutal set piece in a roadhouse, where the vampires linger sadistically over the slaughter of all the assembled humans (the bartender suffers death by spur). The immortal executioners have all the time in the world, but the night is never as young as it seems – Caleb's new pals always lose track of the hours, and end up in a mad dash for shelter as the scorching dawn approaches.

Pumped up with roaring guitars (courtesy of **Tangerine Dream**) and hurtling towards a fiery climax, *Near Dark* carefully assembles a motley crew of ghouls. Severen (**Bill Paxton**) is a wild-eyed yahoo with a Schwarzenegger-esque one-liner for every occasion. Gore on his hands? "Finger-lickin' good!" A hotel clerk about to be blown away? "Check-out time!" As Jesse, the crew's unofficial leader, **Lance Henriksen** has the ancient gaze and fine-carved haggardness of a soul old enough to have served in the American Civil War. (In the role of Diamondback, Jesse's eternal squeeze, **Jenette Goldstein**,

An average night out for the *Near Dark* gang

rounds out Near Dark's triumvirate of *Aliens* alumni – Paxton and Henriksen also appeared in the 1986 blockbuster, directed by Bigelow's future ex-husband, James Cameron.)

Released the same year as **Joel Schumacher**'s silly sleeper hit *The Lost Boys*, *Near Dark* failed at the box office, though it won a strong reputation on home video. Maybe there wasn't room enough in 1987 – several years before the 1990s vogue for vampire flicks – for two movies about a teenager wrested from his family into a gang of blood-sucking hellraisers. But Bigelow's version is a far superior metaphor for chaotic adolescence. Mae is a literally cold-blooded killer, but she's also a histrionic, dippy kid, forever imploring the befuddled Caleb, "Listen … to the night … It's deafening!" Caleb's craving for arterial wine leaves him looking like a heroin addict in the throes of withdrawal, but he fights madly against his natural urges, which provides *Near Dark* with its best sight gag: instead of a sex scene, the movie gives us Caleb sucking rhythmically on Mae's slit wrist.

Night Of The Living Dead

dir George A. Romero, 1968, 96m, b/w

cast Duane Jones, Judith O'Dea, Karl Hardman, Marilyn Eastman *cin* George A. Romero *scr* John A. Russo, George A. Romero

Nineteen sixty-eight was one of the most tumultuous years in American history. Riots raged in Baltimore, Cleveland and Washington, DC. Police clashed with student activists at Columbia University and with protesters at the Democratic National Convention in Chicago. Assassins shot **Martin Luther King, Jr.** and **Robert Kennedy**, and hundreds of Vietnamese civilians died at the hands of American soldiers at My Lai. Added to all this bloodshed, noted the *Chicago Tribune*'s F. Richard Ciccone in 1996, "there was the death of the extraordinarily prosperous, comfortable postwar period … It died in a collision of cultures and a lasting dissolution of American trust in the institutions that nurtured them."

As if rising from the burning wreckage of the American dream, *Night Of The Living Dead* appeared towards year's end, offering an apocalyptic vision of flesh-eating zombies rampaging through the heartland. As J. Hoberman and Jonathan Rosenbaum write in *Midnight Movies*, **George A. Romero**'s low-budget frightener "was not only an instant horror classic, but a remarkable vision of the late sixties – offering the most literal possible depiction of America devouring itself."

Most of the movie's action centres on a deserted Pennsylvania farmhouse, where Barbra (**Judith O'Dea**) seeks shelter after a ghoul attacks her and her doomed brother in a cemetery. Ben (**Duane Jones**) arrives shortly thereafter and takes charge, boarding up the windows and fending off the gathering army of the night as a stunned Barbra becomes almost as catatonic as the predators outside. When another group of refugees materializes out of the basement, cowardly Harry (**Karl Hardman**, also a producer) poses an inept challenge to Ben's authority, though Harry's wife (**Marilyn Eastman**) disapproves: "Those people aren't our enemies," she scolds her husband, underscoring the war within their ranks.

Night Of The Living Dead was shot in thirty days over the course of nine months with the crew often pulling double duty as members of the cast. (Production manager **George Kosana**, who plays Sheriff McClelland, improvised the endlessly quotable line, "Yeah, they're dead, they're all messed up.") The hectic, stripped-down nature of the production intensified the black-and-white film's raw urgency. Director Romero, who also served as cinematographer, co-writer and co-editor, sometimes positions the camera as if it's listening in from behind a piece of furniture or over a character's shoulder, which adds to the movie's fly-on-the-wall immediacy, as do the expository snatches of panicked radio and TV reports.

Romero claims modestly that the harried production team never intended *Night Of The Living Dead* as a bleak national allegory, but then again, he did run his director's credit beneath a shot of the Stars and Stripes fluttering above a grave. Ben's group fends off the staggering mob with Molotov cocktails – then, as now, a device associated with guerrilla warfare and violent protest – but to no avail: brother feasts on sister, child snacks on father, the cute young couple gets burned alive and law-enforcement officials shoot anything that moves. The heroic African-American Ben emerges as sole survivor of the all-night buffet, only to get a cop's bullet between the eyes at daybreak; in the racially explosive America of the 1960s, the allegorical significance of a black man shot down in cold blood by a member of an all-white posse would be difficult to overstate. A grainy montage of newspaper-quality photographs provides the quietly shocking coda, communicating Ben's fate as hard-news reportage.

Frequently cited as the most influential horror film of all time, Romero's debut feature has spawned three fine sequels and informed untold numbers of other zombie parables (most recently the British hit *Shaun Of The Dead*, 2004, and **Joe Dante**'s protest of the second American war in Iraq, *Homecoming*, 2005). *Night Of The Living Dead* ends in flames, and its ever-mutable metaphor for the contemporary American condition shows no signs of burning out.

One False Move

dir Carl Franklin, 1992, 105m
cast Cynda Williams, Bill Paxton, Billy Bob Thornton, Michael Beach, Earl Billings, Jim Metzler *cin* James L. Carter *scr* Billy Bob Thornton, Tom Epperson

A pretty young woman in a sexy frock arrives at the party of some friends in Los Angeles. She steps out almost as soon as she arrives, making some excuse, and two men – one black, one white – burst through the open door, brandishing weapons and demanding to see someone named Marco. Minutes later, the white man and the woman are at the home of said Marco, who receives a kick in the teeth after his girlfriend is doused with lighter fluid and menaced with a flame. Back at the first house, the black man walks over to one of his bound-and-gagged hostages, places a pillowcase over her head and stabs her to death as she squeals in agony and her housemates writhe and moan in horror. On the television set behind them, camcorder footage from the interrupted party plays on.

We are only eight minutes into *One False Move*, which is about as far as some viewers ever got. Director **Carl Franklin** later reported that his own agent walked out of a screening after this brutal overture (Franklin added that this individual wasn't his agent for much

One False Move star and screenwriter Billy Bob Thornton

longer). The movie doesn't sustain this pitch of violence, but its trajectory carries a dreadful inevitability even as Franklin settles into a crosscut rhythm, alternating between the fleeing criminals and law enforcement on the hunt.

On one side, two LAPD cops (**Earl Billings** and **Jim Metzler**) arrive in Star City, Arkansas, supposed destination of the murderous trio's female component, who bears the strip-club sobriquet Fantasia (**Cynda Williams**). This sleepy burg is Fantasia's hometown, and here the city pros are amused by local sheriff Dale "Hurricane" Dixon (**Bill Paxton**), a hayseed blowhard who nonetheless has crucial knowledge of the lay of the land. On the other side, Fantasia (née Lila) makes her halting escape from LA through Texas into Arkansas with her redneck boyfriend, Ray (**Billy Bob Thornton**), and their ominously calm cohort, Pluto (**Michael Beach**).

The script, by Thornton and **Tom Epperson**, deals in neat racial dualities: the black-and-white police duo pursues the interracial Most Wanted; Fantasia is the daughter of a mixed-race union, as is her son. As the LA fuzz mark time in sleepy Star City and their quarry's body count steadily mounts, *One False Move* deepens through slow reveals of characterization and crucial power shifts. Pluto at first appears to be Ray's obedient henchman, a methodical sociopath who does the dirty work. But when Ray crosses a line with a few taunting words, Pluto shows who has the upper hand. Ray and Fantasia are an unlikely love match (as were Thornton and Williams; they married and swiftly divorced after *One False Move* wrapped) and despite Ray's psycho-killer profile, he shows real tenderness and ardour towards his lover.

Fantasia is a fascinating conundrum: she enables the butchering of her friends and eventually becomes a murderer in her own right, but she's also a wounded animal, guarding a secret that could upend Dale's entire shaky persona as adoring family man and scatterbrained pillar of the community. Her reckless downward spiral grants Dale the shot at the big time he craves – but careful what you wish for. The bloody climax sets the scene for a surpassingly strange family reunion, and opens a little shaft of hope among the ruins. *One False Move* is a hard and efficient *noir* update, sleek and chilling, but pumping with warm humanist blood.

Our Song

dir **Jim McKay, 2000, 95m**
cast **Kerry Washington, Anna Simpson, Melissa Martinez**
cin **Jim Denault** *scr* **Jim McKay**

Our Song is an exemplary coming-of-age tale not least because it so gracefully transcends its genre: for all its *vérité* specificity, the film's aches are lifelong and universal. **Jim McKay**'s incandescent second feature, shot on an initial budget of just $120,000, begins with a dateline ("Crown Heights, Brooklyn, USA, late summer") and maintains a loose documentary mode – no score, all hard cuts – in shadowing three friends who cling together and drift apart over the course of a few muggy weeks. With the aid of cinematographer **Jim Denault** (*Boys Don't Cry*), McKay captures the heat-dazed restlessness of a slow-burning August, the inimitable cadences of teenage rapport and a found-sound city symphony: sprinklers on pavements, barking dogs, bass thumping from passing cars, an omnipresent, tinkling ice cream truck. "I watched a lot of Frederick Wiseman when I was writing *Our Song*," McKay told *The Village Voice*, "and I got to a point where I was trying to create something with literally zero plot."

The director and his cast also uncover less tangible emotional streams: the yearning and disappointment found in the best and worst parent-child relationships; the tiny cracks in even the closest friendships that can split open silently, going unnoticed until it's too late to mend them. The film pivots on an asbestos scare that closes a public high school, sending hundreds of kids scrambling for classes elsewhere and splitting up best pals Lanisha (**Kerry Washington**), Joycelyn (**Anna Simpson**) and Maria (**Melissa Martinez**), who perform together in a marching band. (Brooklyn's own Jackie Robinson Steppers punctuate the ambling narrative with boisterous blasts of "Don't Stop Til You Get Enough" and **Lauryn Hill**'s "Doo Wop (That Thing)".) This impending change only thickens the tension growing between the girls. Joycelyn edges shyly towards another pair of friends in a higher social caste. Maria discovers she's pregnant, and confides in Lanisha but not Joycelyn.

Centring on young black and Latina daughters of single mums, *Our Song* is a scarce breed, rarer still for refusing to circumscribe its characters solely by their race, gender, socioeconomic station or purchase-power demographic. McKay abandons the sloganeering melodrama of *Girls Town* (1996), his strident if well-intentioned debut; here he isn't concerned with incident so much as anticipation and between-time: subway rides, party primping, after-school daydreams, shoplifting. (The only eruptive event in *Our Song* is also its sole false note: a murder-suicide that befalls two secondary characters.) Denault's photography matches the adolescent collusion of urgency and ennui – the colours are rich but the picture is a little grainy, just short of crystalline focus. The patient camera leans in closely on the three lead actresses – wonderful first-timers all – as they puzzle out the volatile chemical equations of their lives; Washington's face, even in repose, always seems to be about to break into laughter or tears.

Our Song stays in media res from start to finish. It doesn't end so much as it glimmers and fades out, the pensive last shots striking attenuated chords of sadness and implacable regret, but nothing like resolution. Two friends linger over morning goodbyes at a subway station, knowing that their world will have subtly, irreversibly recalibrated itself by nightfall – which is to say, it's a day like any other.

Poison

dir Todd Haynes, 1991, 85m b/w and colour
cast Edith Meeks, Larry Maxwell, Susan Norman, Scott Renderer, James Lyons *cin* Maryse Alberti, Barry Ellsworth *scr* Todd Haynes

Winner of the Grand Jury Prize at Sundance in 1991, *Poison* crystallized its political and socio-cultural moment in ways that its makers perhaps wouldn't have been able to imagine. **Todd Haynes'** first feature led what would become known as New Queer Cinema (Jennie Livingston's *Paris Is Burning* also set Park City alight that year), bore the imprint of the AIDS pandemic that was then still gathering force and marked a twilight era of public arts funding. The movie received $25,000 (about a tenth of its budget) from the National Endowment for the Arts (NEA), then the American right wing's target of choice. It spurred a pro bono publicity campaign by **Donald Wildmon** of the American Family Association, who alerted Congress to the movie's nonexistent "explicit porno scenes of homosexuals involved in anal sex". Suddenly the 30-year-old Haynes – previously known only for the suppressed all-Barbies featurette *Superstar: The Karen Carpenter Story* (1987) – was making the rounds of the morning talk shows and *Larry King Live*, while chronically embattled NEA chairman **John Frohnmayer** defended the movie. (The first President Bush fired Frohnmayer early in 1992.)

Although it is definitive of the real anguish and manufactured hysteria of the George Bush, Sr. epoch, *Poison* remains current, deriving its timeless potency from the tension between its confrontational imagery and its sinuous meanings. Formally radical and inspired by the writings of **Jean Genet**, the film braids three ostensibly unrelated storylines, each with a distinct style. "Hero" adopts the grammar of a local TV news segment to recount the (fictional) story of Richie Beacon, a bullied Long Island boy who killed his violent father and then, according to his mother (**Edith Meeks**), flew away. In the black-and-white "Horror", crafted like a mad-scientist B-movie from the 1950s, Dr. Graves (**Larry Maxwell**) isolates the human sex drive in a serum and drinks it by mistake, creating a pustular, wildly contagious new disease and occasioning tabloid headlines along the lines of "LEPER SEX KILLER ON THE LOOSE". At once the most lyrical and brutal of the stories, "Homo" (adapted from Genet's *Miracle Of The Rose*, 1946) follows the career thief John Broom through a deceptively Edenic boys' reformatory as well as the dark, cave-like Fontenal Prison. Here, he re-encoun-ters a ghost from his reform-school youth, Jack Bolton (played by **James Lyons**, who also co-edited the film).

Prison blues: from the "Homo" sequence of *Poison*

Poison generates suspense by the frequent switching between stories, which cohere through Haynes and Lyons' suggestive editing, as when they cut from Richie receiv-ing a spanking to one Fontenal prisoner striking another. Love and pain are locked in an inex-tricable embrace. Richie can be read as the masochistic pro-vocateur of his own torments; Dr. Graves knowingly delivers the kiss of death to his sweet-heart; Broom and Bolton's final struggle dissolves any line between sex and violence.

"Prison was not new to me," Broom says in voiceover.

"I lived in them all my life … I could reject the world that reject-ed me." As in much of his work, Haynes here is examining how an outcast – whether the bullied child, the disfigured patient or the criminal/homosexual – tests the boundaries of his unaccom-modating world by accident or design, and how society enacts, and is reshaped by, its rejection of each. At once cerebral and impassioned, *Poison* is a bracing introduction to Haynes' exquisite cinema of outsiders.

The New Queer Cinema: a primer

During the early 1990s, a remarkable concentration of strong gay-themed features by young directors exploded out of the festival circuit, including **Todd Haynes**' *Poison* (1991) and in 1992 alone, Christopher Münch's *The Hours And Times*, **Tom Kalin**'s *Swoon* and **Gregg Araki**'s *The Living End*. Jennie Livingston's documentary *Paris Is Burning* (1990), *My Own Private Idaho* (1991), directed by the established auteur **Gus Van Sant**, and the final works of the renegade British auteur **Derek Jarman** also added to the mix, which *The Village Voice* anointed the "New Queer Cinema" in 1992. Indebted to previous transgressors such as **Andy Warhol**, Jack Smith and Rainer Werner Fassbinder, these young directors worked in the midst of the devastation wrought by the AIDS pandemic, and thus emerged from a moment fraught with political and emotional urgency. *Poison* was an allegorical response to the AIDS crisis, and both Haynes and Kalin were committed members of the AIDS activist groups ACT UP and Gran Fury.

Kalin's *Swoon*, which recounts the infamous Leopold and Loeb murder case, best encapsulates the major themes of the New Queer Cinema. Like *The Hours And Times* (a pensive contemplation of the relationship between John Lennon and his manager, Brian Epstein) and Jarman's *Edward II* (1991), the film inscribes homosexuality into the historical record through its famous protagonists. And like *Poison* and *The Living End*, it examines social deviants who are both victims and perpetrators – all three films feature outlaw lovers literally or figuratively imprisoned by a warped, destruc-tive bond. A fascination with celebrity – or, more pre-cisely, outlaw notoriety – permeates all the films, and none of them seek to present positive role models or martyrs. Neither does **Rose Troche**'s distaff entry *Go Fish* (1994), a romantic comedy starring lesbians. **Kimberly Peirce**'s *Boys Don't Cry* (1999), a little sibling to the NQC contingent, also re-imagines a true-crime tabloid tragedy as a means of investigating desire and identity.

Association with the New Queer Cinema didn't ensure a springboard for a smooth-sailing career. Haynes is a critical favourite but remains commer-cially underappreciated. The quality of Araki's films dipped sharply after his first few insurrections, but he made an artistic quantum leap with *Mysterious Skin* (2004). Münch has only found very limited distribution for his hushed and sombre films and as of 2006, nei-ther Kalin nor Peirce had yet made a second feature. As always, though, mainstream culture took its cues from the cutting edge: **Tom Hanks** won an Oscar as a saintly AIDS casualty in *Philadelphia* (1993) and well into the 1990s a run of "gaysploitation" movies (including 1995's *Jeffrey*, 1998's *Trick* and 1998's *Billy's Hollywood Screen Kiss*) watered down and prettified the NQC approach. Drawing a clear line from era to era, *Poison* and *Swoon* shared a pro-ducer, **James Schamus**, with *Brokeback Mountain*, the gay Western that became the most talked-about movie of 2005.

Portrait Of Jason

dir **Shirley Clarke, 1967, 100m, b/w**
with **Jason Holliday** *cin* **Jeri Sapanen**

One of the few females at the nexus of the New American Cinema movement, **Shirley Clarke** (1919–97) received an Academy Award nomination for her twenty-minute *Skyscraper* (1960) and won the Oscar for her documentary *Robert Frost: A Lover's Quarrel With The World* (1963). Despite mainstream recognition, however, Clarke's sensibilities remained bohemian. Her first feature-length film, the jazz-scored *The Connection* (1962), was an adaptation of a play first performed at New York's experimental Living Theater about heroin addicts waiting in a cramped apartment for their dealer, while a film-maker hovers. *The Cool World* (1963), the first feature shot entirely on location in Harlem, fused documentary and drama in its depiction of a kid's growing involvement with a local gang.

Clarke's equally innovative next feature, the black-and-white *Portrait Of Jason*, continued her interest in the blurred boundaries between art and life, fiction and document – or, more precisely in this case, between performance and personality. For one hundred minutes, her 16mm camera trains on **Jason Holliday**, née Aaron Payne: prostitute, would-be nightclub performer and world-class raconteur. Rattling his cocktail glass, Holliday dishes his autobiographical dirt: his work as a "houseboy" for wealthy San Francisco eccentrics, a stint in prison, his adventures with the immortally monikered "spade queens" Miss Cunt and Louise Beaver. He sings the *Funny Girl* standard "The Music That Makes Me Dance" and tries out his impersonations of **Mae West**, **Miles Davis** and **Butterfly McQueen**. He explains that his long-gestating cabaret show will comprise three sides of Jason Holliday: the cool cat, the bitch and the sad clown. So does the film itself.

As the night drags on and Holliday works his way through a massive joint and most of a bottle of vodka, the deep, vibrating laughter in his voice begins to sound like a sob of pain as he recounts the humiliation of hustling and his relationship with his father, Brother Tough, a bootlegger who beat his son daily with a razor strap. As Holliday's inebriation and exhaustion mount, his wicked camp wit reveals itself as merely a thin line of defence against the debilitating, even deranging, lifetime toll of abuse, poverty, racism and homophobia.

Two years before New York's Stonewall riots ignited the gay-rights movement, to place a black homosexual "stone whore" centre stage in a one-man film was a radical gesture, and it was made by a wealthy white woman to boot. (In a 1985 interview, Clarke suggested that her interest in dispossessed African-Americans may have been a sublimation of her experiences of sexism. "I identified with black people because I couldn't deal with the woman question and I transposed it," she said.) *Portrait Of Jason* also comments upon the *cinéma vérité* movement then being initiated by filmmakers including the **Maysles brothers**, **D.A. Pennebaker** and **Frederick Wiseman** (who produced *The Cool World*). The crewman calling out "Rolling…", the lengthy fading in and out of focus on Holliday's bespectacled face and the sound of Clarke and other offscreen interviewers prompting, goading and eventually heckling Holliday all draw attention to the artifice inherent even in a piece of ostensibly first-person cinema.

Though what begins like a cabaret rehearsal soon becomes an emotional striptease, it's surprising how much of an enigma Holliday, the consummate life performer, remains. When he breaks down late in the film, his offscreen friend Richard scoffs at what he interprets as a cynical ploy for sympathy. Holliday wipes his eyes and concedes his friend's scepticism – and yet aren't those tears real? What do we objectively know of Jason even after his film-length confessional? Perhaps he gives us the answer in his choice of mock-demure catchphrase: "I'll never tell."

Pulp Fiction

dir Quentin Tarantino, 1994, 154m
cast John Travolta, Samuel L. Jackson, Uma Thurman, Bruce Willis, Harvey Keitel, Tim Roth, Rosanna Arquette
cin Andrzej Sekula *scr* Quentin Tarantino

Does *Pulp Fiction* belong in a book about independent cinema? After all, it was produced and distributed by a subsidiary of Disney and it received the kind of marketing blitz only studio money can buy, making a celebrity out of its garrulous director, **Quentin Tarantino**. The movie cost about $8.5 million – little more than small change to a major, but a fortune to an indie outfit – and more than half that sum went to paying the stars, established names all: a drop-dead gorgeous starlet and a steady character actor both in need of their next breakthrough (**Uma Thurman** and **Samuel L. Jackson**), a faded icon looking for a comeback (**John Travolta**) and a bona-fide action superstar in the midst of a string of flops (**Bruce Willis**).

However, reality rarely squares with perception, and *Pulp Fiction* is perceived as the first indie movie to break the magic $100 million figure at the US box office. With its Miramax branding, Godard references and fuck-tastic lingo, not to mention the tireless hustle of its geek-genius auteur, *Pulp Fiction* was an art movie – a Palme d'Or winner, no less – that could play the multiplex.

And it had something for everyone: comedy, action, robbery interruptus, gangster kicks, horror jolts, a **Christopher Walken** cameo, even a piece of slapstick involving a bullet that explodes some poor guy's head. Not forgetting the bestselling soundtrack, a mix tape to die for – featuring **Dusty Springfield**'s sinuous "Son Of A Preacher Man" and **Al Green**'s smoothly persuasive "Let's Stay Together", and switching mid-note from Dick Dale's thrilling surf guitar to **Kool & The Gang**'s irresistible "Jungle Boogie".

Hit men Vincent (Travolta) and Jules (Jackson) banter about European fast-food nomenclature and the erotic potential of foot massage before blowing away their morning appointments. Ganglord's moll Mia Wallace (Thurman) vamps and purrs and does the Batutsi before she inadvertently snorts some pure heroin and ends up with a needle full of adrenaline stuck in her breastplate. Middling boxer Butch (Willis) double-crosses the fearsome crime king Marsellus Wallace (**Ving Rhames**), enjoys a classical motel-*noir* interlude with his twittering-birdie sweetheart (**Maria de Madeiros**) and is spectacularly waylaid both by Mr Wallace and some hillbilly rapists.

Each of the interlocking segments of *Pulp Fiction* hinges on a suspenseful rescue, but by film's end, the Bible-quoting assassin Jules is foremost concerned with saving himself. He believes that he and Vincent survived their morning engagement only by divine intervention and takes this as a sign to quit the gangster life and mend his ways. Tarantino's tossed-salad approach to chronology also works a miracle of sorts: Vincent dies ignobly at the ninety-minute mark, but then the clock turns back to resurrect him for the finale.

There was no turning the clock back on *Pulp Fiction*'s market impact, however. Indie filmmaking had become – or been subsumed into – big business. The major studios built up their boutique divisions, prices soared, opening-weekend grosses became all-important and it got even harder for the little guy to compete. Of course, Tarantino himself had until recently *been* that little guy, a high-school dropout working at a video store and churning out script ideas, and now Miramax was, as **Harvey Weinstein** put it, "the house that Quentin built". But Tarantino has made only a few features in the years since, and it's intriguing to think where his career might have gone had he taken residence in a different house. What if he were cranking out a cheapie B-flick every year like his grindhouse heroes? In any case, if *Pulp Fiction* didn't exist, the Weinstein brothers would have had to invent it.

Return Of The Secaucus 7

dir John Sayles, 1979, 110m

cast Bruce MacDonald, Maggie Renzi, Adam LeFevre, Jean Passanante, Gordon Clapp, Karen Trott, Mark Arnott, Maggie Cousineau, Jean Passanante, Gordon Clapp *cin* Austin De Besche *scr* John Sayles

The name *Return Of The Secaucus 7* suggests a heist team or bandit gang reuniting for one last job, an outlaw connotation reinforced by the film's opening title sequence: a grainy montage of mug shots, accompanied by Spaghetti-Western guitar strains. But writer-director-editor **John Sayles** makes a droll puncture of any further romantic assumptions with the first image of the film: a plunger in a toilet. Domestic partners Mike (**Bruce MacDonald**) and Katie (**Maggie Renzi**), both schoolteachers, aren't planning their next score but prepping their house for a get-together with friends from

Protest music: Adam LeFevre in *Return Of The Secaucus 7*

college. Even the "Secaucus 7" handle is just a fond old joke among
the group, referring to a night spent in jail years ago when, en route
to an anti-war protest, a cop found drugs and a firearm in the trunk
of their borrowed car.

As they edge towards 30, the Secaucus 7 and their associates find
themselves in varying states of flux. Maura (**Karen Trott**) is giving
up acting and ending her relationship with Jeff (Mark Arnott), a
drug-rehab counsellor. Maura rebounds with J.T. (**Adam LeFevre**),
a penniless musician about to light out for Los Angeles; their impulsive coupling on Mike and Katie's living-room floor is hurtful to
Frances (Maggie Cousineau), a medical student with a crush on J.T.

Senatorial aide Irene (**Jean Passanante**) seems the most together of the bunch, arriving with her allegedly square boyfriend, Chip (Gordon Clapp), who doubles as an audience surrogate – the eager-to-please outsider struggles to keep all the criss-crossing life paths and romantic histories straight.

Return Of The Secaucus 7 is loosely structured around a series of set pieces: a basketball game, a round of Charades, a lengthy tavern visit. The movie mostly relies on motionless master shots, which suit the dialogue-driven scenes but also bespeak the tight finances and Sayles' beginner status: he claims that he had "never looked through a camera" before beginning *Secaucus 7* with an initial budget of $60,000. For the 25-day shoot, a ski lodge in New Hampshire served as set, storage facility and sleeping quarters for cast and crew. Mostly, the actors were already acquainted with Sayles through theatrical work, and Sayles' life partner Maggie Renzi served as assistant editor and unit manager in addition to playing Katie. The among-friends intimacy achieved onscreen is perhaps all the more convincing because Sayles was the same age as his characters and shared their background in the 1960s protest movement.

These former college firebrands present a study in ambivalence. The women express hesitancy about the prospect of motherhood, a notion rarely broached in mainstream cinema. (In contrast, an entire plot thread of 1983's *The Big Chill*, which is a Hollywood retooling of the *Secaucus 7* template, concerns an unattached female character's ravenous baby cravings.) No one in *Secaucus 7* has joined up with the establishment, exactly, but none have kept up-to-date with the activist circuit either. Sayles' script is particularly astute in tracing the greying and mellowing of revolutionary energies – the fire has been cooled by adult professional responsibilities and life experience, but Sayles never disowns or belittles leftist ideals as the fancies of sentimental youth. "We want a formula!" a few of Sayles' characters chant, quoting a famous scene from the leftist film landmark *Salt Of The Earth* (1954). But as they've discovered, there is no secret alchemy either for social justice or domestic harmony; each member of the Secaucus 7 remains a work-in-progress.

Roger & Me

dir Michael Moore, 1989, 90m

with Michael Moore, Fred Ross, Rhonda Britton, Pat Boone, Bob Eubanks, Roger Smith *cin* Christopher Beaver, John Prusak, Kevin Rafferty, Bruce Schermer

scr Michael Moore

At early screenings of *Roger & Me*, a seat was always reserved for one **Roger B. Smith**, and alas, it always remained empty. **Michael Moore**'s documentary follows the filmmaker's quixotic pursuit of a face-to-face interview with the elusive General Motors chairman, who oversaw the automotive-plant closings that devastated Moore's hometown of Flint, Michigan. As writer, director, narrator and host of *Roger & Me*, Moore itemizes the human costs of "staying competitive" with varying degrees of snark, whimsy and focused anger: tens of thousands of jobs lost, citizens fleeing their city in droves, a main drag disfigured by boarded-up storefronts and a ballooning crime rate.

Making the festival rounds prior to its 1989 theatrical release, *Roger & Me* won mostly rave reviews, but it acquired a taint of controversy after *New Yorker* film critic Pauline Kael attacked the film's credibility for presenting events non-chronologically. Moore does compress the duration of the city's sharp decline, fudge the opening date of the spectacularly misjudged Auto World theme park and present **President Ronald Reagan** paying a cheer-up visit to the city in what we assume to be 1987, when it was actually candidate Reagan who visited in 1980. These lapses are irksome, but none of them put so much as a dent in Moore's invective against the unnecessary and inhumane sacking of Flint.

What's more frustrating is the overall slackness of the filmmaking. From early glimpses of Moore's family photos and home movies, *Roger & Me* promises a personal journey through the demise of the manufacturing economy that created a prosperous working-class in Flint – the very milieu that Moore grew up in (and, as he admits, couldn't wait to escape). However, Moore loses track of his thesis and the documentary's middle section sags under the weight of desultory, skit-like encounters with various straw men and eccentrics: vapid celebrities, elderly golfers, Miss Michigan ("I'm for employment and working in Michigan," she bravely declares) and an addled woman on government assistance who raises and kills rabbits for extra cash (her sign reads "Pets or Meat"). The movie devotes significant time to **Fred Ross**, a deputy sheriff in Flint who appears to spend his entire week carrying out evictions; Moore's implication is that Ross is so busy evicting families because GM has thrown the breadwinners out of their jobs, but the movie doesn't provide sufficient context to prove it.

Roger & Me is no high-water mark in the art of the documentary, but it doesn't aspire to be any such thing. (It's the record-breaking *Fahrenheit 9/11*, released in 2004, that shows the filmmaker at the peak of his polemical command.) Moore is a popular entertainer who aims right down the middle of the road; he knows that cheap shots work, and they work best when aimed straight to the gut. And he knows how to work the system. The mighty Warner Bros. purchased the distribution rights to *Roger & Me* for a whopping $3 million, which meant corporate-strength marketing and distribution for an independent challenge to corporate hegemony, a movie without stars or a happy ending. The film mourns not only the death of Moore's hometown, but the death of a productive, job-secure working-class in outsourced, downsized America.

Safe

dir Todd Haynes, 1995, 119m

cast Julianne Moore, Xander Berkeley, Peter Friedman, Susan Norman, James LeGros *cin* Alex Nepomniaschy *scr* Todd Haynes

One of the central questions urged by **Todd Haynes**' masterpiece *Safe* is deceptively simple: Who is Carol White? She herself doesn't seem to know. "I'm a housew – a homemaker?" Carol (**Julianne Moore**) says in her thin, uncertain voice, posing the answer as a question. But she does little to make her home, since her maid runs the Whites' big, modern house in the San Fernando Valley. Carol dutifully submits to boring sex with her husband, Greg (**Xander Berkeley**), and has, at best, a peripheral relationship with her stepson. Her days are barely filled out with errands, aerobics, hair appointments and lunch dates. And yet, she feels stressed out, "run down". She gets a nosebleed at the salon. She suffers a coughing fit while driving. She collapses at the dry cleaner's. As her mysterious condition persists and worsens, it's as if Carol has become allergic to her life, as if her immune system were spontaneously rejecting her banal existence.

Influenced by **Chantal Akerman**'s *Jeanne Dielman 23 Quai du Commerce 1080 Bruxelles* (1975) and **Stanley Kubrick**'s *2001: A Space Odyssey* (1968), *Safe* is a film of amazing precision: every camera setup, piece of blocking and line of dialogue carries meaning. When her aerobics classmates notice that Carol doesn't sweat, one says, "I hate you." It's just a joke, but it foreshadows the mounting hostility of Carol's surroundings. Externalizing her alienation, Haynes' *mise-en-scène* maroons Carol in her own living room or strands her at a scene's margins, as the inane white noise of TV chatter and lite-rock FM buzzes around her. At one chilling moment, Carol looks into a reflective sliding door and then, as she pushes the door open, literally wipes herself out of the frame.

Carol's impatient physician seems to think her poor health is all in her mind, and his diagnosis is effectively reinforced when she goes to Wrenwood, a retreat for the "chemically sensitive". The idea for *Safe* originated after Haynes saw a television item about people with "twentieth-century illness", or adverse reactions to everyday

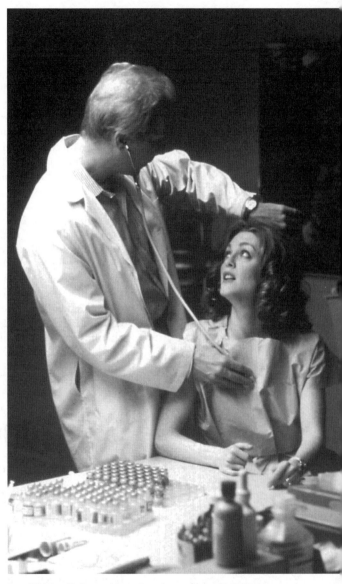

Carol White (Julianne Moore) seeks a diagnosis in *Safe*

chemicals. This ailment was new, controversial and difficult to treat, and the writer-director made a link with experimental therapies for AIDS. Haynes wondered, as he told an interviewer, "why so many gay men seemed to be drawn to people like [self-help author] Louise Hay in the 80s, people who were literally telling them that they made themselves sick, that they could make themselves well if they simply learned how to love themselves."

Likewise at Wrenwood, New Age guru Peter Dunning (**Peter Friedman**) preaches mind over matter, telling a resident, "The only person who can make you get sick is you, right?" His ethos – echoing the cant in Hay's bestselling *You Can Heal Your Life* – is cruelly cunning: faced with the confusion and distress of a confounding illness, Dunning's clients are "empowered" in the act of taking the blame for something over which they have little or no control. He says he's stopped reading newspapers because he doesn't want depressing stories to affect his immune system, and the Wrenwood mantra is similarly isolationist: "I am safe and all is well in my world."

Carol clings to this extremist individualism, even as she becomes dependent on an oxygen tank and a boil-like sore spreads inexorably over her forehead. As her increasingly wasted body dwindles, her "safe" world shrinks too. Even in this remote desert commune, she finds seclusion-within-seclusion, moving into a chemical-proof, pod-like chamber, built for one. In the heartbreaking final shot of *Safe*, Carol gazes into the mirror and makes affirmations of self-love – as if love could heal a sick body, or turn a lie into truth.

Schizopolis

dir Steven Soderbergh, 1996, 96m
cast Steven Soderbergh, Betsy Brantley, David Jensen, Mike Malone *cin, scr* Steven Soderbergh

Despite the disclaimer on the DVD case of *Schizopolis* – "All attempts at synopsizing the film have ended in failure and hospitalization" – let's give it a shot. The first section concentrates on Fletcher Munson (**Steven Soderbergh**), a doleful guy in a dying marriage.

He works for a Scientology-like organisation founded by one T. Azimuth Schwitters (**Mike Malone**), a self-help guru who preaches a dogma called Eventualism. The second part switches to Fletcher's doppelganger, local dentist Dr Jeffrey Korchek (Soderbergh again), who's having an affair with Fletcher's wife (**Betsy Brantley**). The third and final section moves to Mrs Munson, who has dumped Fletcher for the dentist, though not before Jeffrey has fallen in lust with Attractive Woman No. 2 (Brantley again). Meanwhile, the Lothario-cum-exterminator Elmo Oxygen (**David Jensen**) cruises residential neighbourhoods in search of bugs to kill and bored housewives to seduce.

The interwoven betrayals and identity slippage of *Schizopolis* are heady enough even before one factors in the local patois, a surrealist tower of Babel. Elmo Oxygen and his conquests purr at each other in vivid gibberish (choice phrases include "nose army", "mellow rhubarb turbine" and "throbbing dust generation"). Assigned to compose a speech for Schwitters after the death of colleague Lester Richards, Fletcher listens bemusedly as his boss delivers a virtuoso monologue of authoritative blather. (The unfortunate colleague's name nods to director **Richard Lester**, while Schwitters shares a name with Dada-era artist **Kurt Schwitters**.) Small talk is breathtakingly candid, yet delivered in pleasantly perfunctory tones. ("Is your wife coming over tonight?" Fletcher asks a friendly neighbour. "Because her big ass always leaves me satisfied.")

The Munsons' relationship has become so dully routinized that they speak in signifiers: when Fletcher returns home after work, he calls out, "Generic greeting"; when his wife makes an amorous advance, he fends her off with "Really well-rehearsed speech about workload and stress". This is Soderbergh's most tragicomic semiotic switch-up, not least because his real-life marriage to Brantley was falling apart at the time of shooting. Taking its cue from the quasi-religious gobbledygook of Eventualism, the movie is a dizzying hodgepodge of jargon, cant, managerial lingo, cornball puns, Dada pranks and who's-on-first verbal slapstick. *Schizopolis* implies that our means of communication are as dead as the Munsons' marriage; with freewheeling absurdist energy, it dismantles language in order to build a new, working model.

"Being a cult failure is actually a great thing," Soderbergh said in 1997, "because nobody cares what you're doing … If you

The most underrated American indie film: *Schizopolis*

Virtually unnoticed upon its minuscule release in 1997, **Steven Soderbergh**'s *Schizopolis* is easily one of the most radically experimental and startlingly personal works ever made by a mainstream American filmmaker. Pricelessly weird and invigorating on its own, the film is also important for influencing Soderbergh's filmmaking technique – the low-budget, seat-of-the-pants production style of *Schizopolis* later informed the fast-and-loose style of the director's subsequent films, especially 2000's *Traffic*, for which he won the best director Oscar. *Schizopolis* is still largely underseen, although the Criterion Collection did their part to rectify the situation by releasing a handsome DVD release packed with extras in 2003.

always know you're working below a certain level, way below the radar, there's a lot of freedom." Eight years after his extraordinary success with *sex, lies, and videotape*, Soderbergh was generally perceived as a filmmaker of great skill and integrity who had somehow not delivered on the promise of his first, era-defining film. He did not change this perception with *Schizopolis*: shot for peanuts with a five-person crew in Soderbergh's hometown of Baton Rouge, the film all but disappeared upon arrival. A shape-shifting existential experiment in narrative and lingual fragmentation, *Schizopolis* came in well under the radar, but this stunningly dense whatzit represented a crucial artistic and personal breakthrough for its creator. It is Soderbergh's bravest and most fascinating film.

sex, lies, and videotape

dir Steven Soderbergh, 1989, 100m
cast James Spader, Andie MacDowell, Laura San Giacomo, Peter Gallagher *cin* Walt Lloyd *scr* Steven Soderbergh

More than any other single film, *sex, lies, and videotape* crystallizes the American independent renaissance of the late 1980s and early 1990s. Shot in Baton Rouge, Louisiana, for a little over $1 million by first-timer **Steven Soderbergh**, this low-budget "regional" film was cerebral, dense with talk and devoid of cheap thrills (notwithstanding the title and Miramax's racy promotional campaign). Yet it created a sensation in 1989 at Sundance and won the Palme d'Or for its astonished 26-year-old director.

"I was just stunned that people seemed to find something to relate to in the movie," Soderbergh told the *New York Times*. "I thought it was too internal." Given the film's tangle of lust, anomie, sibling rivalry and domestic stagnancy, it would be a rare and lucky viewer who couldn't connect with some of its core emotions. Ann

(**Andie MacDowell**) is a childless housewife who thinks "sex is overrated". Her lawyer husband, John (**Peter Gallagher**), an aspiring Master of the Universe with the power suit to match, secretly fills in the erotic gap with Ann's younger, funkier sister, Cynthia (**Laura San Giacomo**). Betraying her primly perfect sibling works

Andie MacDowell in *videotape* (*sex, lies* not pictured)

like an aphrodisiac on Cynthia, whose relationship with Ann seems based on mutual resentment and near-absolute candour. Both women are drawn to Graham (**James Spader**), a high-school friend of John's who crashes on his old buddy's couch for a short time until he finds a place of his own. By his own account a recovering "pathological liar", Graham doesn't need to work and he can fit all his possessions into his car. He's also impotent, and fulfils his sexual desires by videotaping women as they recount their fantasies.

A mild and soft-spoken conflict-provider, Graham is both a disruptive and magnetic force. He has sidestepped any unnecessary encounters with market capitalism and conventional sexual grati-fication, which marks him out as the polar opposite to the smooth and arrogant John. Both Ann and Cynthia will appear before his camera, which will subtly realign the power dynamic between the four major players. As written and sinuously performed by Spader, Graham remains a fascinating Möbius strip of motivations until late in the film. What kind of threat does he pose? Is he a Machiavellian charmer or a pensive misfit? Does his voyeurism smack of the vampire, or is he performing a kind of benevolent symbiotic therapy?

Soderbergh has spoken frankly of the emotional, autobiographi-cal nature of the movie; Graham, the man with the movie camera, is clearly the writer-director's alter ego, but he's also a stealth film critic. When Ann, rather predictably, snatches up the camera and trains it on the fetishist, he murmurs, "I just don't find the whole turning-the-tables thing very interesting…". A similar self-reflex-ivity can be detected when Graham tells her that he can't encap-sulate his life in a neat narrative that will explain him away – as one would in a typical Hollywood script, via a rousing but tidy speech. *sex, lies, and videotape* builds towards a relatively conventional outcome of comeuppance, reconciliation and romantic union, but Soderbergh questions the means of his own storytelling devices even as he puts them into motion, taking scrupulous pains not to meet all the impossible expectations of love, sex and communication that we learn at the movies.

Shadows

dir John Cassavetes, 1959, 87m, b/w
cast Ben Carruthers, Leila Goldoni, Hugh Hurd, Anthony
Ray, Rupert Crosse, David Jones *cin* Erich Kollmar *scr*
John Cassavetes

The famous end-credit declaration of **John Cassavetes**' first film –
"The film you have just seen was an improvisation" – is a provocative
exaggeration. *Shadows* as we know it was fully scripted, post-dubbed,
edited down from some thirty hours of footage and extensively re-shot
after initial screenings in 1958. (The tireless Cassavetes scholar **Ray
Carney** tracked down the first version of *Shadows*, long thought lost,
in 2003.) Even the fantastic jazz score, originally commissioned from
improv master **Charles Mingus**, was written down. (Alto saxophon-
ist **Shafi Hadi** eventually provided much of the soundtrack.)

However, *Shadows* did grow out of an improvisation, performed
at the acting workshop that Cassavetes taught with **Burt Lane**, in
which a young white man meets his new girlfriend's brothers and
discovers she is black. In the film, Hugh (**Hugh Hurd**) is a struggling
New York jazz singer, indignant that his current stage gig requires
him to introduce a gaggle of off-key chorus girls. Hugh, who is
black, supports his two younger siblings, both of whom can "pass"
for white: Ben (**Ben Carruthers**), a Beat Generation specimen with
comically feckless friends, and Lelia (**Lelia Goldoni**), an impetu-
ous beauty who dabbles in fiction. She loses her virginity to Tony
(**Anthony Ray**), which occasions a post-coital interlude that still
startles for its forlorn candour ("I didn't know it could be so awful,"
she says wonderingly). Back at Lelia's apartment, Tony, so quick to
profess his love, freezes up when his inamorata introduces him to
dark-skinned Hugh. Tony offers lame excuses, makes as if to go, lin-
gers, gets embarrassed, suggests they all get a meal together. Holding
back his anger, Hugh insists that Tony leave and not come back. "I
don't want you to hurt anything of mine," Hugh says, clashing with
Lelia's previous declaration of independence, "I belong to me."

Cassavetes completed *Shadows* in 1959, the year that **Jean-Luc
Godard** shot the similarly jazzy, loose-limbed *A bout de souffle*, which
epitomized the French New Wave much as *Shadows* signalled the

New American Cinema. It was also the year of **Douglas Sirk**'s Hollywood swan song, *Imitation Of Life*, a stinging melodrama of "passing" that, like *Shadows*, showed up the pompous liberal cant with which the studios treated racial issues. *Shadows* has no heroes, villains or canned message; its characters are flawed yet impossible to condemn. Tony is probably as racist as any educated young white man in 1959 Manhattan, and he's callow and manipulative, but he also recognizes his mistakes and tries as best as he knows how to amend them. Lelia's hurt and confusion suffuse the film's later scenes, but Cassavetes refuses to sentimentalize her heartbreak – which she acts out in her abysmal treatment of her next date, Davey (**David Jones**). Tony, to his credit, seems up to the challenge of Lelia's hotheaded, voluble self-regard. Davey, by contrast, seems drawn to it because he'd like to crush it, finding her unacceptably "masculine".

Lelia always plays the diva, waggling her shoulders and batting her lashes (much to her doting brothers' delight), but her actressy extroversion seems rooted in a fundamental anxiety of identity. What role is she to play? Her skin colour is both a fact and a deception; she looks like a pretty girl but she asserts herself "like a man". When Davey sternly orders her to "Be as lovely as you look", it's not worlds removed from Nick Longhetti screaming "Be yourself!" at his unstable wife in Cassavetes' *A Woman Under The Influence* (1974). The filmmaker understood that we are compelled to play contradictory roles in our everyday lives, to negotiate and conceal our zig-zagging emotions with elaborate facades. With unnerving precision, his films pinpoint those pivotal moments when we break character, when the mask slips. Lelia's painful dilemma of identity in *Shadows* introduces one of the great themes in Cassavetes' films: the performance of the self.

Sherman's March

dir Ross McElwee, 1986, 157m
with Ross McElwee, Charleen Swansea *cin, scr* Ross McElwee

Admitting little distinction between making movies and living life, **Ross McElwee** is his own great subject. Through his autobiographical documentaries, he has explored marriage, loss and mortality (1993's *Time Indefinite*), fatherhood and natural disaster (1996's *Six O'Clock News*) and his great-grandfather's role in the advent of the tobacco industry (2003's *Bright Leaves*). However, he remains best known for *Sherman's March*, wherein a retracing of **General William Tecumseh Sherman**'s tear through the south during the American Civil War doubles as a rumination on the women who have passed through McElwee's romantic orbit.

McElwee has just broken up with his latest girlfriend on the eve of his expedition in *Sherman's March*, which is subtitled *A Meditation On The Possibility Of Romantic Love In The South During An Era Of Nuclear-Weapons Proliferation*. (The documentarian tends to have more nightmares about nuclear war when his love life isn't going well.) As he sets out on his quest, friends and family offer grooming tips and try to set him up with prospective sweethearts, and every stop on the Sherman tour seems to produce another female specimen for McElwee to ponder.

Before his camera, throaty-voiced aspiring actress Pat performs "cellulite exercises", which so mesmerize McElwee that he accidentally switches off his tape recorder – a sublime accident of erotic distraction, as satisfying as a pratfall. Dinner with his sister's newly divorced friend, Claudia, leads to a strange detour into the woods and a survivalist settlement modelled on *Little House On The Prairie*, where one resident declares that "the federal government is our mortal enemy". McElwee also journeys to Ossabaw, an island off the coast of Georgia, home of his old friend Winnie, a linguist and nudist; McElwee fantasizes about them living together "in Eden…like Rousseau's savages", but her partner presents an obstacle. McElwee's friend and former teacher, Charleen – a voluble, imperious force of nature who's often the most galvanizing presence in his movies – tries to set him up with DeeDee, but she turns out to be a strict Mormon in search of "a man who can bring the priesthood into her house". McElwee doesn't fit the bill.

Sherman's March derives much of its humour and poignancy from a strain of knowing bathos: the wayfaring, quixotic director strains to draw parallels between Sherman's path of destruction and his own trail of ruined relationships; between the general's business failures and McElwee's failures as a boyfriend. Though he's self-effacing and shambolic, McElwee is trying a bold gambit, one that risks belittling both his own personal bewilderment and a calamitous chapter of his region's history. (And indeed, it's strange to watch a two-and-a-half-hour documentary named for one of the decisive events of the Civil War that scarcely pauses to acknowledge why the war was actually fought.)

Charleen scolds McElwee for his disabling shyness with women, for "hiding behind the camera", and he does concede her point. "It seems I'm filming my life in order to have a life to film," he says. But a film can't last a lifetime. By the movie's end, McElwee is back in his hometown of Charlotte, North Carolina – the city where the Confederacy effectively died – without money, car or girlfriend and with just one roll of film. However reluctantly, he seems resigned to find out what happens when the shooting stops; his quest continues, but *Sherman's March* comes to a halt.

Shock Corridor

dir Samuel Fuller, 1963, 101m, b/w and colour
cast Peter Breck, Constance Towers *cin* Stanley Cortez
scr Samuel Fuller

By the early 1960s, **Sam Fuller** had been long established as a writer-director of sensational intensity for his unvarnished war films and hard-bitten *noirs*, made both within and outside the studio system. He became a permanent Hollywood outsider, however, at the precise moment his sock-in-the-gut style reached maximum potency in the independently produced *Shock Corridor*. The film alienated critics and audiences on its release, but stands today as one of Fuller's signature lurid achievements, busting with salacious encounters, raw violence, quotable hard-boiled repartee and blunt-force social commentary.

Striving newspaper reporter Johnny Barrett (**Peter Breck**) figures his best shot at winning a Pulitzer is to get himself committed to a mental asylum, which is also the site of an unsolved murder. He invents the role of a disturbed man with incestuous longings for his sister and bullies his reluctant girlfriend, Cathy (**Constance Towers**), a stripper, into posing as the menaced sibling. Once he's sectioned, Johnny meets a black university student who believes himself to be

Chaos theory: *Shock Corridor*

a member of the Ku Klux Klan, a Korean War veteran who thinks the Confederacy never died and a Nobel Prize-winning nuclear physicist who's regressed to a childlike state. In what's arguably the movie's most gobsmacking interlude, Johnny inadvertently locks himself in the women's ward and falls prey to a feral pack of mauling "nymphos".

Tougher than the rest: Samuel Fuller

A common criticism aimed at Amerindie movies of the 1990s concerned the incongruity of young filmmakers conjuring up cruel gangster underworlds, when their only experience of criminality came via the vicarious thrills of other films. Their B-movie forefather **Samuel Fuller** (1911–97), however, got his tough-guy attitude through raw experience. Unlike his mostly apolitical descendants, his blunt, dynamic films engage with social issues, posing difficult questions and withering critiques of his beloved USA.

Fuller quit school at 13 to join the newspaper trade, covered the crime beat for the *San Diego Sun* while still a teenager, quit to ride the rails during the Depression and began writing pulp fiction and screenplays in the mid-1930s. After World War II reached the US, he enlisted, fought in North Africa, Sicily and Normandy and received the Silver Star and the Purple Heart; his experiences provided the basis for his war adventure *The Big Red One* (1980; restored in 2004).

Returning to Hollywood after his military service, Fuller signed on with the independent Lippert Productions to shoot his own screenplays on the cheap, including the first of many hard-bitten war films, *The Steel Helmet* (1951). Its commercial success attracted the attention of 20th Century Fox, for which he made another Korean War film, *Fixed Bayonets* (1951), as well as his hard-boiled anti-Communist classic *Pickup On South Street* (1953) with **Richard Widmark**. In between, Fuller made *Park Row* (1952), about feuding newspapers and journalistic integrity under fire in 1880s New York City. Using his *Steel Helmet* payday, Fuller self-financed *Park Row* and lost every last cent.

Fuller alternated between independent and Hollywood ventures for some time, also setting up his own production company for *Run Of The Arrow* (1957),

a Western set in the immediate aftermath of the American Civil War. Another Western from 1957, *Forty Guns* (starring **Barbara Stanwyck**), proved to be one of Fuller's most formally innovative films, and the director began to attract favourable critical attention in Europe, especially France.

Always an envelope-pusher, Fuller exploited his own predilection for lengthy, unbroken shots in the Nazi allegory *Verboten!* (1958), explored internalized bigotry in *The Crimson Kimono* (1959) and mounted a saga of cold-blooded revenge in *Underworld USA* (1961). He surpassed himself with the indie one-two punch of *Shock Corridor* (1963), about a newspaper reporter who commits himself to a mental asylum, and The *Naked Kiss* (1964), about a saintly ex-prostitute trying to start a new life in a hypocritical small town. The latter subversive melodrama wields an unforgettable opening sequence: the hooker beats a drunk relentlessly with her handbag, undeterred even when he yanks off her wig to reveal her bald head.

Fuller was all but *persona non grata* among studios in subsequent years, but he won backing from the indie studio Lorimar for *The Big Red One*, made for $4 million – a tiny sum for a period war film. The ageing director again inspired controversy for *White Dog* (1981), co-written with future director **Curtis Hanson**, which argued that racism is a conditioned reflex that's all but impossible to eradicate. Fuller's anti-racist movie was widely misunderstood to be racist, and thus a filmmaker whose approach was often dismissed as "primitive" managed to make a film so subtle that it was mistaken for the thing it critiqued. It's a regrettable irony, but one that highlights Fuller's genius for cutting right to the heart and bone of an issue.

Johnny acclimatizes to his bizarre surroundings with alarming ease. His paranoia pours out in his dreams, where Cathy taunts him in her showgirl outfit and feather boa, and he becomes convinced Cathy is actually his sister. Electroshock treatment seems to impair both his memory and, intermittently, his ability to speak. In the opening narration, he says, "This is my story, as far as it goes"; by the end of *Shock Corridor*, Johnny is no longer the teller of his own tale – his voice is gone, his personality wiped. The reporter turned madman is a parable of blind ambition, ironically destroyed by his ravenous desire for self-fulfilment.

Fuller's charging style can usually be termed tabloid-intellectual, but the literary bent in *Shock Corridor* is particularly pronounced: Fuller name-checks Euripedes, Dickens, Twain and *Hamlet* in the film's first seven minutes. Although the subject matter is ugly, the arresting black-and-white images are gorgeous, courtesy of cinematographer **Stanley Cortez** (who also lensed 1942's *The Magnificent Ambersons* and 1955's *The Night Of The Hunter*). *Shock Corridor* is a go-for-broke microcosm of American society as a vast mental ward where war, racism, sexual confusion and the threat of nuclear annihilation have deranged social discourse and the body politic. The movie's trashy plot doubles as an editorial cartoon as Fuller conveys his pessimistic vision of America through powerful jolts of pure pulp commotion.

Slacker

dir Richard Linklater, 1991, 97m
cast Richard Linklater, Jerry Delony, Teresa Taylor, Louis Mackey *cin* Lee Daniel *scr* Richard Linklater

Twenty-four hours in the life of the bohemian post-college set and crackpot intelligentsia of Austin, Texas, **Richard Linklater**'s *Slacker* has an idiosyncratic structure and regional specificity that gave a name and profile to an entire demographic. "Before the film even came out nationwide, already it was sucked up into a kind of early-90s zeitgeist thing," the director said years later.

The notion of an anomic, work-adverse age group in its millions had already been floated in the summer of 1990 by

Credit where credit's due

The fun of Richard Linklater's garrulous stroll around Austin, Texas isn't over until the final credits roll – stick around for *Slacker*'s idiosyncratic cast list. Here's a sample:

Richard Linklater	**Should Have Stayed at Bus Station**
Heather West	**Tura Satana Look-Alike**
Daniel Dugan	**Comb Game Player**
Brian Crockett	**Sadistic Comb Game Player**
Jerry Delony	**Been on the Moon Since the 50s**
Teresa Taylor	**Papsmear Pusher**
Sarah Harmon	**Has Faith in Groups**
Louis Mackey	**Old Anarchist**
D. Montgomery	**Having a Breakthrough Day**
Mark Quirk	**Papa Smurf**
Annick Souhami	**Has Conquered Fear of Rejection**
Kevin Thomson	**Handstamping Arm Licker**
Nolan Morrison	**To Be Buried by History**

a *Time* magazine cover story on twenty-something "baby busters". Following *Slacker*, the impression of a lost generation deepened further with **Douglas Coupland**'s 1991 novel *Generation X* and continued with the grunge-rock cash-in of the early 1990s, **Beck**'s ubiquitous 1993 single "Loser" and the movies *Singles* (1992) and *Reality Bites* (1994). *Slacker* has far less in common with those Gen X romantic comedies than with the deadpan comic daisy chains of **Luis Buñuel**'s late career. Linklater's first released feature, shot with non-professional locals, strolls through Austin guided only by a tangential stream of conversation.

Linklater's loquacious films are often characterized as laid-back and low-key, and while it's true that few of the characters in *Slacker* appear to have conventional jobs, they evidently spend a great deal of time and effort *thinking*, and exert a lot of energy trying to get their ideas across. You could say they work quite hard, just not on the capitalist grid. They analyze their dreams, read voraciously and remember what they read, recite statistics and draw inferences from them, and tinker meticulously with conspiracy theories. They hustle to make an off-the-books buck selling Mandela T-shirts or (allegedly) **Madonna**'s pap smear. One guy turns the ultimate slacker pastime, watching TV, into an all-consuming vocation, staying indoors surrounded by a roomful of screens like **David Bowie** in *The Man Who Fell To Earth* (1976) and even strapping a set to his back.

Slacker's loose-limbed ramblings unravel on the street or at the bar. The aforementioned "Papsmear Pusher" is a virtuoso bullshit artist, and elsewhere, a brief discussion of the possible link between the Hindu deity Krishna and Papa Smurf is touching in its stoner pensiveness. But this daydreamer's refuge also incubates dark secrets and bad memories. In the film's second sequence, a young man runs down his mother with a car, then returns to his house to screen home movies until he's arrested by the police. A hum of dread and possible violence is often detected beneath *Slacker*'s breeze-shooting. A fixation on John F. Kennedy's assassination floats freely in the air, as does the ghost of **Charles Whitman**, who in 1966 murdered 16 people, including his mother and wife, and wounded 33 others in a killing spree that ended atop the University of Texas clocktower, where Whitman terrorized the city with uncannily accurate sniper fire. "There was a man!" marvels *Slacker*'s ageing anarchist, who offers a would-be burglar a cup of coffee and a chat while he muses aloud about blowing up the Texas legislature building.

Linklater intended another of the movie's motormouths – the bearded guy in the Batman T-shirt – as a fount of tin-hat paranoia circa 1991, but the fellow's doomsaying remarks about global warming and melting polar ice caps sound like common knowledge in the twenty-first century. In posing timeless existential questions on life, work and self-worth, and in its timely invocations of latent terror and a dying planet, *Slacker* stands apart from most appointed voices of a generation – it hasn't dated a day.

Spanking The Monkey

dir David O. Russell, 1994, 100m
cast Jeremy Davies, Alberta Watson, Carla Gallo, Benjamin Hendrickson *cin* Michael Mayers *scr* David O. Russell

Doing the promotional rounds for *Spanking The Monkey*, **David O. Russell** was often asked if, like his protagonist, he'd ever had sex with his mum. The answer, to the press corps' relief or disappointment, was no, but perhaps the question bespeaks the discomfiting verisimilitude of Russell's movie. He pursued a veritable who's-who of fortysomething stars (including Susan Sarandon, Faye Dunaway, Jessica Lange and Judy Davis) to play the film's self-pitying, pill-popping, incestuous mother – and, unsurprisingly, found no

Oedipus wrecks: *Spanking The Monkey*

takers (the part eventually went to the superb Canadian actress **Alberta Watson**). The lack of a well-known lead left the writer-director with an initial budget of just $80,000, but any qualms about the movie's subject matter were dispelled after *Spanking The Monkey* became one of the more unlikely Audience Award winners in Sundance history.

The film does have autobiographical underpinnings. During his teens in upstate New York, Russell observed a pattern of workaholic, absentee dads and lonely, idle mums among his circle of friends. "We felt really irritated about our mothers because they were too involved with us," Russell told the *San Francisco Chronicle.* "You need that father energy around to kind of break things up after adolescence ... If Dad is not around – emotionally or physically – then things are going to get a little pressurized." The family home becomes a combustion chamber in *Spanking The Monkey.* All of Russell's films build to a lunatic crescendo of improbable circumstance and daffy catharsis, but his debut feature pushes its volatile situation to an unnerving extreme while remaining within the boundaries of black comedy.

Bullied by his coarse friends and his sleazy travelling-salesman father, pre-med student Ray (**Jeremy Davies**, whom Russell first spotted in a car commercial) has to turn down a prestigious summer internship to care for his mother, the sullen but attractive Susan (Watson), who has a broken leg and her own smothered ambitions to stew over. Instead of working in the Surgeon General's office, Ray must carry Mum back and forth to the bathroom, stand by while she showers in case she loses her balance, plunge a hand inside her cast to rub cream on her chafing skin. The whiff of Oedipal tension only thickens the stifling atmosphere. What's more, Ray can't find a moment's peace to experience the pleasures coded in the film's title (the family dog, alas, always takes an interest in his activities), and he botches a possible romance with a high-school senior (**Carla Gallo**). But mother and son are at least united in their miserable imprisonment, and their shared seething frustration boils over into proscribed lust and morning-after revulsion.

Russell recalls that he used to "have these huge screaming fights" with his mother, describing the energy as "sexual, in a way. It's like a fuck-fight. It's very charged." *Spanking The Monkey* captures the family's unique capacity to drive its members crazy, and then forges into nearly uncharted territory by suggesting that blood-borne infuriation can find a taboo erotic release – especially if you're a sexually stymied kid snagged between adolescence and adulthood and your mum looks like Alberta Watson. The filmmaker puns wickedly on this idea when a nosy neighbour asks Ray what he's been up to, and assumes that the reclusive kid has coined a new phrase for spanking the monkey when Ray truthfully replies, "Choking my mother".

Stranger Than Paradise

dir Jim Jarmusch, 1984, 89m, b/w
cast John Lurie, Richard Edson, Eszter Balint *cin* Tom DiCillo *scr* Jim Jarmusch

Jim Jarmusch's films often unfold as a series of cohesive vignettes, like a collection of linked short stories. In the case of *Stranger Than Paradise*, his episodic style was well-matched to a strict economy of resources. The movie began life as a short when German director **Wim Wenders** gave Jarmusch about a half-hour's worth of film stock left over from his previous project. Over a weekend, Jarmusch put together a spare tale of a disaffected young man and his cousin visiting from Hungary, shooting in long single takes so as not to waste film, and later secured German financing to add two more segments. *Stranger Than Paradise* made an astonishing $2.5 million at the American box office, won the Camera d'Or for best first feature at Cannes and, most importantly, helped demystify the idea of the art film, for both audiences and would-be filmmakers.

Willie (**John Lurie**) lives in a blighted patch of Lower East Side New York. He gambles to pay the rent, whiling away much of his

Paradise found? Richard Edson, Eszter Balint and John Lurie (from left)

time with his equally feckless friend, Eddie (**Richard Edson**). His cousin from Budapest, Eva (**Eszter Balint**), arrives for a ten-day stay in his filthy studio apartment before continuing on to their aunt's in Cleveland. (Like Jarmusch, Eva loves the **Screamin' Jay Hawkins** song "I Put A Spell On You" and plays it incessantly.) Willie, who's been in America for a decade, resents her presence, but softens when she shoplifts some food for the household. A year later, Willie and Eddie visit Eva in Cleveland. The trio travel to Florida, where the two men repeatedly leave Eva alone in their hotel room while they place bets at the track. Mistakenly thinking that Eva's returned home, Willie boards a plane to Hungary, but his cousin is in fact still in their hotel room.

Such are the spare events in *Stranger Than Paradise*, which Jarmusch described as "a semi-neorealist black comedy in the style of an imaginary Eastern European film director obsessed with **Yasujiro Ozu** and familiar with the 1950s American television show 'The Honeymooners'." (In case the debt to Ozu wasn't evident in the stationary camera setups, Jarmusch has Willie and Eddie bet on a horse called "Tokyo Story".) Quintessentially American in its multinational lineage and immigrant characters, *Stranger* is a movie about roots. Willie refuses to converse with Eva in Hungarian, though her English is limited, and the words he does use are rude and dismissive ("Don't answer my fucking phone"). His behaviour seems to be a semi-conscious expression of discomfort about his foreign background; he's annoyed when Eddie says, "I didn't know you were from Hungary or Budapest or any of those places." Yet Willie is drawn to Eva, following her to Ohio and even, fruitlessly, to his disavowed birthplace.

"You know, it's funny," Eddie remarks, "you come to someplace new, and everything looks just the same." His sentiments are later echoed in Jarmusch's *Mystery Train* (1989), when a tourist decides that Memphis is a lot like his hometown of Yokohama, and in *Down By Law* (1986), when a trio of convicts on the lam seek shelter in a room that resembles the prison cell they escaped ("Man, this is a little too familiar," one remarks). Shot on location in purposefully drab black-and-white by **Tom DiCillo**, the movie flattens its three different regions into a single underpopulated, derelict landscape. For all its national and physical roaming, *Stranger Than Paradise* traces a frustrated stasis. The characters are going nowhere, and having trouble getting there.

Sweet Sweetback's Baadasssss Song

dir **Melvin Van Peebles, 1971, 97m**
cast **Melvin Van Peebles, Simon Chuckster, Hubert Scales, John Dullaghan** *cin* **Robert Maxwell, Jose Garcia** *scr* **Melvin Van Peebles**

It is difficult in the first decade of the new millennium to gauge the impact that *Sweet Sweetback's Baadasssss Song* had in 1971, when it struck the first blow for the blaxploitation movement. Many of its early viewers had never seen a film made by African-Americans for African-Americans, and it was the first time that any audience had laid eyes on an antihero like Sweetback, a taciturn sex machine who vanquishes Whitey and gets away with it.

"This film is dedicated to all the Brothers and Sisters who had enough of the Man," the opening credits declare. *Sweet Sweetback* is a battle cry – and not just for the rebellion inherent in its bawdy, violent content, which inspired the memorable tagline "Rated X by an All-White Jury". **Melvin Van Peebles** not only directed and starred in the title role but wrote, produced, composed and edited the movie. He bucked the white Hollywood establishment by relying on independent finance (some of it out of his own pocket) and hiring a multiracial, non-union crew. The finished feature rather miraculously emerged from a gruelling production process that entailed arrests, death threats, the temporary loss of the filmmaker's eyesight, fistfights between Van Peebles and his assistant editor and a last-minute financial bailout by **Bill Cosby**. According to Van Peebles, he also got extra money to fund the project after he contracted gonorrhoea from one of his actresses during one of the film's explicit sex scenes and got compensation for on-the-job injury!

Raised in a brothel, Sweetback is thrust onto the path of righteous brotherhood when he witnesses two white policemen savagely beating a black suspect and decides to fight back, pulping both cops with the handcuffs chained to one of his wrists. Thereafter, the minimal plot of *Sweet Sweetback* is easily summarized: Sweetback encounters and eludes cops. He jogs for a while. Encounter, elude, jog. Repeat until Sweetback reaches Mexico. Of course, the very notion that a commercially viable movie would permit Sweetback to cross that border alive – after killing a dog or two and snacking on a lizard – is part of what makes the film such a radical political statement.

One of the impediments to placing the movie in its proper cultural and historical context is that, by virtually every critical standard, *Sweetback* is a dreadful film. The sound is muddy, the performances inept, the images often out of focus and badly exposed, and Sweetback's various, universally satisfied conquests aren't women so much as quivering pairs of spread legs. In an early scene, the figure between two of those legs is none other than Melvin's then-13-year-old son, **Mario**, as the young Sweetback, who loses his virginity to one of his lusty housemates. (Much of this explicit scene is blacked out on the British DVD release of *Sweetback* in accordance with the 1978 Protection of Children Act.) Some thirty years after the fact, Mario would have his own say on *Sweetback* when he directed and starred in the biopic *Baadasssss!* (2003). With the junior Van Peebles once again playing the younger incarnation of his father, the movie was equal parts payback and tribute to his trailblazing dad.

Tarnation

dir Jonathan Caouette, 2003, 88m b/w and colour

with Jonathan Caouette, Renee Leblanc, Adolph Davis, Rosemary Davis, David Sanin Paz *cin* Jonathan Caouette

Not long after 11-year-old **Jonathan Caouette** acquired his first video camera, he filmed a scene of himself playing a battered wife who confesses to shooting her husband. As the addled character – inspired by an episode of *The Bionic Woman* – tugs nervously at her bangs and haltingly delivers her "testimonial", the performance flits almost imperceptibly between drag-queen high camp and soul-scraping Method acting; a child occupies the frame, yet the fact of his youth fades from view.

But Caouette never enjoyed any conventional semblance of a childhood, as he reveals in his film testimonial, *Tarnation*. This scene and seemingly every video, snapshot and answering-machine

The whole truth: indie documentaries

In 2004, the Cannes Film Festival's top prize, the Palme d'Or, went to a documentary for the first time in nearly fifty years: **Michael Moore**'s *Fahrenheit 9/11*, an anguished invective against George W. Bush's presidential administration, which also broke records at the box office. Moore's controversial triumph made the biggest splash in a wave of successful non-fiction films, which included **Jeffrey Blitz**'s *Spellbound* (2002), an improbably riveting tale of young spelling-bee hopefuls; **Andrew Jarecki**'s *Capturing The Friedmans* (2003), a staggering tapestry of a 1980s sex-crimes witch-hunt in suburban Long Island; **Morgan Spurlock**'s *Super Size Me* (2004), a personal investigation into the perils of a McDonald's diet; and *The Fog Of War* (2003), **Errol Morris**'s timely portrait of former US defence secretary Robert S. McNamara.

American independent filmmaking has always boasted a strong documentary component: from the groundbreaking *vérité* work of **D.A. Pennebaker**, Frederick Wiseman and the Maysles brothers in the 1960s, through the searing post-Vietnam docs of the 1970s, to Moore and Morris's own non-fiction hits in the 1980s (*Roger & Me* and *The Thin Blue Line* respectively). The documentary renaissance evident in the 2000s was responding to several specific factors, not least the war in Iraq and the divisive politics and official lies of the George W. Bush era. **Eugene Jarecki** constructed a cogent analysis of American's military-industrial complex, *Why We Fight* (2005), and **Robert Greenwald** cornered the market on quickie polemical docs, including *Uncovered: The War On Iraq* (2004), *Outfoxed: Rupert Murdoch's War On Journalism* (2004) and *Wal-Mart: The High Cost Of Low Price* (2005).

As Greenwald's prolific output makes clear, rapid technological innovations have rendered moviemaking far cheaper and more accessible than ever before. *Spellbound* and *Super Size Me* were shot on inexpensive digital video and **Jonathan Caouette** famously put together his autobiographical film *Tarnation* (2003) for a three-figure budget using iMovie software that came free with his home computer.

Caouette's film points up another trend, whereby compulsive self-documentation over many years becomes a rich archival trove for a documentarian to sift through and stitch together. **Jeff Feuerzeig**'s *The Devil And Daniel Johnston* (2005) revels in the troubled eponymous singer-songwriter's penchant for confessional tape-recorded diaries and artful home movies. The titular family in *Capturing The Friedmans* can be seen as subjects, actors and second-unit directors: the film relies heavily on their enthusiasm for recording their intimate lives, even – or especially – at their lowest and most humiliating ebbs.

As documentaries become more commonplace at the arthouse and even the multiplex, a fruitful mingling of fiction and non-fiction has begun. **Shari Springer** Berman and **Robert Pulcini**'s *American Splendor* (2003) invites the actors and real-life players in comic-book artist **Harvey Pekar**'s biography to share screen space. And for *The Talent Given Us* (2004), first-time director **Andrew Wagner** pushed self-exposure in new directions by casting his own dysfunctional family in a road-trip comedy about a dysfunctional family. Here, truth isn't stranger than fiction so much as the two simply blur together.

message Caouette has ever recorded or possessed enfolds into a confessional collage, pieced together with iMovie software for the famous total of $218.32 (before music rights and post-production, which swelled the budget by several figures). When Jonathan was 4, his mentally disturbed mother, **Renee,** fled their home state of Texas with him to Illinois where she was raped and later arrested. Jonathan went from an abusive foster-care home to the custody of his grandparents, **Adolph and Rosemary Davis,** who gave consent to the electro-shock treatments that presumably short-circuited Renee's brain. At 12, Jonathan smoked two PCP-laced joints dipped in formaldehyde; a subsequent psychotic episode left him with "depersonalization" disorder, whereby the subject feels a strong, dream-like disassociation from the events of his life.

Given Caouette's background, depersonalization sounds less like a malady than a necessary coping tool, one that took practical form through filmmaking. An alternative title for *Tarnation* could be *I Am A Camera.* "Filming things had a critical life or death purpose," Caouette said after the movie's release. "It was always a defence mechanism and a way to have a sense of control over my life." Caouette is a ruthless documentarian, recording his grandmother after she's suffered a stroke, his decrepit and agitated grandfather and, for three excruciating minutes, his mother as she acts out a pathetic routine with a small pumpkin. *Tarnation* offers tantalizing glimpses of Caouette's early, evidently **John Waters**-influenced Super 8 shorts (titles include *The Ankle Slasher; The Goddamn Whore;* and *Rosemary Davis, Rosemary Davis*) as well as footage from the musical he directed in high school (an adaptation of *Blue Velvet* scored to **Marianne Faithfull** songs!). A gifted editor, Caouette weaves an impressionist tapestry of his childhood, interspersing his home movies with film and television clips (*Rosemary's Baby,* the 1970s kids' show *Zoom*) and overlaying a gorgeously melancholy pop soundtrack (including **Magnetic Fields**, Red House Painters and Glen Campbell's "Wichita Lineman"). The filmmaker leaves little doubt that these Proustian artefacts carry as much of a personal significance as his family's travails.

If Caouette's compulsive image-making is a means of self-defence, at times he wields his camera like a weapon at his injured, vulnerable family (*Tarnation* begins when Caouette receives word that his mother has survived a lithium overdose) and the movie is open to charges of exploitation. But if anyone has a right to exploit this material, it's Caouette. *Tarnation* is a kind of pornography, and that's not a dig – nobody since **Courtney Love** in her mid-1990s rock-widow incarnation has performed such a fascinating and fit-fully brilliant strip show of screaming grief, psychic damage and unpretty resilience. The torrential narcissism of *Tarnation* is inextricable from its torn-scab honesty.

The Thin Blue Line

dir Errol Morris, 1988, 103m
with Randall Adams, David Harris, Gus Rose, Edith James, Dennis White *cin* Robert Chappell, Stefan Czapsky *scr* Errol Morris

Dallas police officer Robert Wood was shot dead late one night in November 1976. Sixteen-year-old serial offender **David Harris** later carried the deadly weapon in an armed robbery. Harris was arrested while driving the stolen car in which Wood's assailant had sped away from the murder scene. Harris even bragged to his friends that he had killed the cop. And yet, in the course of events detailed in *The Thin Blue Line*, it wasn't David Harris who was convicted of the crime. Instead, Harris served as chief witness in the prosecution of **Randall Adams**, a so-called "drifter" with no motive and no criminal record, who was sentenced to death for Wood's murder (later commuted to life imprisonment). Adams consistently protested his innocence until, after serving more than twelve years in prison for a crime he didn't commit, he was released in March 1989. *The Thin Blue Line* was submitted as evidence in the hearing that set him free.

Adams "almost overacted his innocence" says a homicide detective in one of the film's many Kafkaesque moments. **Errol Morris**'s documentary strongly suggests that, despite the lack of physical evidence and all the arrows pointing at Harris as the murderer, the state of Texas pursued the 28-year-old Adams simply because he could receive the death penalty and the teenaged Harris could not. (Harris died by lethal injection for an unrelated murder in 2004.) A former private investigator, Morris pieces together the crime and the appalling miscarriage of justice that followed with forensic precision, and his interviews are stunningly incisive. He gets just about everyone involved to talk: Adams, Harris, law-enforcement officials, lawyers for the prosecution and defence, and the three eminently unreliable witnesses whose testimonies sealed Adams' fate. Most chillingly, Harris delivers a tape-recorded virtual confession at film's end. The recording caps Morris's exposé of sheer incompetence and wilful blindness to hard facts as demonstrated by Dallas law enforcement. In a larger sense, the film presents a case study in how the death penalty corrupts the American judicial process. The movie is also an existential howl of anguish. As Morris said at the time of its release, "The terrifying truth at the centre of *The Thin Blue Line* [is] that things happen for no reason."

The Thin Blue Line may have been, as the *Washington Post* put it, "the first movie ever to solve a murder", although that wasn't good enough to earn it an Academy Award nomination. (Morris's film was one among a long and painfully conspicuous streak of critically and commercially successful documentaries inexplicably given the Oscar brush-off, including Michael Moore's *Roger & Me*, **Steve James**'s *Hoop Dreams* and Terry Zwigoff's *Crumb*.) But the movie isn't a landmark solely for its transformational impact on one man's blighted life. *The Thin Blue Line* energized the documentary genre with its nocturnal re-enactments, infusions of ironic black comedy and Morris's idiosyncratic flourishes: at one point, his camera contemplates a fast-food milkshake flying through the air; at another, the movie makes a brief detour so that the original judge in Adams' case can reminisce about his father, an FBI agent during Prohibition who witnessed the death of John Dillinger. Eschewing narration and haunted by **Philip Glass**'s anxious score (Morris has praised the composer for his ability to evoke "existential dread"), the movie is equal parts oral history and *noir*-inflected detective story. Suspenseful and quietly outraged, it shattered established notions of what a documentary could do and be.

To Sleep With Anger

dir Charles Burnett, 1990, 101m
cast Danny Glover, Mary Alice, Paul Butler, Richard Brooks, Sheryl Lee Ralph, Carl Lumbly *cin* Walt Lloyd
scr Charles Burnett

The catalyst for the events of writer-director **Charles Burnett**'s most well-known film is a tried-and-tested dramatic device: the enigmatic stranger on the doorstep, who penetrates the family home and subtly disrupts its established rhythms and power alignments. In *To Sleep With Anger*, the interloper takes form as Harry Mention (**Danny Glover**), who invites himself under the Los Angeles roof of Gideon and Suzie (**Paul Butler** and **Mary Alice**), generous friends from their old days together down south. Harry's hardly had time to put his feet up on the furniture before he's pulling buried secrets and carefully concealed insecurities from under the sofa cushions.

Harbingers of discord presage Harry's unannounced arrival in LA. The superstitious Gideon, patriarch of his middle-class black family, has misplaced his "toby", or good-luck charm. He's infuriated by his younger son, known as Babe Brother (**Richard Brooks**), and Babe's snobby wife, Linda (**Sheryl Lee Ralph**), who treat Gideon and Suzie as de facto nannies for their neglected little boy, Sunny (DeVaughn Nixon). Babe Brother is a feckless whiner who resents the shadow cast by his upstanding elder brother, Junior (**Carl Lumbly**), but Babe's self-pitying inertia thickens considerably under the influence of Harry, a Pushkin-quoting layabout whose courtly manners have an over-practised, predatory edge.

Distending his welcome (he even clips his toenails in the living room), Harry imports playing cards, moonshine and a gaggle of seedy old-timers into Gideon and Suzie's strait-laced abode. His venereal air of contagious corruption is literalized when Gideon falls mysteriously ill. Harry's presence and the consequences of his actions serve as reminders that the fellow members of his southern-rooted generation haven't completely assimilated into their middle-class suburban environs. (In a mordantly funny exchange, the local reverend discovers that Suzie has administered some folk remedies to her ailing husband and scolds her for not invoking the healing powers of prayer instead.) When Harry encounters Hattie (Ethel Ayler), he insists on regarding this pious, white-haired lady as the same promiscuous hellraiser of their youth. A marauding ghost, or an ambassador of hell, he harries his hosts with past memories best left unmentioned.

What's in a name? "Old Harry" is English slang for the devil, and in a popular African-American folk tale, a young boy called Wiley must outfox the menacing Hairy Man. Wiley's analogue is clearly the watchful, taciturn Sunny, who's on to Harry the moment the trickster walks through his grandparents' door. Biblically speaking, Gideon is an instrument of God, and for his sons, (nick)naming is destiny: Junior looks and acts like his father's worthy heir, while Babe Brother is infantilized every time he's addressed (and behaves accordingly). And yet, even a splintering family is a formidable collective force. When a domestic argument turns violent, Junior and Babe Brother are suddenly united in penitent guilt, and the blood drawn – blood they'll always share – acts as a potion to break Harry's spell.

Burnett's film is a modern folk tale imbued with magic and mythic portents, but in its depiction of a hard-won – and perhaps short-lived – family solidarity, *To Sleep With Anger* is also a down-to-earth reflection on the comforts and chafings of blood ties.

Devil's advocate: Danny Glover in *To Sleep With Anger*

Wanda

dir **Barbara Loden, 1971, 102m**
cast **Barbara Loden, Michael Higgins** *cin* **Nicholas Proferes** *scr* **Barbara Loden**

Barbara Loden was inspired to write and direct *Wanda* after reading a newspaper article about a woman, **Wanda Goranski**, sentenced to twenty years in prison for her role in a bank robbery. "When the judge sentenced her, she thanked him," said Loden, who transposes this weird gratitude when the film's Wanda (played by Loden) smiles and thanks the brusque garment-factory manager who's just turned her down for work she badly needs. Penniless and adrift in Pennsylvania coal country, Wanda clings for dear life to a one-night stand who's itching to be rid of her (he finally dumps her at a road-side ice-cream parlour) and sticks loyally by the side of pathetic Mr Dennis (**Michael Higgins**), the middle-aged criminal in a cheap suit who belittles her, slaps her face and forces her collusion in his car-thieving and his doomed bank-heist scheme. And yet, Wanda is capable of letting go. In an early scene, she wanders late into family court (cigarette in hand, hair in curlers), nonchalantly agrees to a divorce and waives all rights and responsibilities pertaining to her children, who are sitting in the courtroom but seem to escape their mother's notice.

As Bérénice Reynaud writes in her valuable essay "For Wanda", the listless protagonist is "a woman who simply doesn't fit within her environment, doesn't belong anywhere (she's never shown as having a home of her own)". The movie itself is a loner too: its theatrical release amounted to a run in a single New York cinema, and the director never helmed another film. Loden was a Tony Award-winning stage actress, best known to moviegoers for her role as **Warren Beatty**'s sister in *Splendor In The Grass* (1961), directed by her husband, **Elia Kazan**. Drawing on the spontaneous *vérité* energies of **John Cassavetes** and **Shirley Clarke**, Loden, editor and cinematographer **Nicholas Proferes** and a skeleton crew shot *Wanda* on hand-held 16mm camera, using available light and non-professional actors with the exception of the two leads, both of whom deliver selfless performances. Loden's Wanda is benumbed, drained of expectation.

By contrast, Higgins' Mr Dennis (as Wanda always calls him) is rigid with fury at his no-exit condition. If you have nothing and want nothing, as he scolds Wanda, "you're not even a citizen of the United States". They are citizens of no place, going in useless circles; at the movie's end, Wanda ends up back where she started, and where she will remain.

Wanda's reputation has grown in recent years; the great French actress **Isabelle Huppert**, for example, arranged for its overdue DVD release in France and chose the film to screen at her Brooklyn Academy of Music retrospective in 2005. What little attention *Wanda* received on its 1971 premiere tended to note its affinities, or lack thereof, to the celebrated *Bonnie And Clyde*. Both films feature a criminal on the run with a girl and a gun, but Loden's hapless duo share little else in common with **Arthur Penn**'s beautiful outlaws in their classic cars and bespoke vintage duds. Painted in wan and grainy colours, *Wanda* is unforgettable for its dinginess; its subcutaneous power comes from its ability to make existential desolation tactile. The slag heaps, the seedy motel rooms, the greasy food, the rarely changed clothes, Mr Dennis's sweaty infuriation – it's all a grimy build-up of dead-end drudgery that will never wash off.

Welcome To The Dollhouse

dir Todd Solondz, 1995, 88m

cast Heather Matarazzo, Matthew Faber, Brendan Sexton Jr, Eric Mabius, Angela Pietropinto, Dimitri Iervolino *cin* Randy Drummond *scr* Todd Solondz

"I wanted the movie to be called *Faggots And Retards*," **Todd Solondz** told a reporter in 1996, "not for the shock value, but because this is the language kids use." However, the writer-director conceded, "I did want the movie to find a distributor, so I didn't call it that." *Welcome To The Dollhouse* loses none of its potency for its polite, accommodating substitute title. The nasty epithets and scarring

Low self-image: Heather Matarazzo in *Welcome To The Dollhouse*

trash-talk of middle-school society whizz around like bullets – most of them hitting Dawn "Weiner Dog" Weiner (**Heather Matarazzo**). Abused by classmates and teachers, cast aside by her parents in favour of her adorable little sister and hopelessly in love with an older hunk, Dawn is the movie's bespectacled face of pubescent pain and forbearance. Solondz's grip on the terror and bewilderment peculiar to the seventh grade never falters from the moment that Dawn all but tiptoes into the gaping maw of hell otherwise known as the school cafeteria.

Solondz's second feature, *Dollhouse* is a uniquely subjective viewing experience. Depending on their memories of early adolescence, audiences may interpret it as an expressionist horror film, a scrupulously accurate representation of the social acid bath that is junior high school, or both. Costume designer **Melissa Toth** dresses the fearless Matarazzo in bright flower prints and happy ruffles that only underline Dawn's miserable estrangement from the sweetness and light of a storybook girlhood. Mum (**Angela Pietropinto**) openly can't stand her own daughter, especially after Dawn refuses to tear down her beloved refuge, the Special People Club – or "that mess in the backyard", as her mother labels it – to make room for her parents' twentieth anniversary barbecue. Resident hood Brandon (**Brendan Sexton Jr**) vows to rape the wretched Dawn, but at least this empty threat stems from a confused affection. He's drawn to his fellow misfit and he's embarrassed by it, just as Dawn is ashamed of the only person who offers her loyal friendship, little neighbour Ralphy (**Dimitri Iervolino**), the sole other member of the Special People Club.

Dawn's internalized capacity for cruelty – she rejects Ralphy as, yes, a "faggot" – is Solondz's psychological masterstroke. Forever fuming, Dawn is not beatified by her suffering. She doesn't seem particularly bright, has no apparent talents or interests of her own and her wish "to be popular" lacks imagination, if not a grasp on reality. *Welcome To The Dollhouse* implicitly invites the audience to identify with the enemy and collude with Dawn's persecutors, which lends the film a discomfiting immediacy, tapping into the same youthful reptile brain as **William Golding**'s *Lord Of The Flies* (1954). It's up to Dawn's college-fixated older brother, Mark (**Matthew Faber**), to let in a sliver of hopeful light. By the time you reach high school, he explains, "They'll call you names, but not as much to your face."

Solondz's steadfast refusal to sentimentalize the resilience of youth only intensifies the chilly desolation of the film's final scene. As Dawn stares out the window of a packed school bus, she pushes out the notes of her school's twee theme song "The Hummingbird Anthem" as if her life depended on it, the soundtrack isolating her thin soprano from the chorus of kids. As ever, Dawn is alone. Of course she will soldier forward and endure, swallowing the insults and absorbing the blows. She's a survivor. But what else could she be?

A Woman Under The Influence

dir John Cassavetes, 1974, 141m

cast Gena Rowlands, Peter Falk, Lady Rowlands, Katherine Cassavetes, Fred Draper *cin* Mitchell Breit (in charge of lighting), Caleb Deschanel (additional photography) *scr* John Cassavetes

Even in the midst of the American cinema renaissance of the 1970s, **John Cassavetes** could find no backers for *A Woman Under The Influence*, which he independently financed and self-distributed. As his wife, **Gena Rowlands**, later explained, "After John had done the screenplay for it, everyone said: 'Why does anyone want to see a picture about a crazy middle-aged dame?'" That's a perfectly valid synopsis of this summary-proof film, and yet, it opens up a question that reaches closer to its heart: just how crazy is this dame?

Mabel Longhetti (Rowlands) certainly looks the part: agitated, dishevelled, muttering to herself as the film's lush opera soundtrack pours out from her radio. She drinks too much, and has a colourful repertoire of tics and strange gestures. She has little or no conception of how to make polite conversation or maintain physical boundaries between herself and others. Yet she's a devoted wife and mother. Her three young children love to be near her and are fiercely protective of her. And though many a "normal" woman would hit the roof if her husband came home at dawn unannounced with a dozen of his co-workers, when Nick Longhetti (**Peter Falk**) does it after a busted water main keeps his construction crew out all night, she prepares a spaghetti breakfast for the lot and does her addled best to be a gracious hostess.

If Mabel is insane, the only concrete threat her insanity poses is to her husband's pride – his self-image as reflected in the gaze of his friends, his blue-collar colleagues and his imperious mother. (The formidable Margaret Longhetti is embodied by Cassavetes' real-life mother, **Katherine**, while **Lady Rowlands**, mother of Gena, plays Mabel's mum; the casting choices lend autobiographical ballast to *Woman*'s volcanic domestic turmoil.) Generally, when Mabel and Nick are alone together, they're fine. But when an audience is watching, they become agitated by the ways Mabel fails at or forgets her role as ordinary housewife. "Tell me what you want me to be ... I can be that," Mabel implores Nick, not long before he commits her to a mental institution. "I can be anything." Nick also clings desperately to the idea that Mabel can snap out of her madness: a destructive illusion that further unhinges them both and is a central source of conflict in the film.

Nick loves his wife deeply and passionately – that's never in doubt – but he oscillates wildly, sometimes in the space of a second, between loyal acceptance of her eccentricities and explosive fury at her unruly behaviour. Once Mabel is sent to an asylum for six months, Nick's emotional instability and dangerous temper become ever clearer. On impulse, he drags his children out of school for a miserable trip to the seaside; on the ride home, he even gets them drunk. After Mabel's release, he stages a disastrous, half-aborted and howlingly inappropriate welcome-home party for his

Crazy middle-aged dame? Gena Rowlands in *A Woman Under The Influence*

fragile bride. She's scarcely been back an hour before he flies into a horrible rage: "I'll kill you, I'll kill those sons a' bitchin' kids!"

Early in the film, Nick directs a similar homicidal threat towards a neighbour and his two children, yet no one in Cassavetes' brilliantly performed film ever raises the possibility that Nick should be committed. Meanwhile, Mabel has endured shock treatments and half a year away from her children, and all for the crime of upsetting social norms and embarrassing her spouse. Her every quirk and outburst taps cracks in Nick's glass ego even when she's nowhere near him. Without compromising its characters' rich nuances and contradictions, without reducing Mabel to a mere martyr or condemning Nick as an uncomprehending bully, *A Woman Under The Influence* lays bare a man's world, where unchecked masculine aggression and violence is normative – a regrettable but sympathetic reaction to the stimulus of female hysteria, however or wherever it may be perceived. It would be enough to drive anybody crazy.

The Icons:
contemporary directors & talent

Michael Moore examines America's gun culture in the ambitious *Bowling For Columbine*

The Icons:
contemporary directors & talent

Paul Thomas Anderson
Writer and Director, b.1970

A low budget and lack of studio affiliation are reliable indicators of independence, but so is a director's right to final cut – a right that **Paul Thomas Anderson** has insisted upon since the adverse experience of his first film. The wunderkind auteur was barred from the editing room after delivering an overlong cut of his debut, *Sydney*, which his production company trimmed and renamed *Hard Eight* (1996) without Anderson's consent. He found a far more hospitable studio in New Line, which championed his breakthrough, *Boogie Nights* (1997). Anderson's only limitations this time around were a $15 million budget and – a tricky proposition for a movie about the porn industry – an R rating, which he earned even though the film ends on an almost-literal money shot.

A grade-school porn aficionado (he discovered his dad's stash around the age of 10) as well as an avid junior filmmaker (he dropped out of NYU film school after a few days), Anderson made a seminal half-hour film, *The Dirk Diggler Story* (1988), when he was in his teens, eventually expanding it into *Boogie Nights*. Famously opening with a bravura, *Goodfellas*-style tracking shot, *Boogie Nights* follows a close-knit group of adult-film personnel from the industry's relatively innocent celluloid 1970s heyday into the crass, cocaine-crazed video era, with the impressionable Dirk Diggler (**Mark Wahlberg**), a sweet kid with a 13-inch dick, centre frame. Drolly hilarious, frank, occasionally shocking and faultlessly empathic, the movie showed Anderson as a major original talent, as well as an ace student of **Martin Scorsese** and **Robert Altman**. Indeed, the through-line from Altman's richly characterized ensembles to Anderson's is so clear that the

Paul Thomas Anderson directs his Rollergirl, Heather Graham, on the *Boogie Nights* set

younger filmmaker was hired as back-up director on the octogenarian Altman's *A Prairie Home Companion* (2006).

Anderson pushed his propensity for domestic grand opera to the limit for his three-hour *Magnolia* (1999) in which a superlative cast (Julianne Moore, **William H. Macy**, Philip Baker Hall, *Boogie Nights'* Melora Walters) sustains high note after high note of explosive ardour, grief and regret; at one point they even break into song (**Aimee Mann**'s "Wise Up"), and the climax of climaxes reaches Biblical proportions. Clearly a work of catharsis – Anderson was mourning his father's death from cancer during production – the movie recruited **Tom Cruise** at his most manic for the role of a misogynist sex guru who reconciles at the last possible moment with his dying dad (Jason Robards).

Smaller in scale but no less unpredictable and unapologetically emotional than *Magnolia*,

Punch-Drunk Love (2002) likewise integrated a trippy score by **Jon Brion**; the music's squeezebox circus melancholy complements and comments upon the action, becoming a personality unto itself. (Brion also scored David O. Russell's *I Heart Huckabees* and **Michel Gondry**'s *Eternal Sunshine Of The Spotless Mind*, both 2004.) Here, however, Anderson for the first time deploys his gifts in the service of a straight-up romantic comedy, improbably casting frat-house comedy favourite **Adam Sandler** against English rose **Emily Watson**. The movie locates its crowning incongruity in harnessing Sandler's soulful-autist persona to a shaggy, irresistible romance of opposites, filmed in widescreen colour like the most sumptuous of MGM musicals. Wherever he goes, Paul Thomas Anderson goes all the way.

 Boogie Nights
dir Paul Thomas Anderson, 1997, 156m

Set during the 1970s and 80s amid the San Fernando Valley porn industry, Anderson's assured movie is a portrait of an extended virtual family, including porn auteur and father figure Jack Horner (Burt Reynolds), motherly leading lady Amber Waves (Julianne Moore) and their surrogate kids Reed Rothchild (John C. Reilly), Rollergirl (Heather Graham) and the stupendously well-endowed Dirk Diggler (Mark Wahlberg). A cornucopia of densely plotted dialogue, superb acting, a terrific period soundtrack and dynamic camerawork and editing, the movie is a coming-of-age tale about a kid and an industry that both grew up too fast.

Charles Burnett

Writer and Director, b.1944

Born in the Deep South but raised from an early age in the Watts area of Los Angeles, **Charles Burnett** has tackled a wide range of subjects and historical periods in his career. He specializes, however, in subtle, incisive portrayals of domestic dissonance, inter-generational conflict and socio-economic anxiety among lower- and middle-class African-American communities in LA. With low-key, deliberate pacing that allows characterizations and moods to expand and deepen, Burnett imbues much of his work with the resentments, claustrophobia and abiding love incubated in the family.

While he was still enrolled in the film program at UCLA, Burnett began his first feature, the landmark work *Killer Of Sheep* (1977). Focusing on a slaughterhouse labourer in an impoverished South Central neighbourhood, *Killer Of Sheep* was one of just fifty films originally selected for the Library of Congress' National Film Registry. Sibling rivalry drove his second film, *My Brother's Wedding* (1983), which was plagued with production difficulties (chief among them the lead actor quitting twice) and the film has been rarely screened. The director had better luck with *To Sleep With Anger* (1990), his first project to employ professional actors, when he secured the participation of producer extraordinaire **Edward R. Pressman** and star **Danny Glover**, a bankable actor after his co-starring role in the blockbuster *Lethal Weapon* (1987).

Despite the critical accolades for *To Sleep With Anger* (which was also later added to the National Film Registry), Burnett's career path has met more than its share of bumps and delays. Miramax declined to put much promotional weight behind *The Glass Shield* (1994), a relatively conventional and surprisingly melodramatic account of racism and corruption within the Los Angeles police force. Although flawed, the movie appeared remarkably prescient after the Ramparts scandal that rocked the LAPD in 1997.

Recipient of many an award, retrospective and even a MacArthur "genius grant", Burnett is widely recognized as an exceptional film artist even as he perpetually struggles to secure financing and distribution for his movies. In recent years, the man hailed as "America's greatest living black filmmaker" (by John Patterson in the *Guardian*) and "the least well-known great American filmmaker" (by Armond White of the *New York Press*) has turned to television. His mini-series *The Wedding* (1998), starring the future Oscar winner **Halle Berry**, carried the imprimatur of "Oprah Winfrey Presents". The Disney Channel was the unlikely venue for one of Burnett's strongest efforts to date, *Nightjohn* (1996), a tale with mythic resonances about a plantation slave who teaches another to read and write, at tremendous risk to them both.

Though Burnett continues to direct regularly, his work is still under-seen and under-appreciated, and his career offers ample evidence that the American independent renaissance of the late 1980s and early 1990s wasn't necessarily an equal-opportunities affair.

Steve Buscemi

Actor, Writer and Director, b.1957

Like no one else among his film contemporaries, actor and director **Steve Buscemi** single-handedly embodies the spirit of American independent cinema. A subtle and unsentimental filmmaker, Buscemi prizes the sort of low-key, character-driven dramas that the Hollywood establishment has rarely championed. As a performer, he has at turns brought jittery energy and wistful pathos to films by **Quentin Tarantino**, **Terry Zwigoff** and the **Coen brothers** (not to mention blockbuster fare such as the *Spy Kids* franchise and various Jerry Bruckheimer productions). As **Jim Jarmusch** told *The New Yorker*, "In the characters

he plays and in his own life, he's representing that part of us all that's not on top of the world."

A onetime firefighter and mainstay of the downtown New York art and performance scene in the 1980s, Buscemi got his first film break via his standout performance in Bill Sherwood's AIDS drama *Parting Glances* (1986). Thereafter he established a seemingly ubiquitous presence as a character actor: as the heist conspirator and bad tipper Mr. Pink in Tarantino's *Reservoir Dogs* (1992), the beleaguered would-be filmmaker of **Alexandre Rockwell**'s *In The Soup* (1992), the beleaguered actual filmmaker of **Tom DiCillo**'s *Living In Oblivion* (1995) and the doleful record collector in Zwigoff's *Ghost World* (2001). He dies in several films by the Coen brothers, who in *Fargo* (1996) built a comic refrain out of repeated descriptions of Buscemi's character: a "little guy, kinda funny-lookin'." In certain lights, Buscemi's features can emanate an askew, spectral beauty, but his oversized eyes, imperfect teeth, slight stature and adenoidal tenor have ensured that he stands aside from conventional leading-man status.

In *Fargo*, Buscemi delivered a selfless performance as the weasely low-life whose body is memorably disposed of in a wood-chipper. The same year, he unveiled his sharply observed, **Cassavetes**-inspired debut feature, *Trees Lounge* (1996), directing himself as a feckless out-of-work mechanic boozing away his days in a Long Island bar. Having also written the semi-autobiographical *Trees Lounge*, he next helmed a script by ex-con **Eddie Bunker** in *Animal Factory* (2000), about a young inmate (**Edward Furlong**) who's new to the trial-by-fire culture of doing hard time and comes under the wing of a tough but sympathetic lifer (**Willem Dafoe**). Buscemi casts a near-anthropological eye on cellblock life, which is fraught with violence and peril and yet also harbours precious corners of refuge and comradeship. Many of the film's extras are actual prisoners, only adding to its rough-and-tumble authenticity. Buscemi returns to *Trees Lounge*'s theme of bewildered adult stasis in *Lonesome Jim* (2005), about a depressed 27-year-old (**Casey Affleck**) who moves back into his parents' house. He continues to focus less on plot mechanics than on conversational rhythms, textures of personality, local custom and the unspoken emotions concentrated in a glance or a gesture.

Parting Glances
dir Bill Sherwood, 1986, 90m

The late Sherwood's sole film is a pivotal day in the life of overtaxed book editor Michael (Richard Ganoung), as he prepares for the departure of his lover, Robert (John Bolger), on a long-term trip to Africa, and also tends to their friend Nick (Steve Buscemi), a musician with AIDS. Bittersweet and acutely observed, this was the first commercial feature to depict the AIDS epidemic, and it gave Buscemi his first major role.

Steve Buscemi, typically beleaguered as *Living In Oblivion*'s indie filmmaker

Two-timers: actor-directors at work

Vanity, thy name may be the actor who "really wants to direct". But for a filmmaker on a tight budget, as **John Cassavetes** demonstrated, casting oneself can be a savvy economic decision (you don't have to pay yourself) and an additional means of maintaining creative control over a project. And often, for autobiographical first features, the writer-director is simply the man closest to the part, as with **Steve Buscemi** in *Trees Lounge* (1996) and **Vincent Gallo** in *Buffalo '66* (1998), both of which draw upon personal history.

Billy Bob Thornton built his star-making, Oscar-winning script for 1996's *Sling Blade* around a character he had developed in a one-man show and an earlier short film. His turn as the mildly retarded, occasionally homicidal Karl Childers is a perceptive example of self-direction:

despite Karl's jutting underbite, hunched gait, gravel-throated drawl and catchphrase-worthy lines, Thornton crafts a fully rounded personality rather than a southern-fried cartoon.

Other two-timers keep a lower profile, including smooth leading man **George Clooney**, who has relegated himself to supporting roles in his directing efforts (2002's *Confessions Of A Dangerous Mind* and 2005's *Good Night, And Good Luck*). **Sean Penn** is a rarity as an actor-director as he has never actually directed himself onscreen, though he can lay claim to guiding **Jack Nicholson** towards two of his greatest late-career performances, in the harrowing dramas *The Crossing Guard* (1995) and *The Pledge* (2000).

Trees Lounge
dir Steve Buscemi, 1996, 95m

After his boss fires him (for "borrowing" money from the till) and takes his girlfriend, lonely mechanic Tommy (Buscemi) slouches towards alcoholism and his ex's restless teenage niece (Chloë Sevigny). Named for the homely bar in working-class Long Island where the protagonist spends too much of his downtime, Buscemi's fine directorial debut never solicits undue sympathy for the feckless but potentially decent Tommy. It strikes an elegant balance between wry comedy and quiet desperation, leaning toward the latter in the lingering, indelible final shot.

Larry Clark

Writer and Director, b.1954

Larry Clark's renowned first book of photographs, *Tulsa* (1971), depicted the seedier side of the heartland's sex-and-drugs subculture. His directing career has similarly drifted into offroad America, documenting sundry penetrations and

effluences of the human body – preferably that of lissome, glassy-eyed adolescents. Since his tabloid-ready first film, *Kids* (1995), Clark's attentions have seldom strayed from the young and the restless, drugging and screwing their way to a halcyon stupor. Scripted by 19-year-old **Harmony Korine**, *Kids* remains the director's biggest critical and commercial success thus far, but his filmmaking instincts and his sense of humour have both improved in the intervening years.

Clark changed gear momentarily for his second work, *Another Day In Paradise* (1998), a serviceable *Bonnie And Clyde* descendant in which a drug dealer (**James Woods** in a sly, nifty performance) and his junkie wife (**Melanie Griffith**) snag a younger couple along for a cross-country crime spree. Despite a cast old enough to buy their own drinks, *Paradise* was a recognizably Clarkian affair for its candid purview of heroin dependency and fondness for the word "fuck" and its variants. Soon enough, however,

Clark delivered another drooling paean to naked, amoral jailbait in *Bully* (2001), a perhaps accidentally hilarious true-crime piece based on a grisly Florida murder case.

His most recent films, *Ken Park* (2002), also scripted by Korine, and *Wassup Rockers* (2005), have celebrated teen sexploits and mischief with not only trademark bluntness (*Ken Park* is far more graphic than *Kids* or *Bully*), but also warmth and cockeyed wit. Saturated with gore, cum and other juices, *Ken Park* revels in adolescent bumping and bloodletting. However, the film's real shock value rests not in its hardcore flourishes – including a dispassionately observed rub'n'tug scored to the grunts and squeals of a women's pro tennis match – but in its unexpected tenderness.

It might have been tempting to give much of the credit for *Ken Park* to Clark's co-director, the brilliant cinematographer **Edward Lachman**, but Clark's next effort was just as inspired. In *Wassup Rockers* (2005), a tight-knit ensemble of Latino skateboard enthusiasts from South Central ("They're like the Mexican Ramones!", an LA scenester coos) rollick through Beverly Hills in pursuit of horny girls and the choicest urban skating arenas, falling foul of racist cops, territorial rich kids and an armed-and-dangerous Clint Eastwood-lookalike. Mostly wiped clean of Clark's characteristic shock tactics and copious bodily fluids, *Wassup Rockers* locates a fertile strain of goofball humanism, and attests that Clark can no longer be pigeonholed as a mere purveyor of titillation.

Patricia Clarkson

Actress, b.1959

Though Amerindie cinema is generally more accommodating to late bloomers and those with unconventional charisma than Hollywood, the road is tougher for women, which makes the relatively recent emergence of **Patricia Clarkson** all the more heartening. Distinguished by her arresting sharp features and throaty, slightly scratched voice, Clarkson was nearing 40 when she won her scene-stealing role in **Lisa Cholodenko's** *High Art* (1998) as Greta, a heroin-addict and former Fassbinder actress. Within a few years of this breakthrough, it seemed every other Sundance premiere reserved a role for the actress, who's ever reliable in adding spark and edge to any film she graces.

Clarkson is flawless as **Julianne Moore's** gossipy, possibly treacherous best friend in **Todd Haynes's** *Far From Heaven* (2002) and sensuously sympathetic as a CBS employee secretly married to one of her colleagues in **George Clooney's** *Good Night, And Good Luck* (2005). She also sunk her teeth into a particularly tasty role in Craig Lucas's *The Dying Gaul* (2005) as the manipulative but wounded wife of a studio executive (Campbell Scott) who's having a gay affair with a penniless screenwriter (**Peter Sarsgaard**).

More often that not, Clarkson had played mothers: a Manhattan therapist whose family finds trouble en route to a weekend in the Catskills in **Larry Fessendon's** indie horror *Wendigo* (2001); a lonely divorcee in **Rose Troche's** suburban-neighbourhood ensemble *The Safety Of Objects* (2001); a sometime clown entertainer who's perhaps too close for comfort to her twenty-something son in **David Gordon Green's** *All The Real Girls* (2003); and the parent of a dead child in both **Sean Penn's** *The Pledge* (2001) and **Thomas McCarthy's** *The Station Agent* (2003).

The actress won a surprise Oscar nomination for **Peter Hedges'** road trip *Pieces Of April* (2003) as the ironically named Joy, a cancer-stricken sourpuss riding shotgun towards Manhattan for Thanksgiving with her semi-estranged daughter

(Katie Holmes). As both written and performed, Clarkson's resentful character corrects – or perhaps overcorrects – moviedom's usual image of the terminally ill patient, beatified by stoic suffering.

High Art
dir Lisa Cholodenko, 1998, 102m

When drug-addict photographer Lucy (Ally Sheedy) meets magazine editor Syd (Radha Mitchell), each sees the other as a potential means of career advancement, but then an unlikely romance develops between them. Cholodenko's moodily photographed character piece provided a comeback for ex-Brat Packer Sheedy, a breakout role for Mitchell and a colourful supporting part for Patricia Clarkson.

Joel & Ethan Coen

Writers, Directors and Producers, Joel b.1954, Ethan b.1957

The actor Jon Polito once said that making a movie with the **Coen brothers** is at times "like being directed in stereo." Although Joel Coen is usually credited as sole director, the breakdown of official titles between him and his younger brother, Ethan – always listed as producer and co-writer – are basically arbitrary. "Co-directed in every sense of the word," as Joel has put it, their movies are collaborations through and through. (They're also co-edited under the shared pseudonym **Roderick Jaynes**.) With a lifetime of cultural and personal experience shared between them, the brothers pack their hyper-referential comedies with verbal and visual quotations from the cinema, literature and pop-cult history they were raised on. Their scripts bear the playful palimpsest traces of two wiseacre kids in their bedroom, acting out scenes from a black-and-white classic they saw on television that afternoon and adding their own gross-out gags and inside jokes.

Their icy, pastiche style invites dismissal of the filmmakers as the mere sum of their influences – but what influences! Onwards from their early *noir* features *Blood Simple* (1984) and *Miller's Crossing* (1990), the hard-boiled pulp of Cain, Chandler, Hammett et al has informed the Coens' entire filmography with its litany of amateur crimes, botched kidnappings and boomerang blackmail schemes. Their 2001 film *The Man Who Wasn't There* most obviously evoked 1940s *noir* in the glittering black-and-white cinematography by **Roger Deakins**. But the Coens also ventriloquize the fizzy verbal wit of Sturges and Hawks and otherwise invoke the disparate likes of Homer, Shakespeare, Hitchcock, Kubrick, **Busby Berkeley**, Kraftwerk, *Night Of The Hunter* (1955) and *The Evil Dead* (1981) (on which Joel served as assistant editor). *Barton Fink* (1991) resurrects *Waiting For Lefty* author **Clifford Odets**, vertiginous curly hair and all, in the form of John Turturro, and also features analogues to Louis B. Mayer and William Faulkner. In *The Hudsucker Proxy* (1994), a toast to 1930s screwball with dazzling Art Deco sets, **Jennifer Jason Leigh** modelled her fast-talking dame on Rosalind Russell in Hawks's *His Girl Friday* (1939).

So is their aesthetic just a fetishist's taxidermy of old stories and modes? Are their films dead things? Sometimes. In *Intolerable Cruelty* (2003) the brothers gluttonously indulge their appetites for sitting-duck targets, broad burlesque, who's-on-first verbal games and infirmity humour (for instance, ulcer, asthma and colostomy-bag jokes). However, they're capable of achieving the screwball humanism of their Hollywood Golden Age heroes when they feel genuine affection for their characters: **Nicolas Cage** and **Holly Hunter** as the baby-napping young couple in the flawlessly hilarious *Raising Arizona* (1987); Joel's wife, **Frances McDormand**, in an Oscar-winning role as the honourable and pragmatic police chief of Brainerd, Minnesota, in the skewed, snow-

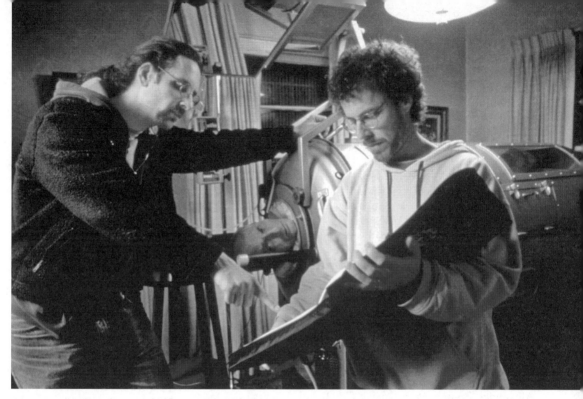

Joel (left) and Ethan Coen confer on the *Big Lebowski* set

bound *Fargo* (1996); and **Jeff Bridges** as Jeffrey "The Dude" Lebowski, "the laziest man in Los Angeles County", in the exhilarating mess *The Big Lebowski* (1998). Given the Coens' reputation as cold-blooded puppetmasters, perhaps it's only apt that their best films are also their most warm-hearted.

 Raising Arizona
dir Joel Coen, 1987, 94m

Ex-convict H. I. McDunnough (Nicolas Cage) and his police-officer wife, Edwina (Holly Hunter), are devastated when they realize they can't conceive, and decide to procure one of the famous "Arizona Quints" because, as Edwina reasons, the babies' parents "already got more than they can handle". The couple's baby quest is complicated by two of Hi's jailbird pals, some nosy acquaintances and a fearsome biker thug in the Coens' madcap, exhilarating comedy.

Hope Davis

Actress, b.1964

A seasoned stage thespian who's made a welcome sidelong entrance into films, **Hope Davis** was unexpectedly well-prepared for the acting life by a degree from Vassar in cognitive science ("It's about getting into somebody's head, and asking why they are who they are," she told the *Village*

Voice in 2003). Davis can telegraph the distress and vulnerability of her often beleaguered characters without demanding to be liked, and their irritable world-weariness is all the more sympathetic for being unsugared.

Imperfect relationships and fractious families are common in the Davis oeuvre. In **Greg Mottola**'s *The Daytrippers* (1996), Davis's fretful wife finds possible evidence that her husband is unfaithful, and her entire family piles into a station wagon to track him down. In Bart Freundlich's *The Myth Of Fingerprints* (1997), she's the ditzy girlfriend of one of the dysfunctional adult children of a domineering father.

Brad Anderson's *Next Stop Wonderland* (1998), which featured Davis in the lead role, became the subject of a proverbial Sundance bidding war (Miramax won). Contrived yet disorganized, the movie is no classic, but the actress is captivating as an unlucky-in-love nurse with a hopeful romantic destiny lying in store for her.

She brought a bracing, plaintive anger to tricky parts as **Jack Nicholson**'s embittered daughter in **Alexander Payne**'s *About Schmidt* (2002) and as the seemingly adulterous wife in Alan Rudolph's *The Secret Lives Of Dentists* (2002). The tall, lovely blonde who routinely effaces her beauty does so most dramatically in Shari Springer Berman and Robert Pulcini's *American Splendor* (2003): donning bug-eyed glasses and a lank brown wig to play the wife of comix artist Harvey Pekar, Davis finds a bedraggled harmony with co-star **Paul Giamatti** to create a cranky, endearing duet.

Next Stop Wonderland
dir Brad Anderson, 1998, 104m

Like *Sleepless In Seattle* and many other modern tales of love, this gossamer film contrives to keep its would-be lovers apart until the last possible moment. Erin (Hope Davis) is a nurse whose meddlesome mum has recently placed a personal ad on her behalf, and Alan (Alan Gelfant) is an aspiring marine biologist. Named for an actual stop on Boston's public transport system and buoyed by a lovely bossa nova soundtrack, this slight romantic comedy is most notable for giving Davis room to shine.

Abel Ferrara
Writer and Director, b.1951

Sticky with spilled booze and cum and covered in spiritual grime, the films of **Abel Ferrara** belong to the often-proud tradition of exploitation filmmaking. But the visceral bursts punctuate deeper social and soulful concerns, and the Bronx-born director is a surprisingly patient observer of his characters and their grim surroundings. Many of his movies compile an anthropological record of pre-Disneyfication New York City: downtown is a menacing wasteland, teeming with all manner of bloodsucking parasites – pushers, junkies, tramps, hoodlums, bad lieutenants – all similarly disfigured by their ravenous cravings. Ferrara most overtly embodied the bloodsucking human condition via the vampire-philosopher played by **Lili Taylor** in *The Addiction* (1995).

Much of Ferrara's work enacts the profound solipsism and physical debasement – whether self-inflicted or projected outward – associated with the throes of religious ecstasy. He often engages with Catholic imagery and dogma, most infamously in *Bad Lieutenant* (1992), in which **Harvey Keitel** played a depraved and desperate New York cop, and most recently in *Mary* (2005), his response to **Mel Gibson**'s blockbuster *The Passion Of The Christ* (2004), with **Matthew Modine** playing a Ferrara-like director making a film about the life of Jesus.

His first film was the epistolary porn flick *Nine Lives Of A Wet Pussy* (1976), which he directed under the pseudonym Jimmy Boy L before taking the lead role in his acknowledged feature debut, *The Driller Killer* (1979), wherein a stressed-out painter blows off steam in the manner suggested by the title. This "video nasty" appeared at a transitional moment in American cinema. It straddled the last days of the sex'n'horror drive-in market (Ferrara made sure to tack on some hot lesbian shower action) and the first stirrings of the American independent renaissance, as did his rape-revenge quickie *Ms. 45* (aka *Angel Of Vengeance*) (1981). The prolific director earned a critical breakthrough with the icy, brutal *King Of New York* (1990), which prowled crime scenes, drug dens and orgies alongside the impassive gang lord played by **Christopher Walken.**

The Abel guy: Ferrara with Zoë Tamerlis filming *Ms. 45* (aka *Angel Of Vengeance*)

(Ferrara has grown to dislike the movie, calling it "fucking fascist filmmaking".)

After the controversial *Bad Lieutenant* and the Keitel-**Madonna** meta-movie *Dangerous Game* (1993) – the director called it *"The Player* meets *Contempt"* and the leading lady called the director a "scumbag" – Ferrara secured his highest budget yet, $20 million, for the spottily distributed remake *Body Snatchers* (1993). He then tried his hand at period melodrama with the histrionic, near-nihilist *The Funeral* (1996), set among a mob–ruled union racket in Depression-era New York, and stumbled over a *Rashomon*-like narrative in *New Rose Hotel* (1998). But Ferrara rebounded with *Cahiers du Cinéma* favourite *'R Xmas* (2001). Taking place during Mayor David Dinkins's final days in office before he was unseated by the Draco-manqué Rudolph Giuliani, this elliptical tale of an aspirational husband-and-wife team of heroin distributors is quintessential Ferrara material, brimming with wry humour and unexpected poignancy.

 Ms. 45 (aka Angel Of Vengeance)
dir Abel Ferrara, 1981, 81m

Thana (Zoë Tamerlis), a mute garment-district employee, is raped on her way home from work, and then raped again that same day – at which point she concludes that enough is enough. Ferrara's potent low-budget revenge fantasy seethes with pointed feminist anger and made a cult heroine out of star Tamerlis (later Lund), who was just 17 at the time of filming; she went on to co-write Ferrara's *Bad Lieutenant*.

Carl Franklin

Director, b.1949

Carl Franklin has an ineffable knack for ambience. Most at home within the flexible confines of neo-*noir*, he can infuse a film with alluring perfume trails of atmosphere, whether conjuring the smoky intrigue of a 1940s LA nightclub or the hazy, horny torpour of hottest Florida. Patient and suggestive, his best work bespeaks a grown-up sensibility all too rare in Hollywood, but perhaps it comes a little easier to a man who made his first feature at 40.

He jobbed as an actor throughout the 1970s and 80s, mostly in television guest spots, before enrolling as a student at the American Film Institute; Franklin directed future star **Don Cheadle** in a short called *Punk* (1986), and made his feature debut for **Roger Corman**'s Concorde Pictures with the forgotten **David Carradine** vehicle *Nowhere To Run* (1989). After helming two more B-movies (both starring future *In The Bedroom* director **Todd Field**), Franklin made his artistic breakthrough with *One False Move* (1992). Winning the Independent Spirit Award for best director, the film moves cagily back and forth between a murderous criminal trio on the road and the goofball rural sheriff to whom they're somehow linked. Equally well-received, but not so successful at the box office, 1995's *Devil In A Blue Dress* was an adaptation of a **Walter Mosley** novel set just after World War II among the jazz clubs on LA's Central Avenue, where newly jobless veteran Easy Rawlins (**Denzel Washington**) becomes an ad-hoc private eye and gets dangerously embedded with unsavoury elements. (The still little-known Cheadle again featured, this time in a flashy supporting turn as Easy's trigger-happy pal.)

Thereafter Franklin made some curious forays: he tried his hand at a dysfunctional-family weepie with *One True Thing* (1998) – for which **Meryl Streep** won an Oscar nomination as an ostensibly flighty woman dying of cancer – and then attempted pulpy legal melodrama with *High Crimes* (2002), starring **Ashley Judd** and **Morgan Freeman**. Franklin returned to form with *Out Of*

Time (2003), which featured Denzel Washington as a south Florida police chief who is framed for murder thanks to a bygone adulterous affair. As in *Devil In A Blue Dress*, Washington must disentangle himself from a sticky web of implication, but here Franklin and first-time screenwriter **David Collard** introduce droll comic elements to the mix, pointing up the existential absurdities of the hard-knock *noir* life.

Vincent Gallo

Actor, Writer, Director, Cinematographer, Editor and Composer, b.1962

Renaissance man **Vincent Gallo** has created an onscreen persona that melds self-obsession with self-loathing, and domination with martyrdom. His extreme multitasking on his second film, *The Brown Bunny* (2003) – he toiled as lead actor, director, writer, producer, editor, cinematographer and set designer – suggests both the narcissistic control freak and the overextended loner, exhausted by his solitude. Like a ragged stray cat, the Gallo alter ego is in desperate need of love and attention, even as he hisses warnings at sympathetic onlookers to stay clear. His persecution complex could feast greedily upon the tremendous criticism heaped on *The Brown Bunny* at Cannes 2003, where observers debated whether or not it was the worst film ever to premiere on the Croisette. (The theatrical-release version of *Bunny* was re-edited and much improved, even winning a thumbs-up from principal Cannes naysayer Roger Ebert.)

A world-class workaholic, Gallo is also a painter and musician, and he seems to spend much of his available free time slagging off his past, present and future colleagues: Abel Ferrara, **Chloë Sevigny** and Anjelica Huston have all been targets of Gallo's hilariously hyperbolic

abuse. He lit out for New York City aged 16 and quickly established himself as a downtown jack-of-all-trades: breakdancer, motorcycle racer and bandmate of a pre-fame Jean-Michel Basquiat. Later a reliable character actor and Calvin Klein model (with his piercing blue eyes and aquiline features, he can look seedy or Christ-like), Gallo appeared in **Alan Taylor**'s Jersey comedy *Palookaville* (1995), as one of three unemployed pals who take up a life of inept crime, and lies in a casket for much of Ferrara's daringly morbid melodrama *The Funeral* (1996). However, Gallo has done much of his most interesting work as an actor outside America, for the great French director **Claire Denis**.

Gallo spent some $100,000 of his own money on his filmmaking debut, *Buffalo '66* (1998), a black-comic finger-salute to his decayed hometown. His protagonist, the vengeful ex-con Billy Brown, is petulant, pathologically touchy and certainly disturbed, yet he's also unaccountably alluring to his kidnap victim, a buxom tap-dance student (**Christina Ricci**). In the road movie *The Brown Bunny*, Gallo's motorcycle racer Bud Clay likewise proves irresistible to seemingly every woman he meets. Anyone sensing a pattern here need not be reminded that *Bunny* famously climaxes during a three-minute sequence in which Chloë Sevigny performs unsimulated fellatio on her director.

 The Brown Bunny
dir Vincent Gallo, 2003, 92m

Morose, unstable motorcycle racer Bud Clay (Gallo) embarks on a cross-country trip to his next competition, and acts as a magnet to a series of different women along the way – all of them lonely, and all of them named after flowers. Gallo's public antics and a graphic sex scene overshadowed this compelling and truly independent film, which is an unflinching, slow-moving journey through truck-stop America in all its quiet desperation.

"Quaffable, but not transcendent": Paul Giamatti (left) with Thomas Haden Church in *Sideways*

Paul Giamatti

Actor, b.1967

Amerindie movies, like the New Hollywood films of the 1970s that so inspired them, have always made room on the marquee for more than just suave heartthrobs and blown-glass beauty queens. Emerging in recent years to join the ranks of Steve Buscemi, **Philip Seymour Hoffman** and other unconventional indie-identified stars has

been **Paul Giamatti**. Vaguely frog-like in aspect, his nasal voice perfectly poised for a fine whine or a cathartic snit, Giamatti onscreen is a consummate schlub, a grumbling underdog who wins our sympathies even as he fends them off.

Son of the late **Bart Giamatti**, the former Yale president and baseball commissioner, Paul Giamatti worked steadily through the late 1990s, contributing fine supporting turns to studio products including *Private Parts* (1997), *Saving*

Private Ryan (1998), *The Truman Show* (1998) and *Man On The Moon* (1999). He made his first significant dip in the indie pool via **Todd Solondz**'s discomforting diptych *Storytelling* (2001), which cast Giamatti as a documentary filmmaker observing a gauche and ghastly suburban family. He is delightfully cantankerous as the grumpy comix artist Harvey Pekar in the imaginative biopic-cum-documentary *American Splendor* (2003), but his richest role to date was in **Alexander Payne**'s *Sideways* (2004). As Miles, a frustrated novelist and alcoholic wine aficionado still reeling from a painful divorce, Giamatti embodies the film's unflinching and often hilarious confrontation with self-loathing and panicked despair.

 ### American Splendor
dir Shari Springer Berman & Robert Pulcini, 2003, 101m

Perpetually disgruntled comix artist Harvey Pekar (Paul Giamatti) survives marriage, cancer and the myriad petty indignities of everyday life in this mordant adaptation. The movie playfully tweaks the stodgy conventions of the documentary and biopic genres by inviting the real Pekar to narrate sections of the film and, delightfully, arranging for the film's actors and the real people they play to interact.

David Gordon Green

Writer and Director, b.1975

Isolated in space and time, **David Gordon Green**'s strange and unclassifiable films transpire over sleepy, semi-rural landscapes littered with rusted debris and ominous portents. Apparently untouched by the incursions of popular culture and recent technological advances, Green's characters sometimes fumble to articulate themselves, yet they all speak his folksy space-cadet patois of teenage poetry and non-sequitur koan, even if the words taste foreign on their tongues. They all seem to have a faintly mythic tragedy or two in their back pages – including, perhaps, the one unfolding onscreen. Situations and dialogue are blatantly contrived, yet Green's movies follow an internal logic that can produce breathtaking moments of emotions stripped and exposed to light. (For some viewers, the films' awkward naiveté and unpractised passion may bring to mind the primitive, powerful oddness of the Shaggs' first album.) Green's films are pretentious, but his pretensions are all his own.

Raised in Texas and based in North Carolina, Green was only 24 when he made his feature debut, *George Washington* (2000). Rejected by Sundance, the movie became a hit – or at least a vivid curiosity – with critics after its Berlin Film Festival premiere. It both beguiled and bemused viewers with its singular mix of dreamy languor and queasying violence, the mood enhanced by the abstracted voiceover and the sun-dappled cinematography by **Tim Orr**, an indispensable collaborator in Green's career to date.

The stiff, even somnambulant acting in Green's films is an important part of their otherworldly ambience, but the young actors in *George Washington* often seem like the director's marionettes. In *All The Real Girls* (2003), however, leading lady **Zooey Deschanel**'s drowsy, sceptical drawl found a perfect cadence with Green's often bizarre dialogue. (She can make "I had a dream that you grew a garden on a trampoline and I was so happy that I invented peanut butter" sound like a breezy ad-lib.) Back home in her North Carolina mill town after several years at an all-girls boarding school, Deschanel's Noel falls in love with Paul (**Paul Schneider**), a twenty-something Lothario who appears to be genuinely regretful about his former love-'em-and-leave-'em ways. Meandering between the languorous and the overwrought, the film nails several indelible moments of passion, disclosure and heart-wrenching communication breakdown.

Observers have often made shorthand references to Green's work as "neo-Southern Gothic", but he only fulfilled the comparison with his third film, *Undertow* (2004), which borrowed openly from **Charles Laughton**'s *Night Of The Hunter* (1955) in setting two boys (Devon Alan and *Billy Elliot*'s Jamie Bell) in flight from their dastardly uncle in rural Georgia. Though the requisite Green-ian quirks are intact here (the younger boy eats mud and paint and organizes his books "according to smell"), *Undertow*'s chase-thriller components make it his most conventional film to date. Still, there's no one remotely like Green working in American cinema today, and the director still retains the rare capacity to surprise and startle audiences.

George Washington
dir David Gordon Green, 2000, 89m

A group of poor, neglected kids in North Carolina attempt to conceal an accidental death among their ranks in Green's debut, shot in gorgeous widescreen 35mm. The voiceover narration and magic-hour images bear the heavy influence of Terrence Malick, but the film also marked out the young Green as a promising talent.

Jake Gyllenhaal

Actor, b.1980

To the Hollywood manner born (mum Naomi is a screenwriter, dad Stephen is a director), **Jake Gyllenhaal** enjoyed a brief tenure as the

Stabs in the dark: Jake Gyllenhaal as Donnie Darko

new millennium's first Indie It Boy. Alongside his more conventional attributes (puppy-dog eyes, carved physique), Gyllenhaal's clenched-jaw diction and air of amiable self-effacement only further augment his appeal. He first came to significant attention with his wondrously sly, soulful performance as the possibly schizophrenic title character in **Richard Kelly**'s *Donnie Darko* (2001). The film also featured Jake's elder sister, **Maggie**, who delivered the memorable first line of this off-kilter period piece, "I'm voting for Dukakis", and became a certified Indie It Girl in her own right as the blooming office masochist in Steven Shainberg's *Secretary* (2002).

Gyllenhaal proved his comic aptitude in a pair of roles as the moony suitor to an older woman: as the ardent teenage photo-processing clerk who pursues **Catherine Keener** at her legal peril in **Nicole Holofcener**'s *Lovely & Amazing* (2001) and as a self-dramatizing Salinger aficionado opposite **Jennifer Aniston** in **Miguel Arteta**'s *The Good Girl* (2002). His Hollywood ascension completed via his starring role in the summer blockbuster *The Day After Tomorrow* (2004), Gyllenhaal made his most daring choice to date in **Ang Lee**'s *Brokeback Mountain* (2005). As a young ranch hand in 1960s Wyoming who falls in socially proscribed love with his fellow sheepherder (**Heath Ledger**), Gyllenhaal won his first Oscar nomination.

Donnie Darko
dir Richard Kelly, 2001, 113m

Unfolding in the Halloween-haunted weeks before the 1988 American presidential election, Kelly's inspired first feature follows a smart, restless, disturbed kid (Jake Gyllenhaal) with a superhero moniker who may or may not have found a wormhole in the time-space continuum. Shaded in autumnal tones of dread and muted grief, unafraid of adolescent emotional violence and perversity and scored to a lovingly curated 1980s pop soundtrack, *Donnie Darko* is one of the most impressive American debuts in a generation.

Hal Hartley
Writer and Director, b.1959

Depending on where you stand on **Hal Hartley**'s work, consistency is either the mark of a true auteur or the hobgoblin of an entire career. Typically set in a strangely depopulated Long Island, his deadpan philosophical comedies often centre on ne'er-do-wells with shady pasts, either on their way to prison or on their way home from it. They speak in aphorisms with Beckett-like taciturnity, delivered in arch monotone. Marked by sudden death, offhand violence, botched crime and family dysfunction, Hartley's films are extremely eventful yet intractably calm. His characters are vessels of ideas, and they rarely react to their electrified circumstances in recognizable ways. At times they hardly seem to react at all.

Often hinging on coincidence, betrayal and startling revelation, Hartley's work (clearly influenced by **Brecht** and **Godard**) transpires in a universe that operates according to its own logic and rhythm. The hermetic quality is heightened by recurring appearances by members of Hartley's unofficial stock company: regulars include **Robert John Burke**, Martin Donovan, Elina Löwensohn and **Parker Posey**. In his first two features, *The Unbelievable Truth* (1989) and *Trust* (1990) – titles indicative of his pet themes – Hartley cast **Adrienne Shelley** in similar parts as a bored, mouthy teen who falls for an ostensibly dangerous suitor. The shadows cast by overbearing or absent fathers loom large in both of these films, as in *Simple Men* (1992), in which two brothers – one a thief, the other a philosophy student – seek out their fugitive dad.

Simple Men is, among other things, a road movie, which gestures towards Hartley's willingness to engage with established genres. *Amateur* (1994) also had the conventional outlines of a *noir*-tinged thriller, sending an oddball pair, Thomas (**Martin Donovan**) and Isabelle (**Isabelle Huppert**), on the run from menacing hit men. But since Thomas is an amnesiac with some nasty business in his recent past and Isabelle is a former nun turned writer of pornography, *Amateur* continues the director's fascination with the nature of identity.

Hartley's propensity for reiteration reached a crescendo with the triptych *Flirt* (1995), wherein an identical story plays out in three different cities. In *Henry Fool* (1997), in which a garbage man (**James Urbaniak**) comes under the dubious wing of a penniless ex-convict (**Thomas Jay Ryan**), Hartley attempted an artistic breakthrough, using unfamiliar actors and working on a broader canvas that included startling scatological humour. In recent years, as well as mounting a sequel to *Henry Fool* (2006's *Fay Grim*), the filmmaker has made forays into science fiction with *No Such Thing* (2001), about the encounter between a journalist and a monster-man, and *The Girl From Monday* (2005), about a hyper-consumerist near-future that looks much like our own present. Both films posted diminishing returns, but Hartley's unmistakeable authorial stamp, for better or worse, has remained intact.

The Unbelievable Truth
dir Hal Hartley, 1989, 90m

A wiseacre star student obsessed with the apocalypse (Adrienne Shelley) falls for mysterious mechanic Josh (Robert John Burke). Recently released from prison, Josh is constantly mistaken for a priest and may or may not be directly responsible for two people's deaths. Establishing many of Hartley's signature touches – knowingly stiff performances, dysfunctional families, rat-a-tat-tat dialogue,

intimations of violence and criminality – this efficient comedy remains Hartley's freshest film, perhaps simply by virtue of being his first.

Todd Haynes
Writer and Director, b.1961

Todd Haynes is arguably the most consistently thrilling director working in the US today. His amazingly fecund movies are shaped by overlapping theoretical frameworks (filmic, literary, cultural and psychoanalytical), meticulously designed, voluminously researched and steeped in lovingly reanimated pop-cult iconography. Yet his intellectual acumen and satirical wit rarely preempt emotional engagement with his characters' typical maladjustment to the surrounding social order, especially in the two films he has made with **Julianne Moore**, *Safe* (1995) and *Far From Heaven* (2002). Haynes's films marry intellect to rapture; they feel as keenly as they think.

Haynes earned a surprising amount of mainstream attention for his brilliant featurette *Superstar: The Karen Carpenter Story* (1987), a semiotician's wrenching elegy for the anorexic soft-rock chanteuse as broken Barbie figurine. Filmed entirely with Mattel dolls on miniature sets, the film was pulled from circulation in 1990 (Haynes hadn't secured clearances for the Carpenters songs on the soundtrack), but remains widely available as a bootleg video. The **Jean Genet**-inspired *Poison* (1991) received a small part of its budget from public funding, and thus attracted the ire of right-wing groups over its homoerotic content. Undaunted, Haynes made his next film for public television, the half-hour *Dottie Gets Spanked* (1993), which explored the vigorous fantasy life of a bullied kid who's obsessed with a Lucille Ball-like TV personality.

Haynes has repeatedly centred on characters who can't or won't assimilate, who aren't quite at home in their social or domestic context, or even in their own skin. In *Safe* (voted the best film of the 1990s in *The Village Voice*'s millennial critics' poll), Moore plays an affluent California homemaker who becomes allergic to her surroundings and escapes to a dubious New Age retreat where her condition deteriorates further. Refusing to offer neat diagnoses or trite affirmations, *Safe* is a uniquely shattering experience. Haynes followed it with his most celebratory film, the musical à clef *Velvet Goldmine* (1998), a fan's valentine to the gender-bending London glam-rock scene of the early 1970s, an era Haynes has called "the last really rich, fertile progressive period, propelled by new ideas."

He moved further into the past with *Far From Heaven* (2002), a lush simulacra of **Douglas Sirk**'s 1950s melodramas wherein Moore's lavishly costumed housewife loses her husband (**Dennis Quaid**) to a man and scandalizes her community through her friendship with her black gardener (**Dennis Haysbert**). Beautifully performed, wild with colour, suffused with loss and yearning, *Far From Heaven* was the best-reviewed film of its year. A muted tragedy, it hinges on a quintessentially Haynesian

conflict between the dominant culture that loathes any disturbance of its fabric and the individual who longs to transcend his assigned category or her ill-fitting persona.

Philip Seymour Hoffman
Actor, b.1967

One of a hybrid breed of performer that might be termed the "Star Character Actor", **Philip Seymour Hoffman** has amassed an eclectic corpus distinguished by evident esteem for auteurs and a heartening lack of vanity. Lending ballast to every film he touches, Hoffman tends to steal a scene or two for himself as well. He

Philip Seymour Hoffman captures Truman Capote's peculiar allure

beams perma-smiling sycophancy as a toady in the **Coen brothers'** *The Big Lebowski* (1998), epitomizes jet-set entitlement as a smug brat in Anthony Minghella's *The Talented Mr. Ripley* (1999) and administers a sorely needed shot of adrenaline to **Cameron Crowe's** *Almost Famous* (2000) each time his gonzo rock critic Lester Bangs blusters onto the screen.

At regular intervals, Hoffman (who got his first big break via a small part in the 1992 Al Pacino vehicle *Scent Of A Woman*) will also add a movement to his ever evolving symphony of sad-sack variations: the pudgy boom operator who makes an unrequited lunge at porn star Dirk Diggler in **Paul Thomas Anderson's** *Boogie Nights* (1997); the heavy-breathing phone stalker in **Todd Solondz's** *Happiness* (1998); Hope Davis's hapless boyfriend in *Next Stop Wonderland* (1998); and the puppyish, put-upon screenwriter in David Mamet's *State And Main* (2000). Mamet's ensemble comedy marked Hoffman's debut as a romantic lead, while *Love Liza* (2002) was his first fully fledged star turn, as a gas-huffing Web designer unhinged by survivor's guilt after his wife's suicide.

In P.T. Anderson's account of illness, grief and regret, the epic *Magnolia* (1999), Hoffman delivered one of his most affecting performances as the empathic nurse who eases the passing of Jason Robards's agonized patriarch. A mainstay of Anderson's films, Hoffman also played the bellowing con man in the director's sublimely goofy confection *Punch-Drunk Love* (2002), loaned strong support as **Edward Norton's** best pal in **Spike Lee's** *25th Hour* (2002) and carried Richard Kwietniowski's arresting character study *Owning Mahowny* (2003), playing a compulsive gambler. Hoffman's adventurous choices – which also leave ample room for stage work as both actor and director – culminated

in a best-actor Oscar for *Capote* (2005), about the genesis of **Truman Capote's** innovative "non-fiction novel", *In Cold Blood*. The film is at once a procedural, portrait of the artist, ethical conundrum, classical tragedy and a case study in voracious ambition, and it all hinges on Hoffman's performance in the title role, which captures the writer's peculiar allure while deftly sidestepping caricature.

Nicole Holofcener
Writer and Director, b.1960

Female filmmakers are conspicuous by their absence in this book, but **Nicole Holofcener** has quietly carved out a likeable niche as a writer and director of character-driven, women-centred ensemble comedies, albeit with long intervals between features (she's also a busy television director). *Walking And Talking* (1996) focuses on two lifelong friends with sharply different romantic trajectories: Amelia (Holofcener regular **Catherine Keener**), though smart and attractive, is unlucky in love, even a little bit desperate, while Laura (Anne Heche) is about to be married to her sweet but somewhat inscrutable boyfriend (**Todd Field**, who would go on to direct 2001's *In The Bedroom*). If *Walking And Talking* examined the rueful strain put on a childhood friendship by the upheavals and imperfect attachments of adult life, then *Friends With Money* (2006) put a socio-economic spin on the same conflict. Again, Holofcener honed in on long-standing girlfriends: three of them wealthy, and one (**Jennifer Aniston**) living from paycheck to paycheck.

Perhaps Holofcener's best film to date, *Lovely & Amazing* (2001) observed a mother and her three daughters at various points of physical or emotional crisis. Mum Jane (**Brenda Blethyn**) suffers complications after liposuction. Eldest daughter Michelle (Keener) is frustrated with her marriage and frozen career, and stumbles into an affair with an ardent teenager (**Jake Gyllenhaal**). Middle kid Elizabeth (Emily Mortimer) is a struggling actress with all the insecurities about her looks, weight and sex appeal that the profession often entails. And the youngest girl, 8-year-old adoptee Annie (Raven Goodwin), must contend with being a pudgy African-American child among all these neurotic white women.

Something of an inside job, *Lovely & Amazing* was partly shot in the house where Holofcener grew up, and she too has a much younger, African-American sibling. The film is admirably frank about the queasier aspects of the acting profession: Elizabeth submits to a supremely uncomfortable session on the casting couch with a famous actor, Kevin McCabe (**Dermot Mulroney**), and doesn't even land the part. More boldly, it doesn't shy away from its characters' tendencies toward masochism which are variously suggested through Jane's elective surgery, Michelle's reiterated pride in having endured childbirth without an epidural and Elizabeth's fling with Kevin: after they go to bed together, she asks him to itemize all her bodily attributes and flaws while she stands before him naked.

Nicole Holofcener's onscreen alter ego, Catherine Keener, in *Friends With Money*

THE ICONS: CONTEMPORARY DIRECTORS & TALENT

Where are the women?

Sofia Coppola's 2004 Oscar nomination for directing *Lost In Translation* was only the third time a female director had been nominated in the category, and the very first time a nod had gone to an American woman. But statistics are never kind to women filmmakers, whose films typically account for a mere ten percent of features made in any given year. Arguably, the situation is even worse in the Amerindie arena. With occasional exceptions such as **Nicole Holofcener** (2001's *Lovely & Amazing* and 2006's *Friends With Money*) and **Mary Harron** (1996's *I Shot Andy Warhol* and 2000's *American Psycho*), who have staked out small patches of Indiewood terrain, and **Kathryn Bigelow**, who has worked in both the independent and action-blockbuster realms, precious few women have mapped out steady careers.

During the 1980s, **Lizzie Borden** (*Born In Flames*, *Working Girls*) and **Susan Seidelman** (*Smithereens*, *Desperately Seeking Susan*) started strong but soon lost momentum. As the 1990s indie juggernaut got rolling, **Julie Dash** (*Daughters Of The Dust*), **Allison Anders** (*Gas, Food Lodging*), **Rose Troche** (*Go Fish*) and **Lisa Cholodenko** (*High Art*) all made their mark at Sundance, but their résumés have since been characterized by television work and lengthy pauses between features. Sundance 2000 was hailed as the "year of the woman", with awards going to **Karyn Kusama**'s *Girlfight*, Jenniphr Goodman's *The Tao Of Steve* and **Maggie Greenwald**'s *Songcatcher*, but none of these directors were able to follow through on the accolades, and as of 2006, **Kimberly Peirce** (*Boys Don't Cry*) had not yet made a second feature.

In his book *Spike Mike Slackers & Dykes*, John Pierson addresses the vexing question of women filmmakers missing in action. He suggests that it's no easier or harder for an untried female director to get her foot in the door than it is for a man, but that a "pattern of bias" seems to emerge after her first feature. Short of a major sociological study devoted to this topic, though, an explanation for the relative scarcity of female directors probably won't be forthcoming. In the meantime, audiences can only hope that **Miranda July** will be able to deliver on the promise of her debut feature, 2005's *Me And You And Everyone We Know*, and that **Debra Granick** (*Down To The Bone*, 2004) and **Kelly Reichardt** (*Old Joy*, 2006) can get more attention for their subsequent movies than they received for their striking but neglected previous efforts.

This proved to be a much-talked-about scene, but Holofcener is an unshowy director with a reticent approach to characterization – she observes closely, but doesn't necessarily interpret. Attuned to the drift and unexpected punch of everyday conversation, Holofcener's films are compact but rich, resisting epiphany and climactic confrontation in favour of tiny increments of personal change and private realization.

Friends With Money
dir Nicole Holofcener, 2006, 88m

Four longtime girlfriends have stayed close into early middle age, and three of them are married and well-off: Franny (Joan Cusack) is an heiress, Christine (Catherine Keener) is a screenwriter with a crumbling marriage and Jane (Frances McDormand) is a clothing designer with anger-management issues. The odd one out is poor, unattached house cleaner Olivia (Jennifer Aniston). Disparity of income between friends is an awkward topic that Holofcener addresses with candid wit and screwball energy.

Ted Hope

Producer, b.1962

One of the most significant American producers of the last fifteen years, **Ted Hope** is a champion of new filmmaking talent whose commitment is readily measured in the number of first features he has produced – fourteen by latest count, including films by Ang Lee, Edward Burns, Nicole Holofcener and Todd Field. Starting out as first assistant director on **Hal Hartley**'s debut, *The Unbelievable Truth* (1989), Hope went on to produce the bulk of Hartley's films.

In 1991, he teamed up with **James Schamus** to form the production and distribution company **Good Machine,** which backed Lee's first effort, *Pushing Hands* (1992), and many more of his subsequent films, most of them scripted by Schamus. Under the aegis of Good Machine, Hope also produced Todd Haynes's *Safe* (1995), Burns's Sundance hit *The Brothers McMullen* (1995), Holofcener's *Walking And Talking* (1996) and Todd Solondz's controversial *Happiness* (1998), which Good Machine released after the film's intended distributor, **October Films**, relinquished it following pressure from corporate parent Universal.

In 2001, the year of Field's exquisite *In The Bedroom*, Good Machine was subsumed into the Vivendi Universal empire. Schamus became head of a new boutique division, **Focus Features**, while Hope and a few fellow Good Mechanics formed a new independent production company, **This Is That**, which secured a first-look deal with Focus. This Is That's early efforts included the harrowing *21 Grams* (2003), the award-winning debut features *American Splendor* (2003) and *Thumbsucker* (2005), the splendidly bittersweet *Eternal Sunshine Of The Spotless Mind* (2004) and **Jeff Feuerzeig**'s terrific documentary *The Devil And Daniel Johnston* (2005), about the mentally disturbed singer-songwriter.

This Is That is a reassuring example of against-the-tide thinking – in an age of vast, faceless mega-corporations, Hope and team have ensured they can still nurture projects with a personal touch. As he told *Indiewire* in 2001, "We definitely relish the idea of a small, intimate company where everybody is intricately involved in all the productions in an artistic way."

Jim Jarmusch

Writer and Director, b.1953

Jim Jarmusch is a true-blue independent, perhaps the last of his tribe. Despite many studio offers after the runaway success of *Stranger Than Paradise* (1984), he has never signed on as a director-for-hire, and he was a quarter-century into his filmmaking career before he availed himself of studio financing in 2005 for *Broken Flowers* (produced and distributed by Focus Features, the speciality-films arm of Universal). The wary distance the longtime New Yorker has kept from Hollywood suits the themes of culture clash and alienated ennui that imbue his work. "I think all my films will be about marginal, outsider people," he said at the time of *Stranger*'s release, and so far his prediction has proved more or less true.

His early films trained their gently mocking gaze on displaced hepcats striking a slouchy pose, too cool for school, gainful employment and just about everything else; this pervading sense of slow drift and droll dislocation has remained a constant theme. Jarmusch's films aren't terribly concerned with plot or character development; they aim squarely for a mood, a moment, a specific place in time that swiftly evaporates in one of his signature fade-outs.

A film student at NYU's Tisch School of the Arts in the late 1970s, Jarmusch put his final semester's tuition fees towards his first film, *Permanent Vacation* (1980), and spent just $125,000 on *Stranger Than Paradise*. His movies cherish displacement: a Hungarian girl marooned in her churlish cousin's Lower East Side apartment in *Stranger Than Paradise*; **Roberto Benigni**'s malaprop-prone Italian jailbird in New Orleans in *Down By Law* (1986); an enthusiastic Japanese girl and her hilariously impassive, Carl Perkins-fixated boyfriend touring Memphis in *Mystery Train* (1989); and **Johnny Depp**'s bookish Ohio transplant out of his depth in the Wild West in *Dead Man* (1995).

After his five-strand taxicab odyssey *Night On Earth* (1991), Jarmusch left the contemporary urban world for *Dead Man*, a monochrome, blackly comic distillation of the Western with Depp as nineteenth-century accountant and accidental outlaw William Blake. One of Jarmusch's strongest films, *Dead Man* is a strange, beguiling (and cameo-rich) mix of searching mysticism and gallows humour, but its distributor, Miramax, didn't release it so much as discard it. Jarmusch soldiered on with *Ghost Dog: The Way Of The Samurai* (1999), which boasted a thrilling score by rapper-producer **RZA** and starred **Forest Whitaker** as a samurai hit man, followed by the all-star, hit-or-miss omnibus *Coffee And Cigarettes* (2003).

His most accessible film to date, *Broken Flowers*, matched Jarmusch with his fellow lanky maestro of minimalist deadpan, **Bill Murray**, as an aging Lothario trying to track down his long-lost son. A bittersweet road movie that subtly intimates a wintry dead end for its lonely protagonist, *Broken Flowers* achieved an emotional depth and transparency unlike anything else in the director's oeuvre. But with its episodic structure, desultory road-tripping and bone-dry sight gags, it's also an unmistakably Jarmuschian bouquet.

Mystery Train
dir Jim Jarmusch, 1989, 113m

Sharing its name with an Elvis Presley record (as well as a Greil Marcus book), this multi-strand comedy spends 24 non-consecutive hours in Memphis, where a young Japanese couple, a bereaved Italian woman and a few seedy types all converge on a hotel where blues musician Screamin' Jay Hawkins presides at the front desk. Loose and strange, the movie revels in Jarmusch's usual deadpan absurdism and weird Americana.

Charlie Kaufman
Writer, b.1958

As focused, imaginative and compassionate a screenwriter as American cinema has ever seen, **Charlie Kaufman** asserts his singular artistry – his independent spirit – through collaboration. Not content simply to hand over his scripts to directors, Kaufman has forged creative partnerships with the music-video whiz kids **Spike Jonze** and **Michel Gondry**. And who knows how much improved George Clooney's so-so *Confessions Of A Dangerous Mind* (2002), helmed from Kaufman's script, might have been had Clooney respected Kaufman's wishes via a little teamwork?

For years, Kaufman toiled as a writer for short-lived television series such as *Get A Life*, *Ned And Stacey* and *The Dana Carvey Show*, while his various movie scripts made the rounds. *Being John Malkovich* (1999) started to come together when **Francis Ford Coppola** happened to show Kaufman's screenplay to Jonze, his daughter's then-boyfriend. From *Malkovich* onwards, all of Kaufman's twisting, sometimes tail-eating stories have dared to treat human consciousness as a living creature, a constructed space, a rich landscape, a wellspring of metaphor. *Malkovich* invaded an actor's brain and populated it with wayward souls seeking new identities or eternal life.

The script for *Adaptation* (2002), which penetrated the interior world of a tormented scribe named Charlie Kaufman (**Nicolas Cage**), is a character unto itself – or rather, a vessel for two diametrically opposed sensibilities: philosophy-damaged screenwriter Charlie and his identical twin, Donald (Cage again), a happy and confident hack. (**Donald Kaufman** is credited as co-writer on *Adaptation*, the film is dedicated to Donald "in loving memory" and Donald received an Oscar nomination for best original screenplay – all this despite the fact that he never existed.)

Kaufman's filmography is a vivid gallery of introverted schlubs: **John Cusack**'s starving-artist puppeteer in *Being John Malkovich*, Cage's lovelorn Charlie in *Adaptation* and **Jim Carrey**'s mopey Joel in *Eternal Sunshine Of The Spotless Mind* (2004), Kaufman's second film with Gondry after the messy farce *Human Nature* (2001). Centred on a couple who erase their memories of each other via a newfangled medical procedure, *Eternal*

Charlie Kaufman (Nicolas Cage) faces down his worst enemy in *Adaptation*

Sunshine leaps audaciously through *Malkovich*-like portals into memory and the subconscious. With its wounded romantic's heart, the script is vintage Kaufman – it works marvel after marvel in imagining the self-preserving amnesia of a broken but hopeful heart, and the bewildering beauty and existential horror of being trapped inside one's own addled mind.

Adaptation
dir Spike Jonze, 2002, 114m

A screenwriter named Charlie Kaufman (Nicolas Cage) struggles to adapt Susan Orlean's *The Orchid Thief*, but his self-doubt and his earnest, confident identical twin keep putting obstacles in his path. Meanwhile Orlean herself (Meryl Streep) begins to question her life choices and feels drawn to her rough-hewn title character (Chris Cooper). Dense with ideas, hilarious and even shocking (what must the real Susan Orlean think of her portrayal here?), the movie demands multiple viewings to fully appreciate its genius and emotional weight.

Catherine Keener

Actress, b.1960

"The more people involved in making a movie, the worse it is, generally," **Catherine Keener** once said, tacitly accounting for her steadfast presence in the stripped-down, auteur-oriented environs of Amerindie film since its early-1990s renaissance. Beloved for her off-kilter sex appeal and sharp comic bite, Keener earned her celluloid chops in several films by **Tom DiCillo**, giving the redemptive love of a good woman to a pompadoured hipster (**Brad Pitt**) in *Johnny Suede* (1991) and projecting a fretful, endearing vulnerability as the insecure actress in *Living In Oblivion* (1995).

Because of her capacity for bringing three human dimensions to spiky-tongued, irritable cynics, Keener has become a go-to woman for filmmakers in need of brittle sarcasm. She is a paragon of emotional cruelty in **Neil LaBute**'s misanthropic *Your Friends & Neighbors* (1998), the fabulously bitchy object of multiple desires in *Being John Malkovich* (1999) and a frustrated homemaker who regresses to a petulant adolescent state in *Lovely & Amazing* (2001). (The latter film was directed by **Nicole Holofcener**, who has cast Keener in all of her features.)

The whiff of typecasting has lessened in recent years, which have seen Keener playing the sympathetic love interest in Judd Apatow's *The 40-Year-Old Virgin* (2005), posing an innocent threat to a strange household's father-daughter harmony in Rebecca Miller's *The Ballad Of Jack And Rose* (2005) and providing the steady voice of reason as Harper Lee in **Bennett Miller**'s *Capote* (2005).

Harvey Keitel

Actor, b.1939

A peerless tough guy capable of surprising tenderness, **Harvey Keitel** is unabashed about stripping either his clothes or his figurative skin for a role. Beginning his movie career as **Martin Scorsese**'s conflicted, soul-searching alter ego in the independent productions *Who's That Knocking At My Door* (1967) and the seminal *Mean Streets* (1973), he was eventually overtaken by **Robert De Niro** as Scorsese's signature collaborator. Although Keitel continued to do incisive work through the golden age of the 1970s, for Scorsese as well as **Paul Schrader** in *Blue Collar* (1978) and **James Toback** in *Fingers* (1978), his career languished in the subsequent decade, then surged again in tandem with the American independent film renaissance of the 1990s.

Having re-established a mainstream presence as the sympathetic cop in *Thelma & Louise* (1991) and the scary boyfriend in *Sister Act* (1992), and having won a supporting Oscar nomination for *Bugsy* (1991), Keitel brought his iconic screen presence to a host of films by maverick directors. He took a chance with an untried filmmaker when he accepted a lead role in **Quentin Tarantino**'s *Reservoir Dogs* (1992), and his committed performance brought the tragic dimensions of Tarantino's proudly derivative script into sharp relief. Keitel also went where most actors fear to tread for **Abel Ferrara**'s *Bad Lieutenant* (1992) as the nameless, spectacularly depraved cop who fumblingly seeks an unlikely redemption. He teamed up again with Tarantino as the redoubtable clean-up man in *Pulp Fiction* (1994) and with Ferrara as the director's virtual surrogate in *Dangerous Game* (1993). Elsewhere, he played the smoke-shop proprietor in **Wayne Wang**'s ensemble comedy *Smoke* (1995), the detective investigating a drug dealer's murder in **Spike Lee**'s *Clockers* (1995) and a corrupt fuzz in James Mangold's *Cop Land* (1997).

Like many of his Amerindie-identified colleagues, Keitel has also ventured further afield in his wide-ranging work for international directors, who more often than their American counterparts envisioned Keitel as something other than a cop or a criminal. Indeed, it's his work with New Zealand director **Jane Campion** – in *The Piano* (1993) as neighbour and pupil to Holly Hunter's mute piano teacher, and in the underrated *Holy Smoke* (1999) as a "cult de-programmer" who takes on hippy chick Kate Winslet – that best demonstrates his fearless onscreen embrace of erotic and emotional frankness.

 Fingers
dir James Toback, 1978, 90m

Both a thug and a sensitive artist, Jimmy Fingers (Harvey Keitel) is an enforcer for his mobster father and a promising classical pianist. His resultant identity crisis becomes more pronounced with the appearance of a macho romantic rival (played by football star Jim Brown). The film foundered on its release but has since gained a strong reputation, and French director Jacques Audiard remade it as *The Beat That My Heart Skipped* in 2005.

Spike Lee
Writer, Director and Actor, b.1957

After his hugely promising and profitable feature debut *She's Gotta Have It* (1986) and the thrilling provocation *Do The Right Thing* (1989), **Spike Lee** was the most controversial and talked-about young actor-director in America. He was certainly the premier black filmmaker in an overwhelmingly white industry and a forceful spokesman for African-Americans fed up with white America's institutionalized bigotry. In his prolific career, Lee has made high art out of button-pushing, tackling nymphomania in *She's Gotta Have It*, internalized racism among blacks in *School Daze* (1988), incendiary racial tension in *Do The Right Thing*, interracial love in *Jungle Fever* (1991), modern-day minstrelsy in *Bamboozled* (2000) and Enron-era corporate malpractice in *She Hate Me* (2005).

A taste for controversy is a key tool in Lee's skill set as consummate showman and self-promoter. He even appeared on the cover of *The Village Voice* in 1986 under the prophetic headline "Birth Of A Salesman." During the high tide of his influence in the early 1990s, he starred with **Michael Jordan** in a series of Air Jordan ads that served as cross-promotion of his own movies, and in the months before the release of Lee's reverent biopic *Malcolm X* (1992), he succeeded in making the "X" logo as ubiquitous as the Nike swoosh.

Born in the still-segregated American South (his family moved to his beloved Brooklyn when he was a small child), Lee is justly renowned for fostering debate on racial pride and prejudice in a country that has bequeathed a terrible legacy to its black citizens. (His stirring 1997 documentary *4 Little Girls* recounted the racially motivated church bombing in Birmingham, Alabama that killed four black schoolchildren in 1963.) Yet he's often been startlingly insensitive to those who don't look like him. Criticized for the anti-Semitic portrayal of the club owners in *Mo' Better Blues* (1990), Lee repeated himself a decade later with the self-righteous Jewish television consultant in *Bamboozled*. Doing publicity for *Jungle Fever* in 1991, Lee guaranteed himself bonus column inches when he said this of white women who date black men: "They be ugly. Mugly, dogs."

A Spike Lee joint typically spills over with enough ideas, characters and subplots to fuel half a dozen movies. To take a recent example, *She Hate Me* begins as a whistle-blowing thriller and abruptly becomes a sex comedy about said whistle-blower, who loses his job and thereafter pays the rent by impregnating wealthy and willing lesbians. The general silliness and confusion of *She Hate Me*, not to mention its retrograde gender politics (ie, every lesbian harbours a deep-down craving for a big slab o' dick) indicated yet again that Lee's career is a case study in arrested development. His latter-day films tend to be visually drab and undernourished, he seems indifferent to his actors and his weaknesses for soapbox didacticism, narrative distension and cartoonish stereotypes have worsened as he has grown older. However, American film culture sorely needs

artists as audacious and resourceful as Lee; here's hoping a career renaissance awaits him. Indeed, it may have started already with *Inside Man* (2006), a breezily enjoyable hostage caper that debuted at the top of the US box office.

 She's Gotta Have It
dir Spike Lee, 1986, 84m, b/w

This episodic comedy chronicles the adventures of Nola Darling (Tracy Camilla Johns), a liberated nymphomaniac who juggles her three dissimilar suitors with some difficulty. Lee's low-budget romp hasn't dated well and smacks of male wish fulfillment, but it's fitfully amusing and significant as a breakthrough for black independent directors.

James LeGros
Actor, b.1962

Formerly an indie-film mainstay, **James LeGros** once occupied a second tier of character actors alongside the likes of Dermot Mulroney, Kevin Corrigan and future *Sopranos* regular Michael Imperioli. LeGros was often cast in roles that required a dark side not immediately evident from his wholesome looks and gentle voice. Early parts included the apprentice junkie thief in **Gus Van Sant**'s *Drugstore Cowboy* (1989), the impotent ex-con who becomes partners in crime with **Drew Barrymore**'s damaged teen in Tamra Davis' *Guncrazy* (1992) and the puppyish but vaguely sinister neighbour in Stacy Cochran's *My New Gun* (1992).

He tapped into a creepy sweetness as a new friend to the environmentally ill protagonist of *Safe* (1995) and found a showcase for his comic acumen in **Tom DiCillo**'s *Living In Oblivion* (1995) as the ditzy, oblivious thespian Chad Palomino. LeGros's performance so strongly evoked DiCillo's previous lead actor, **Brad Pitt**, that many viewers assumed the character to be a parody of the superstar, despite firm denials from the relevant personnel. LeGros's ubiquity has faded since his mid-1990s heyday, though the Indiewood work remains steady, be it as the boyfriend weary of his mate's body-image anxieties in **Nicole Holofcener**'s *Lovely & Amazing* (2001) or the dim fast-food employee in Billy Morrissette's *Macbeth* update *Scotland, Pa* (2001).

 Living In Oblivion
Tom DiCillo, 1995, 90m, b/w and colour

This is a movie-movie after every indie director's heart, hilariously capturing all the tension, drudgery and technical difficulties involved in making a film on a small budget. Amid the usual mess of botched lines and wayward boom mikes, beleaguered auteur Nick Reve (Steve Buscemi) struggles to manage a cast and crew that includes an insecure actress (Catherine Keener), an egotistical male star (James LeGros) and a cinematographer of questionable competence (Dermot Mulroney). Arranged in three movements and alternating gracefully between colour and black-and-white, DiCillo's delightful comedy steadily mounts in screwball mayhem.

Richard Linklater

Writer and Director, b.1960

At the beginning of *Before Sunrise* (1995), Jesse (**Ethan Hawke**) proposes an idea for a cable-access show that each week screens "24-hour documents of real time"; in *Before Sunset* (2004) the same character imagines a novel that transpires within the space of a three-minute pop song. Jesse shares with **Richard Linklater** an affinity for art that's closely circumscribed by duration. Linklater's *Slacker* (1991) and *Dazed And Confused* (1993) both take place over about 24 hours; *Before Sunrise* covers an afternoon stretching into the next morning; *SubUrbia* (1996) and

Tape (2001) compress their drama into a single night; *Before Sunset* depicts less than an hour and a half in slightly tweaked real time. Linklater has an eager ear for the free-associative sidewinding of conversation, often among large character ensembles, and these potentially unwieldy elements gain shape and momentum from their tight temporal constructs – not to mention an undeniable immediacy. As a guy playing pinball in *Waking Life* (2001) declares, "There's only one instant, and it's now, and it's eternity."

Linklater's exuberant comic and intellectual energies and his evident work ethic (twelve features in about fifteen years) aren't what one might expect from the writer-director of *Slacker*, which gave an alternative label to the demographic group-cum-mass media invention known as Generation X. An episodic day-in-the-life shot in Linklater's home base of Austin for about $23,000, *Slacker* led to studio deals for *Dazed And Confused*, a coming-of-age comedy that plays out on the last day of high school in 1976, and the sublime romance *Before Sunrise*. By the mid-1990s, Linklater began turning to existing material and other screenwriters for his movies, with mixed results. *SubUrbia*, adapted by **Eric Bogosian** from his own play, often scanned like a broad, schematic retread of Linklater's previous films, and *The Newton Boys* (1998) was an amiable salute to a prolific real-life crew of relatively scrupulous bank robbers.

In 2001, Linklater's willingness to experiment came to the fore with a one-two punch of sharply dissimilar films: the claustrophobic three-hander *Tape*, based on **Stephen Belber**'s play about a night of reckoning between three old high-school friends, and the underappreciated *Waking Life* (2001), which follows a young man (Wiley Wiggins of *Dazed And Confused*) through a "lucid dream" that may in fact be the

Richard Linklater directs *SubUrbia* star Giovanni Ribisi

beginnings of his afterlife. Like *Tape*, *Waking Life* was shot on handheld digital video, but it was then transformed into Rotoscope animation via a Macintosh G4 computer. The film's pulsing, shape-shifting imagery and existential curiosity act like a tonic – everything in this dream world seems in flux, subject to debate, though the tide of philosophical riffing eventually recedes in favour of a potent, ghostly chill.

The director took a refreshing Hollywood dip with the unambiguously commercial *The School Of Rock* (2003), which managed to be a hilarious crowd-pleaser while remaining unmistakeably a Richard Linklater film; the same couldn't be said for the remake *Bad News Bears* (2005), which failed to conceal its Hollywood-studio origins. Linklater then returned to Rotoscope for the **Philip K.**

Dick adaptation *A Scanner Darkly* (2006) and extracted a thriller out of **Eric Schlosser's** non-fiction bestseller *Fast Food Nation* (2006) – all evidence of a unique, and uniquely driven, filmmaker who's made a workable peace with mainstream forces.

Waking Life
dir Richard Linklater, 2001, 100m

Like a haunted animated version of Linklater's *Slacker*, this sinuous hallucination of a movie tracks a stream of consciousness, moving from one dream to another towards many small philosophical epiphanies and a larger, more troubling realization for its young voyager. It's no criticism of the film that its gorgeous oneiric imagery and constant intellectual chatter may make some viewers sleepy – indeed, it seems custom-made to inspire fabulous dreams.

Julianne Moore
Actress, b.1960

In her memoir *Shooting To Kill* (1998), **Christine Vachon** writes, "Producing *Safe*, I had an opportunity to watch **Julianne Moore** at work. In the role of a woman who felt as if her environment was attacking her, she lost twenty pounds, and she was thin to begin with. She walked around weak from hunger, and she began to acquire an almost luminous fragility. Seeing up close what truly great actors do to their bodies – and their minds – brings it home: *Actors are not like other people.*"

And Julianne Moore is not like most other actors, given her near-flawless instincts and resources. Beginning as a New York stage actress who paid her dues in television soaps, Moore attracted serious attention in the early 1990s for a battery of roles, notably her alluring interpretation of Chekhov's Yelena in **Louis Malle's** final film, *Vanya On 42nd Street* (1994), and as part of

Robert Altman's ensemble in *Short Cuts* (1993), in which she famously played a scene naked from the waist down. She won her first Oscar nomination via **Paul Thomas Anderson's** *Boogie Nights* (1997) as adult-film actress Amber Waves, who acts as coked-up mother hen to a de facto family of porn associates but has little contact with her own young son. Her turn as an icy bitch in *The Myth Of Fingerprints* (1997) marked the first of several collaborations with her future husband, the indie director **Bart Freundlich**; Moore was pregnant with their first child when she played an eccentric artist in *The Big Lebowski* (1998), donning a Viking costume for one of the movie's loopy Busby Berkeley production numbers.

The versatile Moore can appear radiantly gorgeous or nakedly plain; she can be sexy or prim, but never spins cartoonish variations on either. Her timing and technical skills are stunning, especially her ability to modulate her voice according to the part. She can unleash magma bursts of unchecked emotion and vulnerability, as in the floodgates of keening blather at the end of **Todd Haynes's** *Safe* (1995) or in her profane arias of grief as a guilt-ridden trophy wife in Anderson's *Magnolia* (1999).

At the same time, few performers can match Moore's ability for conveying repressed pain and passion in near-subliminal flickers of expression, a gift she demonstrated in 1999 as the adulterous wife in *The End Of The Affair* and twice in 2002, when she played housewives trapped by their prescribed social roles in Haynes's *Far From Heaven* and **Stephen Daldry's** *The Hours* (all three films earned her Oscar nominations). Like many of her indie-icon cohorts, Moore switches easefully between high-profile studio moneymakers and low-budget labours of love. When she works with Haynes, she accepts a tiny fraction of her usual fee, and for good reason: their

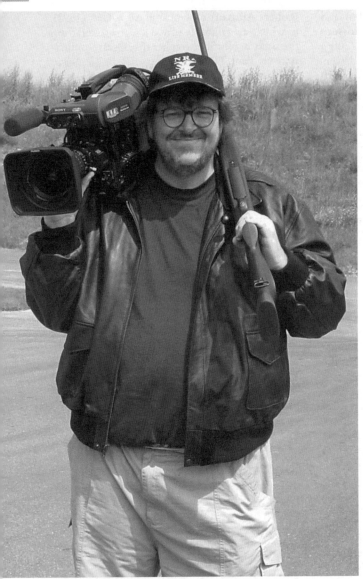

Muckraker Michael Moore and his weapons of choice

collaboration could shape up to be one of the great actor-director partnerships of the age.

Michael Moore
Writer and Director, b.1954

Michael Moore is a documentarian of many gifts. He combines an investigative reporter's nose for scandal and corruption, a curator's eye for found footage, a *Candid Camera* acumen for the comic ambush and a committed activist's sense of outrage. Launching his formidable self at corporations and presidential regimes, Moore is the self-styled champion of the working class, the befuddled voice of reason who narrates his films in a sarcastic *yeah-right* twang. He's a guerrilla muckraker, waddling through plutocratic sleaze to get his viewers the ugly facts, but he sweetens the deal with humour. No matter how dead-serious his subject – corporate downsizing, deadly gun violence, war in Iraq – Moore can fashion his material into a laugh-out-loud comedy without trivializing the issues.

A former journalist, Moore began filmmaking with *Roger & Me* (1989), a documentary about the devastating impact of General Motors closing their plants in his hometown of Flint, Michigan. He followed up with his sole fiction feature to date, *Canadian Bacon* (1995), a broadly staged, hit-or-miss farce wherein the American president, eager to distract his citizens from a poor economy, decides to invade Canada (an idea that 1999's *South Park: Bigger Longer & Uncut* would later elaborate). Moore returned to the documentary format in 1997 with *The Big One* (and also pursued two short-lived news series, *TV Nation* and *The Awful Truth*). *The Big One* echoed the central gimmick of *Roger & Me*: just as he once fruitlessly pursued GM chairman **Roger Smith**, he now chased a series of elusive CEOs, eventually scoring an awkward chat with Nike honcho **Phil Knight**.

Portly and nasal-voiced, Moore is the anti-star of his documentaries, and often makes for an overbearing emcee. His films suffer a weakness for narcissism and maudlin sentiment, and he's susceptible to minor but irritating manipulations of facts and chronology. *Bowling For Columbine* (2002) featured all of the above flaws, but it advanced an ambitious, soul-searching argument about the causes and consequences of America's gun culture, its focal point being the 1999 Columbine high-school massacre (also the subject of **Gus Van Sant**'s fictionalized *Elephant*, released the following year).

Bowling For Columbine not only won the Oscar for best documentary, but also became the highest-grossing documentary of all time – a record that Moore's next effort, the Palme d'Or-winning *Fahrenheit 9/11* (2004), beat in its opening weekend alone. Moore's anguished invective against the Bush administration won free publicity when Disney refused to let its subsidiary, Miramax, release it. Nevertheless, the movie debuted at the top of the US box office, a first for a non-fiction film. For the liberal moviegoer, however, *Fahrenheit 9/11* proved to be at once an energizing rally and a heartbreaker, because at the end of the 2004 election season, **George W. Bush** remained in office. Moore pulled out all the stops and yet his art, or his agitprop, still couldn't change the world.

Errol Morris
Writer and Director, b.1948

One might say that **Errol Morris**'s filmmaking career was secured on a dare. When he told his friend **Werner Herzog** about the difficulties he had financing his projects, Herzog replied that Morris should simply forge ahead, "and the day I see the finished work," the German director added, "I am going to eat my shoe." The finished work turned out to be *Gates Of Heaven* (1980), a droll and richly detailed portrait of the proprietors and clients of two pet cemeteries. Herzog also held up his end of the bargain, immortalized in **Les Blank**'s 1980 short *Werner Herzog Eats His Shoe*.

Morris brought new strains of ironic comedy to the documentary format, an innovation that would inform the work of non-fiction filmmakers including **Michael Moore** and **Chris Smith** (1999's *American Movie*). Even in the unsettling *Mr. Death: The Rise And Fall Of Fred A. Leuchter, Jr.* (1999), about the titular capital-punishment technologist and Holocaust denier, Morris incorporates touches of the blackest humour. The opening-credits sequence, lit by lightning, casts Leuchter as a mad scientist out of a 1950s B-horror picture. But Morris's deadpan sensibilities rarely cheapen his material. *Gates Of Heaven* is at once amused and impressed by its subjects' sometimes overwrought dedication to their deceased cats and dogs, and his second film, *Vernon, Florida* (1981), is a tapestry of eccentric Floridians that never descends into snide grotesquerie.

Appropriately for a former philosophy student who once paid the rent by working as a private investigator, Morris has consistently produced work that poses questions about the very limits of knowledge and self-knowledge. *A Brief History Of Time* (1991) is a delightful elucidation of **Stephen Hawking**'s cosmic best-seller and *Fast, Cheap & Out Of Control* (1997), a brilliant four-hander on a disparate group of specialists (a topiary artist, a mole rat expert, a robot scientist and a lion tamer), melds scientific and philosophical inquiry to reach cockeyed epiphanies. Meticulous and quietly shocking, *The Thin Blue Line* (1988) virtually solved a murder and helped set free Randall Adams, a Texas man serving a life sentence for a crime he didn't commit.

Winner of an overdue documentary Oscar for Morris, *The Fog Of War: Eleven Lessons From The Life Of Robert S. McNamara* (2003) incorporated many of his instantly recognizable motifs: no narration, an agitated **Philip Glass** score (the director favours the composer for his gift of evoking "existential dread"), a revelatory treasure trove of archival footage and its use of the "Interrotron". This is Morris's name for a filming setup that enables the subject – in this case, former US Secretary of Defence **Robert S. McNamara** – to speak directly into the camera. Depending on the context, the much-vilified McNamara comes across as both mediator and warmonger; with characteristic reticence, Morris allows the viewer to deliver the final judgment.

Gates Of Heaven
dir Errol Morris, 1980, 80m

Funny, ironic and poignant, often all at once, Morris's first documentary listens to the stories of various animal lovers associated with a pet cemetery in California. As in most of Morris's films, the ostensible subject matter is only the entry point for a larger, unresolved investigation into, among other things, love, consciousness, being and nothingness.

Parker Posey
Actress, b.1968

After she'd racked up more than thirty film credits in mostly independent productions over a mere eight-year span, **Parker Posey** was anointed "queen of the indies" in *Time* magazine – a label that would prove as much an albatross as a medal of honour. Whippet-thin with a tomboy-ish beauty, Posey is a deft comedienne with a line in flighty loudmouths and quirky downtown hipsters; often her characters teeter on the edge of hysteria and strain to keep their balance. Such is the case in the high-school flashback *Dazed And Confused* (1993), where Posey made a unforgettable early impression as Darla, the senior sadist who brings unduly fearsome commitment to freshman initiation proceedings. Posey ascended to cult star status with the sleeper hit *Party Girl* (1995), a wisp of a comedy given stature and flair by Posey's turn as a chic-dressing good-timer who holds rent parties in her loft in lieu of finding a job – that is, until she improbably resolves to become a librarian.

Though she's appeared in a couple of **Nora Ephron** comedies and other mainstream fare, Posey has long concentrated, by happenstance or design, on more narrowly targeted, low-budget projects. Only a few of her movies are particularly good, but her inimitable presence always brings added energy to the proceedings. She played a sex killer's conspirator in *Frisk* (1995), a frank adaptation of **Dennis Cooper**'s disturbing novel, and has appeared in several features and shorts by indie stalwart **Hal Hartley**, including *Henry Fool* (1997), in which she played the slatternly layabout who marries the eponymous drifter. She reprises the role in the sequel *Fay Grim* (2006), so named for Posey's maturing character.

Like *Henry Fool*, **Mark Waters'** *The House Of Yes* (1997) focused on a troubled sibling relationship: the incestuous bond between Jackie O (Posey), an obsessive devotee of the former First Lady, and her twin brother (Josh Hamilton). Posey climbed into the station wagon with another dysfunctional family in Greg Mottola's *The Daytrippers* (1996), and in Jill Sprecher's *Clockwatchers* (1997), she was one of a clique of office temps (including **Toni Collette** and **Lisa Kudrow**) mired in an increasingly poisonous work environment. More recently, Posey anchored the strongest segment in **Rebecca Miller**'s triptych *Personal Velocity* (2002), and has continued working with the informal acting ensemble that staffs **Christopher Guest's** hilarious mockumentaries, including *Waiting For Guffman* (1996), *Best In Show* (2000) and *A Mighty Wind* (2003).

The House Of Yes
dir Mark Waters, 1997, 85m

Long before she snagged a role in TV's *Boston Legal*, Posey was the flinty yet adorable star of numerous indie sleepers, perhaps epitomized by Waters' black comedy about a Jackie O fetishist with a thing for her own brother. Like many a Sundance premiere, the movie observes a highly dysfunctional family convening for the holidays. The flat script doesn't transcend its stage origins, but Posey throws herself headlong into her kooky, kinky role.

The Kennedy curse: Jackie O (Parker Posey) eyes her brother (Josh Hamilton) in *The House Of Yes*

Christina Ricci

Actress, b.1980

Though she first came to moviegoers' attention as a saucer-eyed youngster in the *Addams Family* movies and other all-ages fare, **Christina Ricci** eluded the child-star trap and graduated to wiseacre indie princess by her late teens. Her transition role was in **Ang Lee's** *The Ice Storm* (1997) as sardonic teenager Wendy Hood, one of a multi-generational group of confused hedonists in a wealthy enclave of suburban Connecticut. Seducing a dissimilar pair of brothers, Wendy enjoys some heavy petting in a rubber Richard Nixon mask – a good indicator of Ricci's developing taste for kink and quirk.

The following year, Ricci hit her stride with a fusillade of films including **John Waters'** *Pecker* (1998) and Morgan J. Freeman's *Desert Blue* (1998), in which she played a small-town maker of bombs. Newly blond, milky-skinned and ripe for the plucking in a baby-doll dress and glitter

Blonde faith: Christina Ricci in *Buffalo '66*

make-up, Ricci glowed with voluptuous purity as the sweetly willing hostage in **Vincent Gallo's** *Buffalo '66* (1998), especially in a dreamy tap-dancing sequence set in a grimy bowling alley. The same summer that *Buffalo '66* was released in the US, a platinum-haired but otherwise completely different Ricci could be seen in **Don Roos'** satirical black comedy *The Opposite Of Sex* (1998) as a dangerous, nasty brat who schemes to rip off her half-brother Bill (**Martin Donovan**) by seducing his witless boyfriend.

Notwithstanding the occasional bright spot, such as her supporting part as serial killer Aileen Wuornos' girlfriend in **Patty Jenkins'** *Monster* (2003), Ricci has seemed miscast or unmoored in recent years. But given the dense onrush of her early adult career, perhaps the lull can be chalked up to belated growing pains.

David O. Russell

Writer and Director, b.1958

The inhabitants of **David O. Russell's** excitable comedies plunge into bewildering swamps of addled moral confusion, and must talk or fight their way out. Like his American contemporaries **Spike Jonze** and **Charlie Kaufman**, Russell wagers that the most refined medium for picking apart the big quandaries – the fiction of the self, the definition of necessity, the possibility of leading a meaningful life – is the wacky comedy, and he has thus far located ample humour in incest, war and existential anxiety.

Russell spent his twenties as a labour and literacy activist in Nicaragua and the American northeast. His first film was a short video documentary about Central American immigrants in Boston, where he taught English as a second language. His audacious first feature, *Spanking*

The Monkey (1994), concerned a college student (**Jeremy Davies**) who disastrously overreaches his role as round-the-clock carer to his injured mother. Fractious family dynamics also powered the delightfully unhinged *Flirting With Disaster* (1996), a splendid screwball comedy in which adoptee and new father **Ben Stiller** criss-crosses the US in a constantly thwarted search for his birth parents.

Russell's next two films not only harnessed the slapstick, absurdist energies of *Flirting With Disaster*, but also revealed Russell's political acumen. In *Three Kings* (1999), which Russell made for Warner Bros, a cynical heist plot engineered by a crew of Desert Storm soldiers becomes a humanitarian rescue mission after they stumble upon the ugly aftermath of the war they've ostensibly finished fighting. Dark and morally inquisitive, this was the first major American studio release to question seriously the motivations behind the first American invasion of Iraq and the deadly chaos left in victory's wake. (In 2004 Russell completed a documentary follow-up called *Soldiers Pay*, which Warner Bros refused to append to the *Three Kings* DVD reissue; it eventually found a home with tiny distributor Cinema Libre.)

During the making of *Three Kings*, Russell and star **George Clooney** sniped at each other incessantly and once came to blows. Appropriately for a maestro of onscreen disorder, Russell can be an aggressive and destabilizing force on his sets – in the *New York Times*, reporter Sharon Waxman depicted the set of *I Heart Huckabees* (2004) as equal parts encounter group and unsupervised playground. In the unclassifiable (and poorly received) finished movie, earnest environmental activist **Jason Schwartzman** (in a role Russell based on his younger self) hires a husband-and-wife team of "existential detectives" (**Lily Tomlin** and **Dustin Hoffman**) to investigate his inner and outer life. Like *Flirting With Disaster*, *Huckabees* is a go-for-broke identity-investigation that exemplifies Russell's filmmaking spirit: voluble, a bit nuts and tireless in its metaphysical questing.

John Sayles
Writer and Director, b.1950

John Sayles' name is synonymous, for better or worse, with conscience-raising cinema. A staunch leftist who mourns the lost art of socialist solidarity (his first film name-checks the 1953 landmark of the blacklist, *Salt Of The Earth*), Sayles specializes in liberal-humanist filmmaking that often attracts more praise for its good intentions than for its style or substance. He possesses a gentle skill for drawing wry, world-weary characters, but they often become unconvincing mouthpieces for a social or political stance.

Doggedly independent, often eschewing larger budgets to retain final cut, Sayles got his start as a screenwriter for **Roger Corman**, and put his fees for writing the B-flicks *Piranha* (1978) and *The Lady In Red* (1979) towards the financing of his debut, *Return Of The Secaucus 7* (1979). (Throughout his directing career, Sayles has continued a sideline as a writer-for-hire, most recently penning *Jurassic Park IV*.) In subsequent films, Sayles showed a penchant for stories about people who are estranged from, or at odds with, their milieu. The title character of *Lianna* (1983), stuck in a stale marriage, falls for another woman. In the endearing if occasionally clunky comedy *The Brother From Another Planet* (1984), **Joe Morton** plays a mute alien whose spaceship lands just off hospitable Harlem.

Sayles turned to historical drama next: he based *Matewan* (1987) on a real-life 1920s strike

by an interracial coalition of West Virginia miners, and *Eight Men Out* (1988) centred on the infamous Chicago White Sox scandal of 1919. The tireless writer-director showed himself incapable of being neatly categorized with his disparate next ventures, *Passion Fish* (1992), about an embittered white paraplegic and her black nurse, and *The Secret Of Roan Inish* (1994), based on a Celtic fable.

One of Sayles's signature formats is the shaggy ensemble narrative that doubles as an oral history of a community, fecund with anecdotal nuance and inconvenient details. *City Of Hope* (1991) is a mosaic of a New Jersey city, *Lone Star* (1996) is a flashback-laden murder mystery set in a Texas border town and *Sunshine State* (2002) looks on as real-estate developers descend upon a sleepy Florida town. The domineering past with all its ghosts is often his de facto protagonist, and Sayles's good-guy characters often share a mix of resilience and disillusionment. "Oh, shit happens, you know?" **Edie Falco**'s character says in *Sunshine State*. "And a lot of it happened to me."

Sayles's directorial strategy occasionally amounts to throwing what happens against a wall and seeing what sticks. His compositions are usually perfunctory and his allegiance to everyday verisimilitude tends toward messy sprawl, hanging threads and an odd uncertainty of tone. However, there are exceptions to these rules, as in **Haskell Wexler**'s evocative photography for *Matewan* and in the trajectory of *Limbo* (1998), an ambitious experiment in asymmetrical structure. In the end, the success of his films rests on the strength of the writing; when Sayles is at his best, his characters embody the inextricable links between mammoth social forces and the small words and acts of everyday life.

Lone Star
dir John Sayles, 1996, 135m

Chris Cooper plays the haggard and decent sheriff of a Texas border town where there are skeletons in the closet, or rather in the dirt – the discovery of human remains opens a can of worms that implicates his legendary lawman father (played in flashbacks by Matthew McConaughey). Heartfelt and bittersweet, this is one of Sayles's most successful attempts to put a large ensemble and a multi-thread narrative in the service of a sweeping history play and a down-to-earth, character-driven story.

James Schamus
Producer, b.1959

Both screenwriter and producer, **James Schamus** has mapped out an adventurous career substantially guided and shaped by his association with two major talents: the producer **Ted Hope**, Schamus's longtime partner in the company Good Machine, and filmmaker **Ang Lee**. Schamus has been a producer on all of Lee's films to date and screenwriter of all but two. From Lee's first feature, the low-budget *Pushing Hands* (1992), in which an aging Chinese *tai chi* master relocates to upstate New York to live with his son's family, Lee and Schamus have evinced a particular interest in cultural and generational conflicts within and between individuals, and the frequent incompatibility between emotional instinct and social convention.

Schamus and Good Machine also provided invaluable support to young filmmakers, including Edward Burns, **Todd Haynes**, Nicole Holofcener and Todd Solondz. After the conglomerate Vivendi Universal purchased Good Machine in 2001, Schamus became head of the new speciality division Focus Features. Under his stewardship, Focus is arguably the best among the studio boutiques – their terrific résumé of vibrant, intelligent movies

includes Haynes's *Far From Heaven* (2002), **Sofia Coppola**'s *Lost In Translation* (2003), Fernando Meirelles' *The Constant Gardener* (2005) and Lee's *Brokeback Mountain* (2005). Given that Schamus served as executive producer on two of the signature films of the New Queer Cinema, Haynes's *Poison* (1991) and **Tom Kalin**'s *Swoon* (1992), it's fitting that he was also a key player in making *Brokeback Mountain*: a plangent, epic romance perceived as a belated breakthrough for Hollywood in its frank portrayal of a gay relationship.

Martin Scorsese
Writer and Director, b.1942

Although his career spans five decades, ranging from micro-budgeted indie productions to major-studio extravaganzas, **Martin Scorsese**'s movies still sweat and quake with the determination of men obsessed. It's a state of body and soul that the famously single-minded director knows intimately, and it finds explosive expression in film after film: Travis Bickle's deranged kamikaze odyssey in *Taxi Driver* (1976), **Jake LaMotta**'s pitiful self-annihilation in *Raging Bull* (1980), Rupert Pupkin's desperation for fame in *The King Of Comedy* (1983) and the revenge missions pursued in *Cape Fear* (1991) and *Gangs Of New York* (2002). All but the last of these starred Scorsese's defining actor: as the critic Peter Rainer wrote, **Robert De Niro** "is at the centre of so many of Scorsese's films because he is a genius at monomania – and monomania is the engine that, for good or ill, keeps these films on track."

Although Scorsese's typical protagonist is a loner with tunnel vision, he often burns just as feverishly with the inner conflict and self-doubt that can befall a deeply spiritual quest. *The Last*

Martin Scorsese (right) guides his actors through *Mean Streets*

Temptation Of Christ (1988) was attacked as blasphemous for daring to imagine Jesus Christ as flesh and blood (Scorsese's other great religious biopic is 1997's underappreciated *Kundun*, about the Dalai Lama). In Scorsese's breakthrough film, the independently produced *Mean Streets* (1973), the unbreakable bond of loyalty that church-going Charlie (**Harvey Keitel**) feels towards the redemption-proof Johnny-Boy (De Niro) goes beyond tribal allegiances or Catholic guilt to become a self-sabotaging idée fixe.

Growing up in New York's rough-and-tumble Little Italy, Scorsese seriously considered entering the priesthood, which puts an intriguing gloss on his filmography's sexually repressed brotherhood of men. Even when they're beating each other to pulp, the guys always seem to prefer each other's company to that of their women. Indeed, the conflict at the core of Scorsese's first feature, *Who's That Knocking At My Door?* (1967), is the Madonna-whore complex of Keitel's young protagonist after he discovers his girlfriend has been raped. The homosocial volatility of Scorsese's world reached its apotheosis in *Goodfellas* (1990), a brutal, riveting gangster *Bildungsroman*. But, the filmmaker had already proven his versatility earlier in his career when, as director-for-hire on *Alice Doesn't Live Here Anymore* (1974), he guided **Ellen Burstyn** to a best-actress Oscar for her role as an aspiring singer with serial man trouble.

One of Scorsese's greatest films, the Edith Wharton adaptation *The Age Of Innocence* (1993), has the rare distinction within his oeuvre of depicting a relationship between a man and a woman (played by **Daniel Day-Lewis** and **Michelle Pfeiffer**) that holds a credible promise of intellectual, emotional and sexual fulfilment for both parties – until, that is, it's quashed by the rigid social codes of 1870s New York's high society, which Scorsese observes with forensic, even fetishistic precision.

Scorsese didn't turn his back forever on independent filmmaking after *Mean Streets*. When production on *Last Temptation* stalled, he returned to his indie roots for *After Hours* (1985), a bizarre nocturnal odyssey through New York that he shot quickly on a tight budget. At the turn of the millennium, Scorsese entered a possibly Faustian pact with **Harvey "Scissorhands" Weinstein** that foretold a clash of bull-headed indie titans, but *The Aviator* (2004) became Scorsese's first $100-million grosser, and *Gangs Of New York*, however muddled, could boast Day-Lewis's magnificent turn as Bill "the Butcher" Cutting. The performance seemed

to crystallize so much of what's great in Scorsese's films: a masterful rendering of criminal passion and soulful pathology, scary and sympathetic in equal measure, and pureblood New York.

Chloë Sevigny
Actress, b.1974

Chloë Sevigny was the subject of a *New Yorker* profile by Jay McInerney before she was out of her teens or had ever made a movie. Though such an early anointment of niche stardom might have proved too-much-too-soon for a lesser talent, Sevigny's acting skills, glowing screen presence and intrepid tastes have carried the day. The actress never flinches from tough, even sensational material, but no matter how sordid or turbulent her screen surroundings might be, she emerges with her earthy luminescence intact.

As the HIV-positive teenager combing New York for the boy who infected her, Sevigny gave a much-needed centre of gravity to **Larry Clark**'s scandalous *Kids* (1995), which was scripted by her longtime on-off boyfriend, **Harmony Korine**, who also directed her in his mucky curiosities *Gummo* (1997), for which she designed the costumes, and *Julien Donkey-Boy* (1999). Charming and vulnerable as the accidental teen temptress in **Steve Buscemi**'s *Trees Lounge* (1996), Sevigny was fruitfully cast against type as the uncertain newcomer to Manhattan in **Whit Stillman**'s *The Last Days Of Disco* (1998), and won a supporting Oscar nomination as the steadfast lover of a young man with a dangerous secret in **Kimberly Peirce**'s *Boys Don't Cry* (1999).

An actress of unusual integrity who's clearly not in the business to make an easy buck, Sevigny has eschewed big-money roles in favour of small-scale productions with European directors such

The eyes have it: Chloë Sevigny in *Trees Lounge*

as Volker Schlöndorff (*Palmetto*, 1998), Olivier Assayas (*Demonlover*, 2002) and **Lars von Trier** (*Dogville*, 2003; *Manderlay*, 2005). She also took an arguably foolhardy risk when she accepted a part in **Vincent Gallo's** *The Brown Bunny* (2003) that required her character to perform unsimulated fellatio on the writer-director-star. (Sevigny's take on *Bunny* was coolly sensible: "It's an art film. It should be playing in museums. It's like an **Andy Warhol** movie.") The scene drove the prestigious William Morris agency to drop Sevigny as a client, but she moved on unscathed,

landing parts in **Woody Allen's** *Melinda And Melinda* (2004) and Jim Jarmusch's *Broken Flowers* (2005), as well as a starring role as one of three wives to a Mormon polygamist in the HBO series *Big Love* (2006).

Gummo
dir Harmony Korine, 1997, 95m

The first feature directed by *Kids* screenwriter Korine follows the misfits and miscreants of a small Ohio town (including Chloë Sevigny and *Days Of Heaven* star Linda Manz) where a devastating tornado twenty years ago has warped the entire community. His episodic onslaught of weirdo depravity (kids kill cats and euthanize a grandmother, while the director himself sexually intimidates a midget) is numbingly self-indulgent, but the movie is certainly one of a kind, and counts Gus Van Sant and Werner Herzog among its admirers.

Kevin Smith
Writer and Director, b.1970

Using a creative toolbox that's long on stoner repartee and pop-culture minutiae and short on visual imagination and narrative momentum, **Kevin Smith** has been making student films for his entire career. He'll never be a master of light, shadow and mise-en-scène, but his movies scrape by on scrappy, motormouth energy – most entertainingly in his debut, *Clerks* (1994), a strenuously profane comedy transpiring in and around a convenience store that's a magnet for slackers,

weirdos, burnouts, accidental necrophiles and the occasional cigarette-smoking 4-year-old. Shot for an initial budget of $27,575 in the same New Jersey convenience store where Smith worked as a cashier, *Clerks* won an enthusiastic distributor in Miramax and made its young director, alongside *Brothers McMullen* director **Edward Burns**, one of the frat-boy darlings of the mid-1990s Amerindie scene.

Although Smith's major-studio follow-up, *Mallrats* (1995), bombed badly, it established what his fans would come to dub the "View Askewniverse" (so named for Smith's production company, **View Askew**), a unique world unto itself defined by its recurring actors and characters, references to Smith's past films and invocations of *Star Wars*, *Jaws* and other Smith favourites. (In *Clerks*, the cashiers discuss the sad fate of independent contractors who perished

The most overrated American indie film: *Clerks*

One of the virtues of independent cinema as an ideal is that it's an essentially democratic enterprise. Despite the overwhelming power of a handful of corporate entities to decide what we see, the fact remains that anyone with a few credit cards and some indulgent friends can make a movie, and with a little courage and a lot of luck, he can get it distributed too. This was the case with **Kevin Smith**'s *Clerks* (1994), a film about an eventful day among the trash-talking cashiers and eccentric customers at a New Jersey convenience store.

Shot in black-and-white for a pittance, the movie won the crucial endorsement of the *New York Times*, whose lead critic, Janet Maslin, praised "a buoyant, bleakly funny comedy … an exuberant display of film-student ingenuity [that] is a classic example of how to

spin straw into gold." Really? Gold? Perhaps in the literal sense, since *Clerks* benefited from an extravagant Miramax publicity campaign and made a huge profit on its meager budget.

In terms of moviemaking, however, *Clerks* falls short on every count: the sound is bad, the camera setups ugly, the line-readings flat and grating, and the humour pubescent. Worse, an arrogant mood of posturing self-congratulation pervades everything – the movie is never more obnoxiously pleased with itself than during a clumsy bit of business pertaining to a woman having sex with a corpse. Reissued on DVD in a lavish three-disc package on its tenth birthday, *Clerks* is perhaps the most unlikely film to get the box-set treatment – unless you count the tenth-anniversary collectors' edition of Smith's ill-fated *Mallrats*.

on the Death Star; in 1997's *Chasing Amy*, a character condemns **George Lucas**'s franchise as white-colonialist propaganda.) The inseparable supporting duo of Jay and Silent Bob (respectively played by **Jason Mewes** and Smith himself) have appeared in almost every one of the director's movies. Despite his moniker, Silent Bob delivers a passionate monologue on lost love in *Chasing Amy*, wherein an immature comic-book artist (**Ben Affleck**) falls for a nominal lesbian (Joey Lauren Adams) with surprisingly downbeat results.

Smith bolstered his reputation as an envelope-pusher with *Dogma* (1999), about a disillusioned Catholic (**Linda Fiorentino**) who's recruited by a heavenly squad trying to avert Armageddon as perpetrated by a pair of fallen angels (Affleck and **Matt Damon**). Featuring a heroine who works at an abortion clinic and **Alanis Morissette** as God, the movie piqued the ire of the Catholic League, which staged protests at theatres and drove Miramax to bow out of distribution duties (Lions Gate subsequently stepped into the fray).

Strangely, Smith followed the daring if visually static *Dogma* with his worst film, the excruciatingly self-reflexive *Jay And Silent Bob Strike Back* (2001), a gormless and gay-baiting devotional to the titular louts. (A parody website featured in the movie, the vividly named Moviepoopshoot.com, later launched as an entertainment site under Smith's seal of approval.) *Jersey Girl* (2004) marked another hairpin turn, spinning a sentimental yarn about a workaholic Manhattanite (Affleck) who loses his wife and livelihood and resolves to become the best father a reduced income can buy. Perhaps Smith recognized that his arrested-development edge had dulled, since he then returned to his roots with *Clerks II* in 2006.

Steven Soderbergh
Writer and Director, b.1963

"I guess it's all downhill from here," **Steven Soderbergh** famously quipped during his Palme d'Or acceptance speech in 1989. He was 26 years old, and his first feature, *sex, lies, and videotape*, had won the top prize at the world's premier film festival. For the better part of a decade, his self-deprecating line appeared to be accurate: in commercial terms, at least, Soderbergh entered a decade-long slump after the box-office success of *sex, lies*. His adventurous career has come to represent all the triumphs and perils of auteurist filmmaking in America. As he climbed his way back to the top directorial ranks with the one-two punch of *Erin Brockovich* and *Traffic* in 2000, Soderbergh has brought an idiosyncratic touch to familiar genre material. As both director and producer, he strikes an implicit détente between the arthouse and the mainstream, whereby aesthetic integrity and bottom-line exigencies meet halfway.

Soderbergh followed *sex, lies* with *Kafka* (1991), a nightmarish yet playful thriller that mixed biopic and adaptation, and *King Of The Hill* (1993), a poignant Depression-era story of a boy coping without his parents. Both films flopped (*Kafka* especially suffered a critical drubbing), hampered by unreasonable expectations and uncommercial subject matter. Even Soderbergh himself disliked *The Underneath* (1995), a chilly remake of **Robert Siodmak**'s *Criss Cross*. The director had reached an impasse, and what followed was a painful self-administered shot of adrenaline called *Schizopolis* (1996), in which writer-director-star Soderbergh dismantled narrative, identity, language and his own collapsed marriage.

After *Schizopolis* and a collaboration with **Spalding Gray**, *Gray's Anatomy* (1996), the

Steven Soderbergh on the set of *Ocean's Eleven*

revitalized Soderbergh delivered a pair of sinuous, witty thrillers: the sexy-cool *Out Of Sight* (1998), with **Jennifer Lopez** and **George Clooney** as a federal agent and her bank-robbing quarry, and *The Limey*, with the great **Terence Stamp** as a Cockney avenging angel seeking the truth about his daughter's mysterious death. Both lost money for their distributors, but were widely considered terrific films that simply hadn't found their

audience – not a problem for the $100-million-plus grossers *Erin Brockovich* and *Traffic. Brockovich* won **Julia Roberts** the best-actress Oscar for her brassy turn as a crusading legal secretary, while *Traffic*, which weaves three colour-coded storylines from various battlefields in the US drug war, won Soderbergh an Oscar for directing.

After *Traffic*, Soderbergh could write his own ticket (not to mention serve as his own

DeViation: Steven Soderbergh's digital experiment

Always thinking outside the box, **Steven Soderbergh** made one of his most innovative gambits to date in 2005 with the release of *Bubble*, a no-budget, partly improvised love triangle captured on handheld digital video. Shot on location in and around a West Virginian doll factory (one of just three of its kind left in the US) with non-professionals in the lead roles, the completed film was released almost simultaneously in theatres, on DVD and on the digital cable channel **HDNet Movies**.

The move essentially collapsed the usual release window between a film's theatrical run, DVD release and television premiere, an experiment backed by the billionaire entrepreneurs **Mark Cuban** and **Todd Wagner**, who own the Landmark chain of art-house cinemas, Magnolia Pictures and HDNet. However, non-Landmark exhibitors resisted this new release model, believing it was harmful to their business – in Baltimore, for example, not a single cinema screened the movie.

Since *Bubble* is a work of narrow appeal, its limited launch can't be said to have revolutionized film distribution in North America. But Soderbergh – whose partnership with Cuban and Wagner will extend to six movies – thinks it's a sign of things to come. When theatre chains have completed the transition to digital projection, he told the *Independent*, filmmakers will be able to skip over the studio middleman. "You'll see [well-known] film-makers self-distributing their own films," Soderbergh said "...I'll just go right to the theatres and make a deal with them. I'm certainly going to pursue that."

cinematographer, under the pseudonym Peter Andrews). He's since used his clout to aid other independent-minded filmmakers through **Section Eight**, the production company he set up with his frequent star Clooney, and to spearhead innovative projects, such as his partnership with **HDNet Entertainment** to direct six features on high-definition video with non-professional actors, starting with *Bubble* in 2005.

Otherwise, Soderbergh has drawn on his informal ensemble company (including Clooney, Roberts, **Don Cheadle** and **Luis Guzmán**) and pragmatically alternated between crowd-pleasing cash cows and more eccentric endeavours: from the jaunty all-star pageantry of *Ocean's Eleven* (2001) and its self-reflexive 2004 sequel to the avant-garde misfire *Full Frontal* (2002) and *Solaris* (2003), a plangent retelling of Polish author **Stanislaw Lem**'s sci-fi spin on the Orpheus myth. Pensive, elegant and moving (not qualities one would expect from a film co-produced by **James Cameron**), *Solaris* crashed commercially, but proved once again that Soderbergh hasn't yet sacrificed art for industry.

King Of The Hill
dir Steven Soderbergh, 1993, 109m

In Depression-era St. Louis, 12-year-old Jesse (the talented Jesse Bradford) finds himself alone when his mum becomes ill and his father hits the road to look for work, leaving the boy to fend for himself in a seedy hotel. Based on the memoir by A.E. Hotchner, Soderbergh's third feature is a subtle, quietly moving story that avoids easy sentiment.

Todd Solondz
Writer and Director, b.1959

Everybody's either a bully or a weakling, and the weaklings will gladly become bullies if given half the chance: such is the human strain seen through the microscope of **Todd Solondz**, cinema's Bard of the New Jersey suburbs. The geek's-revenge passion play *Welcome To The Dollhouse* (1995) made its dorky whipping post, Dawn Weiner, as capable of cruelty as her tormenters – a brave choice that showed the writer-director's keen grasp of the nastier aspects of human psychology. In the yet chillier climes of *Happiness* (1998), Solondz choreographed a deadpan freak show in which the most rounded character happened to be a child molester.

In his youth, Solondz considered becoming a rabbi and later taught English to Russian immigrants. Before he was 30, he wrote, directed and starred in his first feature, the barely released *Fear, Anxiety & Depression* (1989). His debut was the derivative product of a **Woody Allen** acolyte, though its title neatly encapsulated the dominant moods of his more successful future films. *Dollhouse* (still Solondz's best film) won the Grand Jury Prize at Sundance, and *Happiness* – comprising murder, suicide, paedophilia and an obscene phone caller in the shape of **Philip Seymour Hoffman** – earned an unexpected PR boost when its usually adventurous distributor, October Films, dropped the film under pressure from new corporate parent Universal. Though less heartfelt than *Dollhouse*, *Happiness* followed through on Solondz's potential for misanthropic rabble-rousing.

After *Happiness*, Solondz had to push ever harder to offend, and the strain began to show. In the schematic, self-reflexive *Storytelling* (2001), a black teacher and his white creative-writing student engage in rough, indeterminately consensual sex while he orders her to scream, "Nigger fuck me hard!" Split into two unrelated narratives called "Fiction" and "Non-fiction", *Storytelling* was the first of Solondz's films in which the abstract purity of his inimitable cruel world is broken by self-reflexive winks and nudges.

The discipline of its formalist framework held promise for his future offerings, but *Palindromes* (2004) proved to be a minor atrocity with a major gimmick: protagonist Aviva is played by eight different actors, including four girls, a 12-year-old boy and **Jennifer Jason Leigh**. Aviva longs to be a mother, but after her parents force her to have an abortion, she escapes to an orphanage-cum-Bible camp for disabled kids. The rotating cast may be intended to indicate the universality of Aviva's desires – for love, physical affection, creation – but the conceit ensures that she's little more than a wheedling cipher. It would appear that the blistering satire typical of Solondz's earlier work has subsided into canned sentimentality and snide contempt.

Happiness
dir Todd Solondz, 1998, 134m

In its matter-of-fact misanthropy, Solondz's cavalcade of dysfunction is less Chekhovian than Buñuelian, despite its three-sisters template: Joy (Jane Adams) is a miserable ESL teacher, Helen (Lara Flynn Boyle) is an ice-queen poet and Trish (Cynthia Stevenson) is a smug, deluded soccer mum. Sampling multiple flavours of pathology and perversity, *Happiness* is most wilfully inflammatory in its portrayal of a paedophile (Dylan Baker) as a sympathetic suburban dad doing his best – a brattish stunt on Solondz's part, but also darkly comic proof that human monsters have souls.

Whit Stillman
Writer and Director, b.1952

"If J. D. Salinger and F. Scott Fitzgerald had mated and had a child," the actor **Chris Eigeman** told the *New York Times* in 1990, the result would have been his voluble old-money character in **Whit Stillman**'s first film, *Metropolitan*. This vivid literary pedigree might also illuminate Stillman's small oeuvre, a suite of urbane, well-wrought comedies that also evinces the writer-director's love of Jane Austen and the cinematic influence of **Woody Allen** and **Eric Rohmer**.

Stillman's subjects are sons and daughters of privilege, handsomely appointed and educated but not yet sufficiently self-enlightened. In delineating their small trials and triumphs, the filmmaker sustains a delicately balanced tone, pitched between warmth and irony, between dry-eyed sympathy and gentle satire. His droll, referential screenplays (dropping names from Tolstoy to Thorstein Veblen to Scrooge McDuck) carry a theatrical lilt, since his characters tend to speak with precision and literary finesse even when they're being trivial or ridiculous. Following Austen's example, Stillman's work aspires to cultural anthropology, where much more is at stake than first meets the eye, and like Austen, his pointed wit can both tickle and draw blood.

All of Stillman's films draw to some extent on autobiographical experience. He's a product of the same upper-crust, Ivy League-school set that he lovingly sent up in *Metropolitan* (1990), a film financed in part with family loans and the proceeds of a Manhattan apartment sale. He worked in Barcelona as a producer's representative in the early 1980s, a setting revisited in his second film, *Barcelona* (1994). Here, he cast two of *Metropolitan*'s principals, **Chris Eigeman** and **Taylor Nichols**, as dissimilar American cousins – Eigeman is a naval officer, Nichols a salesman – posted in Spain during "the last decade of the cold war." *The Last Days Of Disco* (1998) centres on two young women who work at entry-level publishing jobs by day and frequent a Studio 54-like discotheque at night, much as Stillman did when he first lived in New York after graduating from Harvard.

It's not a fact he advertises in his work or interviews, but Stillman is a rarity in the Amerindie film world for his apparently rightward political outlook. He was formerly an editor at *The American Spectator*, and a headline in the Manhattan Institute's *City Journal* in 2004 hailed him as "A Great Conservative Filmmaker". However, Stillman's touch is too light to accommodate any grinding of ideological axes, even if the ugliest realities of the sexual revolution are conveyed with blunt force in *The Last Days Of Disco*, when a character's very first sexual encounter leads to gonorrhoea, herpes and humiliation.

Barcelona pokes equal-opportunity fun at its American expats and their Spanish girlfriends, and although all three of Stillman's films are set in an era on the wane, the wistful tenor of his coming-of-age movies *Metropolitan* and *Last Days Of Disco* doesn't express any reactionary nostalgia for lost innocence. Rather, Stillman excels at capturing the growing pains, heart-fractures and general absurdity endemic to just about any stage of life, whatever your bank balance or party affiliation might be.

David Strathairn

Actor, b.1949

Lean and ruggedly handsome with a voice that exudes sonorous authority, **David Strathairn** is equally equipped to play social pillars or saturnine villains. A graduate of Ringling Brothers Clown College, Strathairn has remained closely associated with **John Sayles**'s loyal stock company of actors (which also includes **Chris Cooper**, Mary McDonnell and Joe Morton) even as his profile in higher-budget studio pictures has steadily grown.

Beginning with his role as the obnoxious mechanic in Sayles's debut, *Return Of The Secaucus 7* (1979), Strathairn has worked many times for

Smoke and mirrors: David Strathairn says *Good Night, And Good Luck*

his fellow Williams College alumnus. He made a deft comic duo with Sayles himself as the "men in black" on the trail of **Joe Morton**'s mute alien in *The Brother From Another Planet* (1984), and played the tough-skinned police chief in the mining-strike drama *Matewan* (1987). Other key roles in Sayles's oeuvre include playing the pitcher for the disgraced 1919 Chicago White Sox in *Eight Men Out* (1988); a strong component of the urban mosaic *City Of Hope* (1991); a love interest for **Mary McDonnell**'s paralyzed soap actress in *Passion Fish* (1992); and an Alaskan journeyman burdened with guilt over a past boat accident in *Limbo* (1999).

Outside of Sayles's corpus, Strathairn has gained attention for parts in **Curtis Hanson**'s *L.A. Confidential* (1997) and in HBO's TV series *The Sopranos*. He won his first Oscar nomination as the CBS newsman Edward R. Murrow in **George Clooney**'s low-budget *Good Night, And Good Luck* (2005), set in the waning days of the McCarthy era. Strathairn doesn't merely impersonate the legendary newscaster Murrow so much as channel his solemn gravitas.

Quentin Tarantino

Writer, Director and Actor, b.1963

Casting an eye over the diner-cum-Hollywood shrine called Jack Rabbit Slim's in *Pulp Fiction* (1994), hit man Vincent Vega quips, "It's like a wax museum with a pulse", which might apply equally well to **Quentin Tarantino**'s cinema. Tarantino is not an originator of ideas and images so much as an expert curator and assembler of them; he constructs an entire universe out of quotation, reanimation, judicious borrowing and outright theft. His movies are anthologies of stolen moments: from 1940s *noir*, **John Woo**'s action symphonies, martial-arts throwdowns, badass blaxploitation, Godard's breathless outsiders, Leone's Spaghetti Westerns and much more. Giving voice to Tarantino's fanboy disquisitions on the hidden meanings of "Like A Virgin" or the Superman/Clark Kent dichotomy, his characters are pop-culture artefacts filling his personal gallery of favourite films.

What gives the museum its thumping pulse are Tarantino's manifold talents: his aptitude for profane banter and perfect soundtrack choices; his adroit staging of blood-splattered action; his relatively unsung gifts as a director of actors and reviver of faded careers; and his keen eye for clean compositions. The director's many visual imprints include the car-trunk point-of-view shot and the torture or violent death that's filmed from afar, or heard but not seen. The latter device is ably illustrated in his first film, *Reservoir Dogs* (1992), when the sickened camera turns away just before Mr. Blonde (**Michael Madsen**) slices off a cop's ear.

An all-male crime caper about a jewel heist gone awry (Tarantino lifted the crew's colour-coded nicknames from the 1974 B-classic *The Taking Of Pelham One Two Three*), *Reservoir Dogs* provided a hard and efficient introduction to Tarantino's line in quotable repartee and scrambled chronology, as well as his appetite for artery wine. (**Tim Roth**'s Mr. Orange spends much of the film writhing in a pool of his own blood.) The film won a devoted following on video, and its ill-fated criminals in their shades and skinny ties had become pin-ups on millions of students' walls by the time *Pulp Fiction* (1994), an exuberant suite of interconnected *noir* comedies, reached theatres for its phenomenally successful run. (In the meantime, the Tarantino-scripted *True Romance* (1993) and **Oliver Stone**'s *Natural Born Killers* (1994), which began life as a QT script, had also come and gone.)

Pulp Fiction was a hard act to follow, and Tarantino wisely stepped into a lower key for *Jackie Brown* (1997), an adaptation of an Elmore Leonard novel. Despite considerable longueurs and a fixation on the word *nigger* that carried an extra dosage of poison coming from the pen of a white man, the film soared in its portrayal of the soulful, thwarted mid-life attraction between **Pam Grier**'s money-smuggling flight attendant and **Robert Forster**'s weathered bail bondsman.

By the late 1990s, Tarantino had become dangerously overexposed, especially in his ill-considered acting endeavours, and by the turn of the millennium he all but disappeared from public sight. However, his wilderness years ended with a bang. Having paid homage to blaxploitation goddess Grier in *Jackie Brown*, he now worshipped at the altar of a movie star that he himself had helped create. **Uma Thurman**, whom Tarantino dressed as Anna Karina in *Pulp Fiction*, now donned Bruce Lee's banana-yellow track suit as the vengeance-seeking Bride in *Kill Bill Vol. 1* and *2* (2003/2004), a homage to the **Shaw Brothers** and many a grindhouse past master. Fulfilling

Tarantino's fantasy of playing filmmaker Josef von Sternberg to Thurman's Marlene Dietrich, the *Kill Bill* films represent the apotheosis of their maker's chopsocky celluloid dreams.

Lili Taylor

Actress, b.1967

Equally convincing as the spunky best friend, the comic-relief eccentric or the dangerous woman, **Lili Taylor** can be sweet or scary, ordinary or otherworldly. Cutting her teeth on coming-of-age tales such as *Mystic Pizza* (1988), which proved to

Heart and Solanas: Lili Taylor in *I Shot Andy Warhol*

be **Julia Roberts**'s launch pad to stardom, and *Say Anything* (1989), where she played best pal to the romantic hero, Taylor moved on to small parts in the prestigious ensembles *Short Cuts* (1993) and *Mrs. Parker And The Vicious Circle* (1994). Beneath the radar, she blossomed as an actress in **Michael Fields**' overlooked indie flick *Bright Angel* (1991), where she struck an intriguing balance between hardness and naïveté as a young wayfarer in perilous territory. Taylor also thrived under the direction of **Nancy Savoca**: as the resilient victim of a cruel prank in the barely released *Dogfight* (1991) and as the radiantly devout young Catholic in *Household Saints* (1993).

Taylor committed herself body and soul to **Abel Ferrara**'s *The Addiction* (1995) as Kathleen, the philosophy grad student whose world is turned upside down after she's bitten by a frightening temptress (**Annabella Sciorra**) on a downtown New York street. As cerebral Kathleen realizes that her new status as a vampire is a visceral metaphor for the human compulsion for violence and bloodshed, Taylor handles the difficult task of both playing a character and explicating the film's themes. The following year, she had her best role yet in **Mary Harron**'s *I Shot Andy Warhol* (1996) as the infamous **Valerie Solanas**, author of the *S.C.U.M. Manifesto* and attempted assassin of the scenester artist. By a small miracle, Taylor's compassionate performance fully humanizes a murderous and most likely deranged extremist who's custom-made for caricature.

In subsequent years, Taylor drifted among a forgettable flood of indie product (*Illtown*, 1996; *Kicked In The Head*, 1997; opposite love interest **Courtney Love** in the virtually unscreened *Julie Johnson*, 2001). However, her onscreen presence has remained steady and welcome, whether it's a recurring part in HBO's *Six Feet Under* or a juicy supporting role in Bent Hamer's *Factotum* (2005)

as barfly girlfriend to a character based on gutter poet Charles Bukowski.

 I Shot Andy Warhol
dir Mary Harron, 1996, 100m

Militant feminist author of the *S.C.U.M Manifesto*, Valerie Solanas (Lili Taylor) won her Warholian fifteen minutes of fame by shooting Andy Warhol (hilariously impersonated by Jared Harris), an event revisited in Harron's accomplished first film. The movie strikes a delicate balance: it's understandably aghast at Solanas's spiral into violent madness (and, to a lesser extent, at Warhol's studious vacuity), but it's also sympathetic toward the woman's desperation and mental distress.

Christine Vachon

Producer, b.1962

With all due respect to the brothers Weinstein, **Christine Vachon** is *the* definitive American independent film producer. Though auteurism has conditioned us to think of the director as a film's author, many a smart, challenging, hard-to-finance movie would never have seen the light of day without her. "At times when I would've given up," **Todd Haynes** has said, "she kept fighting, and very few directors can really claim that kind of relationship with a producer who is so determined and committed to their vision."

Starting out as assistant editor on **Bill Sherwood**'s *Parting Glances* (1986), Vachon formed an experimental-film production company called Apparatus in 1987 with fellow Brown grads Haynes and Barry Ellsworth, and she has served as producer on every one of Haynes's films since. Her early producing résumé is a virtual roll call of New Queer Cinema: Haynes's *Poison* (1991) and *Dottie Gets Spanked* (1993), **Tom Kalin**'s *Swoon* (1992), Rose Troche's *Go Fish* (1994) and Steve McLean's *Postcards From America* (1994).

A fierce advocate of cutting-edge cinema, Vachon has stood at the front-lines of many a celluloid controversy. *Poison* was financed in small part by government arts funds, thus drawing the ire of the Christian right for its homoerotic content. Two of Vachon's projects have famously frightened off their corporate parents: **Larry Clark**'s *Kids* (1995), for its copious underage sex, drugs and violence, and **Todd Solondz**'s *Happiness* (1998), for its portrayal of a child molester and its general air of hopeless depravity. (Vachon also produced Solondz's equally seditious next feature, *Storytelling*, in 2001.) A loyal friend to the fledgling director, Vachon has helped get a first shot for Troche, Mary Harron (1996's *I Shot Andy Warhol*), artist **Cindy Sherman** (1997's *Office Killer*), Kimberly Peirce (1999's *Boys Don't Cry*) and New York's downtown theatre sensation **John Cameron Mitchell** (*Hedwig And The Angry Inch*, 2001).

A paragon of steely fortitude, pragmatic know-how and discerning taste (and, like many a renowned producer, known for her hot temper), Vachon is the guardian angel of an indie director's wildest dreams. Take just one example: when lawsuits pending against true-crime tragedy *Boys Don't Cry* made the Toronto Film Festival nervous about screening it, Vachon took the kind of calculated risk that a studio executive wouldn't even consider – she personally indemnified the festival at the peril of millions of dollars, and first-timer Peirce was floored. "That night she

Christine Vachon with director Tom Kalin on the set of *Swoon*

was pure John Wayne of *The Searchers* – fearless, relentless and apparently calm," Peirce told the *Los Angeles Times*. "She is Vachon."

Swoon
dir Tom Kalin, 1992, 82m, b/w

This gleaming black-and-white take on the infamous 1920s child murderers Nathan Leopold (Craig Chester) and Richard Loeb (Daniel Schlachet) examine what director Kalin called "a critical reading of official history."

Gus Van Sant
Writer and Director, b.1952

Gus Van Sant is cinema's poet laureate of motherless boys on the fringes of the law, the straight life or civilization itself, wandering America's highways, woods and deserts beneath rushing time-lapse clouds (the director's high-lonesome motif). The **Kurt Cobain** doppelganger, Blake, played by **Michael Pitt** in *Last Days* (2005), is a summation of Van Sant's protagonists to date. Like **Matt Dillon**'s junkie bandit in *Drugstore Cowboy* (1989), the beautiful and doomed Blake is a passionate connoisseur of pharmaceuticals, and he's also a bewildered fellow traveller in the Land of Nod with **River Phoenix**'s narcoleptic, lovelorn hustler from *My Own Private Idaho* (1991). As with **Matt Damon**'s working-class math prodigy in *Good Will Hunting* (1997), Blake's remarkable gifts are a blessing as well as a curse – they're the source of a profound alienation that's perhaps the dominant condition in Van Sant's films.

For his acutely observed first feature, *Mala Noche* (1985), Van Sant adapted a novella by **Walt Curtis** about a grocery-store owner's unrequited longing for a Mexican teenager. Shot in the director's home base of Portland for less than $30,000, the movie previewed early-1990s New Queer Cinema and won critical raves, as did Van Sant's much-laurelled breakthrough, *Drugstore Cowboy*. Some reviewers were taken aback, however, by *My Own Private Idaho*, a melancholy and amusingly off-kilter update of Shakespeare's *Henry IV*, while *Even Cowgirls Get The Blues* (1993) proved to be an unmitigated critical and commercial disaster.

Van Sant bounced back quickly with *To Die For* (1995), a black comedy about a ruthlessly ambitious television reporter that gave **Nicole Kidman** a splendid opportunity to prove she was more than just a superstar's wife. The film also signalled Van Sant's first full-body dip into the mainstream, which continued with the Oscar-winning *Good Will Hunting*, a bizarrely pointless remake of *Psycho* (1998) and the lifeless *Hunting* retread *Finding Forrester* (2000).

The filmmaker had reached a career impasse, or so it seemed, but then came *Gerry* (2002), the first entry in a fascinating trilogy of true-death films that privilege real-time drift, oneiric sound design and experimental chronology. All three films locate their rhythms in their characters' perambulations. In *Gerry*, two young men embark on a desert trek and only one returns. In the eerily calm and meditative Palme d'Or winner *Elephant* (2003), a reckoning with the 1999 Columbine high-school massacre, the camera strolls down endless corridors of a high school that becomes a sprawling death trap. The camera in *Last Days* often stalks Blake from behind as he tramps through the forest or his own backyard like a man escaped – from rehab, from his family and friends or even from his looming appointment with oblivion. All of Van Sant's cowboys get the blues, seeking refuge inside private Idahos of their own design; the emotional heft of his movies derives from a fundamental loneliness, one that's treatable but incurable.

 Last Days
dir Gus Van Sant, 2005, 97m

Here is a person you know – or rather, a simulacrum of the late grunge icon Kurt Cobain – performing commonplace acts that are filtered through the dream-state prisms of drug addiction, depression and fame. A nature documentary shot through a disorientating cloud of heroin and *musique concrète*, Van Sant's film considers the final week before Cobain's suicide via his doppelgänger Blake (Michael Pitt), a zonked-out musician who shares his blond hair, junk habit, bug-eyed sunglasses and haunting, solitary demise.

John Waters

Writer and Director, b.1946

Long before David Lynch and Todd Solondz exposed the livid underbelly of American suburbia, Baltimore-based **John Waters** giddily celebrated the violence, perversity and poor hygiene to be found just beyond the white picket fence. The cracked epitome of the hometown boy made good, Waters has made all of his films in Baltimore, from his first short, *Hag In A Black Leather Jacket* (1964), shot on the rooftop of his parents' house with an 8mm camera his grandmother gave him for his seventeenth birthday.

Any film from his 1970s run of no-budget underground movies will serve up some permutation of cannibalism, incest, intravenous drug use, death by electric chair, religious blasphemy and sex with chickens. In *Multiple Maniacs* (1970), leading lady **Divine** (né Harris Glen Milstead) snarfs down human organs and is raped by a lobster. (Perhaps even more shocking

America's sweetheart: Divine in John Waters' *Pink Flamingos*

Guiding lights: the cinematographers

Behind every great film is a great cinematographer, who sculpts light and shadow to make a director's vision into glowing reality. In looking over the unofficial honour roll of groundbreaking American films to emerge in recent decades, the names of several directors of photography stand out.

• One of the elder statesmen of American independent cinema is **Frederick Elmes**, who handled the black-and-white photography for the hilariously horrific David Lynch short *The Amputee* (1974), as well as Lynch's feature debut, *Eraserhead* (1977); Elmes continued working with Lynch and his knack for painterly composition made him a favourite of Ang Lee and Jim Jarmusch.

• **Jim Denault**'s early work included two films for Michael Almereyda, and he's since ranged all over the indie map, his credits including the lyrical, grainy verite-like images in *Our Song* (2000), *The Believer* (2001) and *Maria Full Of Grace* (2003), and the gorgeous nocturnal landscapes of *Boys Don't Cry* (1999).

• **Harris Savides** was a key player in the mounting of Gus Van Sant's trilogy of films about young death (*Gerry, Elephant* and *Last Days*), in which the camera's movements took their cue from the characters' wanderings. However, his most stunning work can be found in Jonathan Glazer's *Birth* (2004). Savides lit the interiors entirely from above through muslin wraps and then radically underexposed them, conjuring a dusky ghost world of candlelit apparitions, granular light and tactile shadows.

• Notable for the gleaming black-and-white images she honed for *Swoon* (1992), **Ellen Kuras** forged a partnership with Spike Lee for several films, but most memorably in her sun-bleached, kinetic cinematography for *Summer Of Sam* (1999). She also conjured a wintry dream-light for *Eternal Sunshine Of The Spotless Mind* (2004).

• **Lance Acord** created a similar dream-light effect for another Charlie Kaufman-script, *Being John Malkovich* (1999), directed by Spike Jonze. Acord also lensed Jonze's *Adaptation* (2002) and two films by Jonze's former wife, Sofia Coppola (*Lost In Translation*, 2003, and *Marie-Antoinette*, 2006). In *Lost In Translation*, Acord's gauzy, slightly colour-bleached imagery sees Tokyo through the eyes of the puzzled, beguiled characters, capturing their jet-lagged wistfulness.

• Sofia Coppola turned to veteran cinematographer **Edward Lachman** for her melancholy first feature, 1999's *The Virgin Suicides*. His early credits included the valedictory *Lightning Over Water* (1990) and the valuable punk document *The Blank Generation* (1980), and he has since worked on films by Steven Soderbergh, Larry Clark and Todd Haynes. As is the case for all these talented cinematographers, versatility is crucial to Lachman's craft. "What I love about my job is getting to move between different worlds," he told this writer in 2002. "The challenge is not to have a signature camerawork or lighting, but to be more of a chameleon."

is that Waters made the movie for a mere $7,000.) In the midnight-circuit blockbuster *Pink Flamingos* (1972), Divine eats a poodle dropping, then grins for the camera. "If someone vomits watching one of my films," Waters once wrote, "it's like getting a standing ovation."

The fearless Divine was the unrivalled star of stars in the informal repertory company of

Waters' underground years. This included **Mink Stole**, Mary Vivian Pearce, David Lochary and the ample and elderly **Edith Massey**, resplendent in a revealing dominatrix ensemble in the surprisingly coherent *Female Trouble* (1974), which sends schoolgirl Divine on a rampage after she's denied a pair of cha-cha heels for Christmas. *Polyester* (1981) provided the opportunity for

Waters' first piece of star casting – 1950s teen idol **Tab Hunter** as Divine's unreliable love interest – and a somewhat resistible gimmick: the film was presented in "Odorama," with scratch-and-sniff cards to be inhaled by audience members at assigned moments.

Waters toned down the spectacular bad taste of his previous output with the PG-rated *Hairspray* (1988), a Day-Glo slice of irreverent 1960s nostalgia about a "pleasantly plump" teen (**Ricki Lake**) who dreams of strutting her stuff on a local dance show. The director's sweet-souled mainstream breakthrough was also the swansong of the irreplaceable Divine, who died just a few weeks after *Hairspray*'s Baltimore premiere. The director soldiered on with *Cry-Baby* (1990), a spoof on *Grease* with **Johnny Depp** sending up his teen-pinup image, and *Serial Mom* (1994), with **Kathleen Turner** as a model housewife driven to murder by bad manners and faux pas.

Ten years later, Waters returned to his outlaw roots with the aptly titled *A Dirty Shame* (2004), featuring **Tracey Ullman** as a concussed nymphomaniac and **Selma Blair** sporting Russ Meyer-worthy breasts. *A Dirty Shame* continued a theme in Waters' films that stretches back to *Pink Flamingos*: in the face-off between trash culture and the "straight" world, the ostensibly upstanding citizens are truly the most depraved.

Pink Flamingos
dir John Waters, 1972, 108m

In Waters' grotesque underground hit, made for a relatively lavish $100,000, two families compete for the coveted title of the "Filthiest People Alive": it's Divine's trailer-trash clan versus the Marble family, who run a baby-production factory out of their basement. The movie leaves no doubt about where its sympathies lie in this particular contest, and crowns Divine's triumph in the notorious coda wherein she eats dog shit.

Bob & Harvey Weinstein
Producers, Bob b.1954, Harvey b.1952

Old-school studio executives who ushered in a new era of filmmaking, Miramax founders **Bob** and **Harvey Weinstein** make a fascinating study in yin-yang symbiosis. Bob is the enigmatic, media-wary businessman who makes the fatter income with his cheap, niche-market genre fare, while Harvey is the blustering, attention-hungry cineaste who courts the press and brings home the prestigious awards. The elder Weinstein brother's shortcomings are abundant and well-documented: spiteful hardball tactics; a nuclear temper; a compulsion for acquiring lots of movies, only to leave many of them mouldering on the shelf; and an invasive post-production presence that earned him the nickname "Harvey Scissorhands". For years, Harvey's thuggish personality easily overshadowed his brother's activities, though it couldn't quite obscure their profitable good works in distributing fresh, vital cinema from all over the world. But as the New York-based **Miramax** (named after the brothers' parents, Miriam and Max) proved itself eminently capable of taking on the big Hollywood studios, it became increasingly indistinguishable from them; perhaps the die was cast when mighty Disney acquired the Weinsteins' home-grown organization in 1993.

Moving from music-events promotion in Buffalo into film distribution in the early 1980s, the brothers from Queens scored a sleeper hit with the British concert film *The Secret Policeman's Other Ball* (1982) and made an ill-advised foray into writing and directing with the reportedly dreadful teen comedy *Playing For Keeps* (1986). Sticking thereafter to other people's movies, the Weinsteins showed their knack for savvy, aggressive promotion and the fine art of misrepresentation with their

Profiles in chutzpah: Harvey Weinstein (left) and Quentin Tarantino

early successes. They marketed **Lizzie Borden**'s *Working Girls* (1986), an acerbic feminist polemic, as a saucy romp, and their campaign for **Errol Morris**'s *The Thin Blue Line* (1988) discreetly concealed that the film was a documentary – a commercial kiss of death in the 1980s.

Nineteen eighty-nine was a banner year for Amerindie film and also for the Weinsteins, who distributed **Steven Soderbergh**'s epochal *sex, lies,* *and videotape*, as well as a host of splashy acquisitions from abroad. They won plenty of column inches in 1989 with the daring British arthouse favourites *Scandal* and *The Cook, The Thief, His Wife And Her Lover*, and the Miramax-distributed *My Left Foot* (1989) and *Cinema Paradiso* (1988) earned an armful of Oscars between them. Miramax persisted in promoting superb foreign-language cinema to an American audience allergic to subtitles, with Chen Kaige's *Farewell My Concubine* (1993) and **Krzysztof Kieslowski**'s *Three Colours* trilogy both benefiting from handsome campaigns.

Into the 1990s, Miramax barrelled past one milestone after another. They backed the first independent film to gross $25 million (*The Crying Game*, 1992, which blew the record away with a $60-plus million gross) and the first "independent" film to gross $100 million (*Pulp Fiction*, 1994, which went into production eight months after the Disney purchase). They won their first Oscar for Best Picture courtesy of *The English Patient* (1996), followed two years later by *Shakespeare In Love*. **Kevin Smith**'s *Clerks* (1994) racked up one of the highest profit-to-budget ratios of all time, and the *Scream* horror movies provided the brothers with their first franchise under the aegis of Bob's money-making genre division, **Dimension**.

A strange dichotomy of the aesthete and the vulgarian, Harvey Weinstein was the subject of a much-discussed *New Yorker* profile in 2002, which itemized many of his public eruptions, observed that "Miramax staff suffers from something akin to battered-spouse syndrome," and quoted a studio head saying that many of Weinstein's partners leave a project feeling "'raped' – a word often invoked by those dealing with him." By this point, the Miramax tradition of quality had dropped off sharply (with notable exceptions such as **Todd Field**'s 2001 masterpiece *In The Bedroom*), and Harvey was endlessly distracted by his political activities, bouts of ill health and a short-lived venture into publishing with *Talk* magazine.

The brothers' professional fortunes looked ambiguous after Miramax's deal with Disney soured, and in September 2005 they left their home-grown organization to found a new regime, the **Weinstein Company**, where their early slate of releases was decidedly spotty. These days, the accuracy of one of Harvey's most infamous sound bites needs reconfirming: "You know what? It's good that I'm the fucking sheriff of this fucking lawless piece-of-shit town."

Terry Zwigoff
Writer and Director, b.1948

When Seymour, the doleful record geek in **Terry Zwigoff**'s *Ghost World* (2001), complains, "I can't relate to 99 percent of humanity," he's unwittingly paraphrasing **Robert Crumb**'s sardonic closing comments in Zwigoff's *Crumb* (1994) – and no doubt both of these disgruntled loners speak volumes for their director too. Zwigoff has often acknowledged the influence of the cracked comix artist Crumb ("The way I see the world was largely formed by knowing him as a friend," he told London's *Independent*).

Seymour, a depressive hoarder of old blues 78s, is effectively the filmmaker's self-insertion into the deadpan realm of Daniel Clowes' comic book on which the film is based (the character doesn't appear in the original strip). Given a tragicomic gravitas by **Steve Buscemi**, Seymour can be interpreted as an act of simultaneous self-deprecation and wish-fulfilment on Zwigoff's part. The character may be an object of ridicule, but he also attracts the sexual advances of the movie's fresh-out-of-high-school protagonist, Enid (**Thora Birch**), an eye-rolling aspiring artist whose drawings were provided by Crumb's talented young daughter, Sophie. (Zwigoff was later annoyed when his old pal Crumb snickered to *The New Yorker*, "A middle-aged record collector who gets laid by a teen-aged girl is one of Terry's big fantasies.")

A former comic-book publisher, Zwigoff first channelled his musical connoisseurship in his debut feature, the documentary *Louie Bluie* (1985), a portrait of the aged members of the African-American string band Martin, Bogan and the Armstrongs. The movie won a rave review from Roger Ebert, but eight years passed before Zwigoff made his critical and commercial breakthrough with his next film, *Crumb*. Since this extraordinary and long-gestated documentary, Zwigoff's forte has been sarcastic outcasts who regard their surroundings with fascinated disgust, and his position as a late bloomer amid a youth-obsessed American mass culture may only strengthen his iconoclastic stance. Zwigoff was well into his 40s at the time of *Crumb*'s success, and was 53 when his melancholy comedy about teen-girl anomie, *Ghost World*, reached US theatres. At the time, he also reported turning down a $10,000 offer from clothing chain the Gap to pose for their campaign featuring what Zwigoff called "young hip film directors".

The middle-aged hip film director reunited with *Ghost World* creator Clowes for another comic-book adaptation, the poorly received *Art School Confidential*, in 2006. The director's only non-comic-related movie of recent years features his most hilariously misanthropic outsider: Willie T. Stokes (**Billy Bob Thornton**), dyspeptic drunk and department-store St. Nick, in the riotous *Bad Santa* (2003). Scripted by **Glenn Ficarra** and **John Requa** (with uncredited revisions by Zwigoff and **Joel** and **Ethan Coen**) the movie borders on the symphonic in its virtuosic insults and bottomless variations on the word "fuck". A weirdly exhilarating wallow in booze-marinated degeneracy, *Bad Santa* eventually reveals its inner softie, but not before tickling your inner Grinch, and its mix of scalpel-sharp cynicism and unexpected humanism is vintage Zwigoff.

Ghost World
dir Terry Zwigoff, 2001, 112m

An acerbic, melancholic chronicle of teenage ennui in American suburbia, Daniel Clowes' comic book enters the third dimension in the capable hands of Zwigoff – whose previous subject, comix elder statesman Robert Crumb, is recalled in the tetchy jazz aficionado Seymour (Steve Buscemi). As bespectacled ironist Enid, Thora Birch deftly reveals layers of vulnerability and alienation; the film is empathic and often laugh-out-loud funny in observing a young woman's discovery of how to hurt and be hurt.

Conduct Unbecoming:
the American underground

Boys and their toys: Peter Fonda and
company in *The Wild Angels*

Conduct Unbecoming: the American underground

Many of the films that appear in the narrative of Amerindie cinema fit, however loosely or awkwardly, into one upstanding genre or another: drama, comedy, thriller, documentary. But there's another juggernaut in this tale; one that occasionally roars onto the American main street but more often keeps to the underlit side streets and alleyways of the national culture. Horror, porn, midnight movies and their otherwise weird or sleazy brethren comprise an important chapter in the American independent story. Proudly crude, sometimes legally problematic and often extremely profitable, this is the sight and sound of the underground.

Immoral and notorious: porn in the USA

Paul Thomas Anderson's *Boogie Nights* (1997) recreates the golden age of American porn in the 1970s and its ugly comedown in the 1980s, but the genre began around 1907, when the earliest pornographic motion picture is believed to have surfaced in Argentina. The Kinsey Institute dates its first American counterpart, a silent "stag film", at circa 1917–19. Also called "blue movies", stag films were made and viewed under risk of arrest; they were typically screened without sound accompaniment in smoke-filled rooms to men-only crowds, assembled through hushed word of mouth. To escape legal scrutiny, the actors often performed in disguise, and cast and crew were typically credited under evocative pseudonyms such as "Ima Cunt" and "R.U. Hard".

The informative six-part documentary *Pornography: A Secret History Of Civilisation*

The Carrie Nations in repose in *Beyond The Valley Of The Dolls*

Breast in show: Russ Meyer

"I'm in it for lust and profit," said **Russ Meyer** (1922–2004), the inimitable director who cut his teeth on gigs both hard-boiled and softcore. He worked as a combat photographer during World War II and made a transition into cheesecake portraiture before finding his calling with his first feature, *The Immoral Mr. Teas* (1959). Hitting his stride in the anything-goes second half of the 1960s, Meyer established multiple trademarks: Amazonian women, fast cars, startling violence, spicy one-liners, deadpan performances, leering camera angles and, most famously, large and lavishly displayed boobage, whether spilling out of a low-cut top or straining against a tight angora sweater – not for nothing did Meyer title his 1,213-page autobiography *A Clean Breast* (2000).

Certainly prolific, Meyer made more than twenty films in as many years, always cheaply and almost always outside of the studio system. Yet from a technical standpoint, his movies – brimming with *vroom* and *va-voom* – were far more crisply shot, carefully composed and kinetically edited than most trash-movie connoisseurs would ever expect, especially his best-known film, *Faster, Pussycat! Kill! Kill!* (1966) and the X-rated *Vixen!* (1968), a surprisingly explicit fuckfest revolving around a racist, incestuous, sexually insatiable pilot's wife, played by the avid **Erica Gavin**.

Incredibly, despite his salacious track record, Meyer was signed to a three-picture deal with the ailing studio 20th Century Fox in 1969. As Chicago film critic **Roger Ebert** later marvelled, Meyer was even "given carte blanche to turn out a satire of one of the studio's own hits" – this being the uproarious *Beyond The Valley Of The Dolls* (1970), written by Ebert and featuring a formidable trio of rocker girls who fall under the sway of a gender-bending Svengali figure. "I deal with women who are archetypes – in fact, they're *beyond* women," Meyer once boasted, and, at their best, his gobsmacking trash epics are *beyond* movies.

(1999), made for British television, points out that stag reels were as close to a sex-education film as many young men could get in the early decades of the century. By the 1940s, as *Pornography* shows, blue movies had entered "the age of the do-it-yourself pornographer", with fledgling hardcore directors developing film in their bathtubs and perhaps exhibiting the footage in a "pay-and-spray booth" for 25 cents a snippet.

During the 1950s, pin-up icon **Bettie Page** reigned as queen of the peep show, and her bondage photographs even instigated a Senate inquiry. (Page earned her own Amerindie biopic, **Mary Harron**'s *The Notorious Bettie Page*, in 2005.) However, the popular nudist-camp movies of the decade were able to circumvent obscenity laws and avoid similar inquiries because of their supposedly educational content, but they couldn't show any genitalia.

Onwards from his first film, *The Immoral Mr. Teas* (1959), smut swami **Russ Meyer** worked independently, often self-financing his pictures and usually turning a profit. He became a sexploitation godfather with trash classics such as *Faster, Pussycat! Kill! Kill!* (1966), *Vixen!* (1968) and *Beyond The Valley Of The Dolls* (1970), starring many a top-heavy dominatrix.

Meyer never made a bona fide porno movie, perhaps because he didn't want to turn over his handsome earnings to the Mafia, whose associates produced many adult films and owned most of America's porn theatres in the 1960s and 70s. The **Colombo crime family** even had their own facility in Brooklyn, All-State Film Labs, for processing 8mm skin flicks. Meyer's *The Immoral*

Mr. Teas was, however, a direct ancestor of the hardcore industry, which seized on the new "X" rating as a seal of approval after the Motion Picture Association of America (MPAA) introduced the ratings system in 1968. (Thus the Best Picture Oscar for 1969's X-rated *Midnight Cowboy* isn't as remarkable a piece of anything-goes 1960s lore as it may seem: the rating didn't become a scarlet-neon letter until the porn business had a chance to commandeer it.)

Hardcore porn marked its first mainstream phenomenon in the form of *Deep Throat* (1972), starring **Linda Lovelace** (née Boreman) as a sexually frustrated nurse who embarks on a career of world-class fellatio administration after discovering that her clitoris is located in her throat. At once juvenile and coarsely progressive, the film both enacts the ultimate male fantasy and puts female sexual pleasure at centre stage. *Deep Throat* finally ushered porn out of the stained-raincoat closet, and became a must-see for New York's hip cognoscenti – initiating a trend that the *New York Times* famously labelled "porno chic".

The film's director, **Gerard Damiano**, had ties to the Mafia through his co-producers (and the Mob predictably vacuumed up all of the movie's massive profits). And yet, when federal investigators sought a scapegoat for the allegedly obscene movie, they didn't prosecute the producers, the compromised Damiano or the sword-swallowing heroine Lovelace. Instead, they went after male lead **Harry Reems**, an automatically sympathetic figure given that he spends much of *Deep Throat* nursing his overtaxed, bandage-swaddled member. (Reems' conviction on obscenity charges was later overturned). Lovelace, meanwhile, became a household name – although she was later involved in anti-porn activism and claimed that she was forced at gunpoint to perform in the

Sound investments: the most profitable movies

A tally of the biggest-grossing movies of all time makes a familiar list of behemoths such as *Titanic*, *Jurassic Park*, and the various *Star Wars* and *Lord Of The Rings* installments. But what about the most *profitable* films – the movies that returned the largest gains on the smallest budgets?

The poster for the documentary *Inside Deep Throat* (2005) claims that the $25,000 porno flick grossed $600 million, making it "the most profitable film in motion picture history". There's no doubt that 1972's *Deep Throat* pulled gargantuan profits, but since the Mafia-affiliated Peraino family handled its distribution and box office receipts, there's no way to confirm exact numbers. ("Whatever you've heard about how much *Deep Throat* earned, it's underestimated," a Peraino lawyer told the *Los Angeles Times* in 1982, but his guess was $100 million.)

Among films that reached audiences through more conventional channels, champions of the US box office include 1969's *Easy Rider* (which made about $47 million domestically on a $500,000 budget) and 1978's *Halloween* ($47 million on $325,000), while *Teenage Mutant Ninja Turtles* became the highest-grossing independently released film of all time in 1990, with a domestic take of more than $135 million. The famously no-budget movies *El Mariachi* (1992) and *Clerks* (1994) both posted exponential returns on their initial costs, but the movie to blow all precedents out of the water was *The Blair Witch Project* (1999), the DIY horror movie with the five-figure budget that snapped up more than $135 million in the US alone.

film. (Other cast and crew members strenuously denied this charge.)

Deep Throat started a wave of porno chic films. *Behind The Green Door* (1972), directed by brothers **Jim** and **Artie Mitchell**, cast **Marilyn Chambers** in the demanding role of a young woman abducted and ravished, somewhat consensually, by a variety of patrons in a sex club. (Tragically, Jim Mitchell shot and killed his brother in Artie's home in 1991.) The lithe and athletic Chambers – the face of laundry detergent Ivory Snow – later starred as a promiscuous heiress in the popular *Insatiable* (1980). *Deep Throat* director

Damiano also continued to make films about insatiable women, including the surprisingly existential *The Devil In Miss Jones* (1973), about a chaste woman (**Georgina Spelvin**) who commits suicide and is born again as an ardent hedonist. Director **Radley Metzger**, who worked under the *nom de film* Henry Paris, took an almost elegant approach to skin flicks, especially with his erotic retelling of the Pygmalion legend, *The Opening Of Misty Beethoven* (1976).

The American porn industry thus enjoyed a fleeting Hollywood moment, with its own A-list of stars and directors, until the dawn of the

Hard to swallow: picketers object to *Deep Throat*

video age put hundreds of porn cinemas out of business in the early 1980s. Cheap video technology meant that production increased exponentially and hardcore porn became a home-viewing experience – a multi-billion-dollar industry with little inclination towards Damiano and Metzger's ragged aspirations to art. The state of California legalized adult-film production in 1988, and now the vast majority of American hardcore films are produced in the San Fernando Valley, also known as "Porn Valley".

The Immoral Mr. Teas
dir Russ Meyer, 1959, 63m

The eponymous salesman enjoys the ability to see through women's clothing in Meyer's six-reeler, which is considered to be the first bona fide American "nudie cutie" – a forerunner of the sexploitation genre with which Meyer became synonymous. Ever resourceful, the director shot the flick for about $24,000, and filmed most of in a dentist's office on loan for the weekend.

Beyond The Valley Of The Dolls
dir Russ Meyer, 1970, 109m

Meyer tracks the naïve rise and deadly fall of The Carrie Nations, a voluptuous all-girl rock group – lead by former Playmate of the Month Dolly Read – who head out to LA in search of fame and fortune. Originally devised as a sequel to the accidental campfest *Valley Of The Dolls* (1967), Meyer's garish, violent tour de force is an outlandishly hilarious riff on Jacqueline Susann's beach-read bestseller, packed with bons mots and bountiful bosoms.

Inside Deep Throat
Fenton Bailey and Randy Barbato, 2005, 92m

This fun documentary examines the scrappy little skin flick, *Deep Throat*, that became a mainstream phenomenon in 1972, thanks in part to a pan-American litigious assault that inadvertently doubled as a publicity campaign. Bailey and Barbato's effort toasts a moment when a sense of erotic freedom and experimentation seemed to beckon, albeit in the form of a low-grade porn movie.

The gay underground: flaming creatures of the pleasure dome

In her pioneering study of moving-image pornography, *Hard Core* (1989), the academic Linda Williams draws mischievous parallels between the musical and the porn film, pointing out that the latter genre can offer up sexual set pieces as highly choreographed and narrative-propulsive as any musical sequence in a Gene Kelly classic. Her point brings to mind **Jack Smith**'s orgiastic *Flaming Creatures* (1963); as J. Hoberman and Jonathan Rosenbaum write in *Midnight Movies*, "the film ends, like a Busby Berkeley musical, with a series of ensemble and solo dance numbers." Appearing the same year, **Kenneth Anger**'s erotically charged, pop-scored *Scorpio Rising* (1963) originated the grammar of MTV with its proto-music video elements.

Smith and Anger were two of the visionary gay artists whose thrillingly subversive films lit up the underground circuit long before the 1969 Stonewall uprising in New York catalyzed the gay-rights movement. Anger's 1947 short *Fireworks* (the first of nine films in his *Magick Lantern Cycle*) is an extraordinary debut, for both its teenage author's filmmaking talents and for his astonishing boldness in imagining same-sex longings at a time when homosexuality was still the desire that dare not speak its name. Full of phallic visual puns (including a Roman candle), the movie stars young Anger as "the Dreamer", who is beaten and, it's suggested, raped by a gang of sailors.

An oneiric haze of Dionysian hallucination or baroque nightmare suffuses all of Anger's movies, including the fetishist's fantasia *Scorpio Rising*. The film examines the social and criminal life of a smouldering, speedfreak biker thug whom Anger compares – with characteristic irreverence – to both Jesus Christ and Adolf Hitler. Winking with shiny leather and glinting chrome, the movie inspired **David Lynch** with its ironic use of crooner Bobby Vinton's "Blue Velvet".

Scorpio Rising spurred a California obscenity trial, and Smith's *Flaming Creatures* likewise attracted the unwelcome attentions of law-enforcement officials. From New York to Texas to Michigan, screenings were raided and prints seized. *Village Voice* columnist **Jonas Mekas** received a suspended prison sentence for screening *Flaming Creatures* at the New Bowery Theater on St Marks Place, and the New York Supreme Court banned the film outright for its male nudity and transvestitism. Filmed on the roof of a downtown Manhattan

theatre with a hodgepodge of local artists, burnouts and colourful characters, *Flaming Creatures* was a seminal work that influenced the likes of filmmakers **Andy Warhol** and **John Waters**, who were no doubt delighted by its criminal status.

Taking his cue from the polar amazements of Meyer's macho skin flicks and Smith's queer bacchanalia, Waters spent much of his career trying to outdo his own shock tactics. And his greatest star, the vast and fearless drag queen **Divine**, was clearly the child of *Flaming Creatures*. Warhol's career also emulated Smith's, in both the outrageous brio of his ramshackle films and the legal complications they provoked. Later in the decade, Warhol found himself under investigation by the FBI for the interstate transport of obscene material – his own *Lonesome Cowboys* (1967). An anti-Western of

Kenneth Anger: magick man

Though his entire filmography only adds up to about three hours of screen time, **Kenneth Anger** (born 1927) has exerted a powerful influence on filmmakers as diverse as **Martin Scorsese**, **Derek Jarman** and **Roger Corman**. British director **Isaac Julien** also credited Anger's movies with "develop[ing] the vocabulary for the New Queer Cinema".

Anger (né Anglemyer) was a precocious child of the dream factory: his grandmother was a Hollywood wardrobe mistress, and he appeared as an 8-year-old in the 1935 film version of *A Midsummer Night's Dream*. Steeped from birth in Tinseltown lore, Anger first found fame when he wrote *Hollywood Babylon* (1959), a grimly fascinating compendium of sordid celebrity lives and deaths, replete with autopsy and crime-scene photos. (A second volume followed in 1981, and he has long dangled the possibility of a third installment, but nothing has yet materialized.)

At the tender age of 17, Anger made his first surviving piece, *Fireworks* (1947), in his parents' home while they were away. From his teens onwards, he was also fascinated by the writings of English occultist **Aleister Crowley**, to whom the young director dedicated his *Inauguration Of The Pleasure Dome* (1954), which took its title from **Samuel Taylor Coleridge**'s opiate-befogged poem "Kubla Khan". His influential short *Scorpio Rising* (1963) conjured a pop-scored fever dream of biker boys and their toys.

In the late 1960s, Anger started work on *Lucifer Rising* (1981), which took more than a decade to complete, hindered foremost by the theft of original footage and camera equipment. Featuring Marianne Faithfull and Donald Cammell as gods and a soundtrack recorded in prison by Manson Family associate **Bobby Beausoleil**, *Lucifer Rising*, despite its lengthy gestation, is Anger's most fast-paced film, an associative collage that spins into a vortex.

lamentable technical quality, but brimming with pretty boys, *Lonesome Cowboys* was confiscated by Atlanta police in 1969. That same year, Warhol's 1968 two-hander *Blue Movie* (aka *Fuck*) ran into similar trouble in godless Gotham, where police confiscated the film and arrested the employees of the movie theatre showing it.

Perhaps Warhol was a natural-born pornographer because he was such a devoted connoisseur of the everyday. He redefined celebrity and sowed

Cuddle party: Joe Dallesandro and friends in *Flesh*

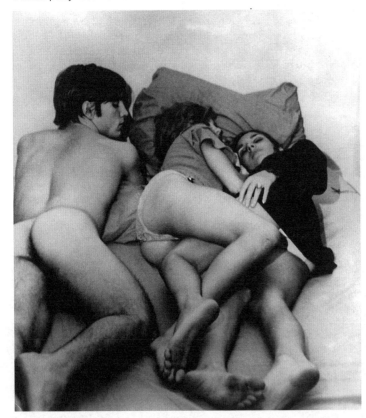

the seeds of reality television with his *Screen Test* series (1965-66) and feature films such as *Chelsea Girls* (1966). The latter showcased the various friends, deadbeats and personalities ("Warhol superstars") who hung out at his studio-home, The Factory, chatting, fucking, taking drugs and generally passing the time.

Warhol's film work in the second half of the 1960s added sex and sensation to his earlier, more conceptual movies. His first film, *Sleep* (1963), was a five-hour silent document of stockbroker-turned-poet **John Giorno** snoozing (a conceit that Sam Taylor-Wood lifted for her 2004 video portrait of superstar footballer David Beckham). That same year's *Eat* looks on for 45 minutes while a man consumes a mushroom. With his early movies, Warhol discarded established notions of what makes a film, just as artist **Marcel Duchamp** (subject of one of the *Screen Tests*) created a new art paradigm with his readymades.

Warhol's audaciously boring aesthetic reached a literal peak with *Empire* (1964), an eight-hour antecedent of the webcam stream and a document of what was then the world's tallest skyscraper, the Empire State Building. As with *Sleep*, *Empire* asks us to ponder the image as we would a painting, an invitation perhaps better extended in a shorter Warhol film of 1964 which carried the self-explanatory title *Taylor Mead's Ass*.

In later years, especially after he was shot and nearly killed by Valerie Solanis (subject of the 1996 **Mary Harron** biopic, *I Shot Andy Warhol*), the artist delegated directorial authority to his assistant director **Paul Morrissey**. Morrissey helmed by far the best of the movies to carry the Warhol brand, including *Flesh* (1968), *Trash* (1970), *Women In Revolt* (1971) and *Heat* (1972). He also worked as a director outside the Warhol fold, most memorably on *Mixed Blood* (1985), a witty, violent tale of a teenage gang war that is an invaluable time-capsule document of New York's Lower East Side before gentrification.

Chelsea Girls
dir Andy Warhol and Paul Morrissey, 1966, 210m, b/w and colour

Shot largely in New York's Chelsea Hotel with Factory superstars (including Nico, Edie Sedgwick and Brigid Berlin) just being themselves, Warhol's split-screen epic unspools three and a half hours of gabbing, drugs, abortive sex, hairdressing, tears, role-playing and naked confession. An exhaustive document of a certain strand of downtown bohemian nihilism, *Chelsea Girls* is also a case study in Warholian real-time voyeurism.

Flesh
dir Paul Morrissey, 1968, 105m

Factory hunk Joe is a passive hustler trying to scrape together enough cash for his wife's abortion in Morrissey's first film, "presented by Andy Warhol" and featuring Warhol associates Jackie Curtis and Candy Darling. Forming an informal trilogy with Morrissey's *Trash* (1970) and *Heat* (1972), *Flesh* displays plenty of flesh, while its rough real-time rhythms belie its thematic rigour. Exploring sex as a form of financial and emotional barter, the movie is funny, engrossing and unexpectedly plangent.

Mixed Blood
dir Paul Morrissey, 1985, 98m

Rita La Punta (Marilia Pera) is manager and mama bear to a gang of teenage drug runners in lethal conflict with their equally youthful rivals in Morrissey's overlooked gem

of camp vérité. The grainy visuals match the rough-and-tumble narrative of this hard-edged yet often funny film, and the amateurish acting only heightens the occasional overtones of street-level documentary.

Ray Cohn/Jack Smith
dir Jil Godmilow, 1994, 90m

This film alternates between two monologues by actor Ron Vawter: in one he is Cohn, the ethically compromised lawyer and aide to witch-hunting senator Joseph McCarthy; in the other he is Smith, the underground filmmaker who here wears garish pharaoh garb. What these diametrically opposed historical figures had in common was homosexuality and death from AIDS, and Godmilow's editing teases out a complementary diptych of repression and expression, cold logic and hot-blooded irrationality.

Badass songs: the blaxploitation era

Far from seeking acceptance or assimilation, underground films by gay artists celebrated outlandish behaviour, voracious libidos and criminal instincts, which meant they had much in common with another flamboyant phenomenon of the 1970s: blaxploitation.

Mostly contained in a rush of some two hundred films produced in the first half of the 1970s, the black exploitation genre spilled over with flashy gangsters, drug-addled pimps, sleazy pushers, depraved cops and vampy whores, most of them upholstered in ghetto-fabulous costumes and backed by irresistible soul-funk soundtracks. In their larger-than-life tales of heroes (or occasionally heroines) out for justice or vengeance – and often caught between the rock of oppressive white society and the hard place of the disenfranchised black ghetto – the movies reinforced stereotypes of black male violence, lawlessness and over-amped sexuality. Black civil-rights organizations, including the National Association for the Advancement of Colored People (NAACP), protested that the movies were denigrating to African-Americans, and the genre soon faltered – though not without leaving a permanent stamp on the sensibilities of many a future filmmaker and musician.

The first inklings of the genre could be seen in **Ossie Davis**'s *Cotton Comes To Harlem* (1970), which deployed violent action and broad humour in adapting **Chester Himes**' 1965 novel about a team of Harlem detectives hunting down a stash of stolen money. The following year, **Melvin Van Peebles** threw down the gauntlet for blaxploitation with *Sweet Sweetback's Baadasssss Song* (1971), wherein the eponymous anti-hero loses

his virginity to a prostitute before the credits roll (and, it would seem, before the character has completed puberty). He grows up to be a lone, nearly mute black rebel: a cop-killer, a ladies' man (his workman-like technique unaccountably drives the women wild) and finally an enigmatic soul rebel. The closing credits predict a revolution: "A baad asssss nigger is coming back to collect some dues."

Peebles, who starred as the laconic Sweetback as well as directing, writing and handling most of the main technical duties, kept costs down by using a small, non-unionized crew. He kept the unions at bay with the ruse that he was shooting a porn movie – hence the film's abundant but obviously bored copulations. The movie's startling scenes of sex and violence became the norm

Another day at the office for Shaft

Pam Grier: queen of blaxploitation

Pam Grier's film persona easily eclipses the patchy B-movies and grindhouse fodder that make up much of her résumé. In the blaxploitation films that made her a legend, she's a well-coiffed, sharply dressed badass mama, equally adept with a gun, her fists, a damning quip and any other available weapon ("I got my black belt in bar stools," she snarls after whomping a karate expert in *Foxy Brown*). A tough-talking, street-smart warrior with a regal bearing and massive reserves of primal fury, the gorgeous Grier projected feminine fortitude and attitude in films often mired in misogyny.

Her first screen credit was a walk-on role in **Russ Meyer**'s *Beyond The Valley Of The Dolls* (1970), and while she was certainly statuesque enough to take on any of Meyer's Amazonian goddesses, she instead joined the illustrious ranks of the **Roger Corman** fold. She took roles in a few of the women-in-prison movies that Corman outsourced to the Philippines, including *Women In Cages* and *The Big Doll House* (both 1971) for Corman's New World Pictures and, for AIP, *Black Mama, White Mama* (1971), a distaff rendition of the 1958 prison-break drama *The Defiant Ones*. Boasting a story by **Jonathan Demme**, *Black Mama, White Mama* has intimations of racial and class conflict, but they are mostly secondary to reliable doses of nudity and violence.

Grier went on to play the titular angels of vengeance in the AIP productions *Coffy* (1973) and *Foxy Brown* (1974), both directed by *Black Mama, White Mama*'s **Jack Hill**, who had a practised eye for showcasing Grier's impressive cleavage (not to mention her glorious shoulders). AIP's *Scream Blacula Scream* (1973), a so-so sequel to the previous year's *Blacula*, cast Grier as a voodoo priestess recruited to transplant the blood-thirsty Count back to his native land. And in *Friday Foster* (1975), she played a photojournalist who uncovers a conspiracy to kill successful African-Americans.

After her mid-1970s heyday, Grier continued to have a steady stream of film and television work, including a striking turn as a drug-addicted prostitute in *Fort Apache, The Bronx* (1981), a stint on *Miami Vice* and a regular role on *The L Word*. However, it was **Quentin Tarantino** – who had previously reverently name-checked her in *Reservoir Dogs* (1992) – that gave the middle-aged actress the role of a lifetime. In Tarantino's *Jackie Brown* (1997) she is the eponymous leading lady, a resourceful flight attendant who keeps her cool when caught between a gun-runner, a Fed and a bail bondsman. Guided by her clearly adoring director through a part of unusual richness and nuance, Grier was impeccably poised and more beautiful than ever, displaying a new gravitas brought by the passage of time.

Too close for comfort: Pam Grier gets collared in *Foxy Brown*

for blaxploitation flicks, and so did its signature music. *Sweetback*'s reiterative theme consisted of a terse synth-and-sax refrain by funk group **Earth, Wind & Fire** freshened with liberal doses of the hymn "This Little Light of Mine", and it paved the way for more accomplished blaxploitation scores.

Longtime Stax Records musician **Isaac Hayes**, whose *Hot Buttered Soul* album was a hit in 1969, won an Oscar for his unforgettable theme song to *Shaft* (1971), which posed the immortal question, "Who's the black private dick that's a sex machine to all the chicks?" The answer is John Shaft (**Richard Roundtree**), the cool and mighty detective with a suitably phallic name, who strides coolly through the dangerous city streets heralded by the wah-wah riff and horns of Hayes' jazzy soul instrumentals. **Curtis Mayfield**'s soundtrack for *Superfly* (1972) was even better, its tight, ominous grooves and socially charged lyrics fuelling the singles "Pusherman" and "Freddie's Dead". Like *Shaft*, *Superfly* spun a swaggering tale about a sharply dressed man who must negotiate a smooth path between the white and black worlds, but it told its story from the other side of the law: the protagonist (**Ron O'Neal**) is a cocaine dealer – a pusherman – trying to score one last big deal to secure his retirement.

Shaft and *Superfly* epitomized the black exploitation genre, and they kept it in the family: the pioneering filmmaker behind *Shaft*, Gordon Parks, was the first African-American to direct a picture for a major studio (1969's *The Learning Tree*) and **Gordon Parks Jr** helmed *Superfly*. (Although the elder Parks also directed the 1972 sequel, *Shaft's Big Score*, he was disdainful of the blaxploitation tag.) Both *Superfly* and *Shaft* were products of major studios, MGM and Warner Bros. respectively, who belatedly saw that profits could be made from onscreen representations of the black experience, however glamorized or ghettoized those representations might be.

Many of the signature blaxploitation films, however, were independent ventures, including **Michael Campus**'s iconic hustler story *The Mack* (1972) and **D'Urville Martin**'s cult classic *Dolemite* (1975), starring oddball comic **Rudy Ray Moore** as a hustler turned narc. A fair number of blaxploitation films did make some kind of departure from the cops-and-criminals template. Black cinema got a martial-arts master of its own in **Jim Kelly**, who led the cast of the kitsch favourite *Black Belt Jones* (1974), while **Tamara Dobson** threw kung-fu kicks as the eponymous heroine of *Cleopatra Jones* (1973). Though blaxploitation was a uniquely macho and often misogynistic field, it had its share of female heroines, including Dobson and the magnificent **Pam Grier**, who headlined several of American-International Pictures' black-exploitation features (see more on AIP later in this chapter).

Richard Fleischer's studio-financed *Mandingo* (1975), released in the twilight of the blaxploitation heyday, moved from the usual gritty urban milieu to the American South in the 1840s, where a slaveowner's plantation is a place of avarice, rape, violence and murder. Condemned by many mainstream critics as crude sensationalism of the lowest order (*The New York Times*' Vincent Canby likened the film to pornography, adding, "This one is strictly for bondage enthusiasts"), *Mandingo* nonetheless won a healthy following at the box office.

The Mack
dir Michael Campus, 1972, 110m

In one of the most enduring and influential products of blaxploitation, Max Julien plays a kind-hearted pimp who's just trying to keep a tight rein on his girls, make a luxurious living and give something back to the community.

Featuring a fine performance from Richard Pryor as a cocaine-tongued hustler, *The Mack* – with its glitzy, gaudy fashion sense and profane repartee – left its mark on many a hip-hop musician as well as Quentin Tarantino and Dave Chappelle, and was a clear influence on Craig Brewer's *Hustle & Flow* (2005).

Coffy
dir Jack Hill, 1973, 91m

The incomparable Pam Grier plays amateur detective while seeking justice for her sister's heroin overdose among a succession of pimps, gangsters and motley lowlifes. Essentially a series of sex-and-violence set pieces, the movie is significant in the annals of blaxploitation for placing an ass-kicking female at centre stage – as did the following year's *Foxy Brown*, a cruder rendition of *Coffy*'s revenge plot, also starring Grier as a vengeful sexpot.

Dolemite
dir D'Urville Martin, 1975, 90m

A veteran of the nightclub circuit, Rudy Ray Moore stars in this frankly inept, weirdly endearing staple of stoner cinema. After his release from prison, the eponymous mack daddy reconnects with his de facto harem and tries to collaborate with the police. Much of the film's arguable appeal derives from Moore's stolid conviction as a pudgy, forty-something stand-up comic lumbering his way through the role of a prize stud.

Wild angels and scary monsters: the Roger Corman factory

Had the prolific producer-director **Roger Corman** been able to convince a young Italian-American director to make a foray into blaxploitation, a classic of American independent cinema might have been a different movie altogether. When **Martin Scorsese** – who had previously

directed *Boxcar Bertha* (1972) for Corman – was seeking funds for *Mean Streets* (1973), Corman offered to put up $150,000, but only if Scorsese promised to recruit an all-black cast. Scorsese demurred, but paid grateful homage to his mentor by including a scene from Corman's **Edgar Allan Poe** adaptation *The Tomb Of Ligeia* (1964) in the film. "What Corman gave us was the discipline of how to make a film," said Martin Scorsese, who appreciated that the busy producer "did leave you alone, provided you played it within the genre and didn't get too crazy."

An exploitation entrepreneur bar none, Roger Corman rarely met a cheap yet decadent genre he didn't like: monster movies, Gothic frighteners, juvenile-delinquency melodramas, biker flicks, true-crime adventures, black comedies, softcore romps and more. Corman was a resident director at **American-International Pictures** (AIP), a studio without its own lot – the company rented its stages, just like the Poverty Row studios of yore. He was also a budgetary magician who used leftover sets and kept to absurdly compressed shooting schedules, cranking out factory-issue schlock for speedy delivery to the drive-in circuit.

Corman's filmmaking ethos is summed up by the title of his 1990 autobiography, *How I Made A Hundred Movies In Hollywood And Never Lost A Dime*. The sheer breadth, depth and extent of his oeuvre as director can be gleaned simply from a scan of his credits: *Swamp Women* (1955), *Naked Paradise, Attack Of The Crab Monsters, The Saga Of The Viking Women And Their Voyage To The Waters Of The Great Sea Serpent* (all 1957), *She Gods Of Shark Reef, Teenage Cave Man* (both 1958), *A Bucket Of Blood* (1959) – and that's just a sample of his 1950s run. However, his attempt at hard-hitting social drama – *The Intruder* (1961), starring the young **William Shatner** as a white supremacist in a small town – was met with disappointment.

Several of Corman's films that hold up best come from his Edgar Allen Poe cycle, which cast the legendary **Vincent Price** in the aforementioned *Tomb Of Ligeia*, as well as adaptations of *The Pit And The Pendulum* (1961), *The Raven* (1963) and *The Masque Of The Red Death*

(1964). *The Raven* boasted a particularly sterling cast, including Price, **Boris Karloff**, **Peter Lorre** and regular Corman collaborator Jack Nicholson. For *Bloody Mama* (1970), Corman directed the irreplaceable **Shelley Winters** as the infamous Kate "Ma" Barker, who led her four sons on a homicidal crime spree in the 1930s. In *The St. Valentine's Day Massacre*

"Would you excuse us?"

(1967), **Jason Robards** played Al Capone (a role Corman originally intended for **Orson Welles!**).

There's a case to be made that more prodigious film talents have "graduated" from the various production companies associated with Roger Corman and AIP than any of the more formal institutions. Corman had an unrivalled, even prophetic eye for promising youngsters – Scorsese is just one of many future luminaries who got their first break working in the Corman fold. Another was **Peter Fonda**, who starred in two of AIP's most profitable Corman-directed films: *The Wild Angels* (1966), a violent saga about the Hell's Angels biker society, and *The Trip* (1967), an LSD odyssey scripted by **Jack Nicholson**.

Tall, strong-jawed and golden-haired, Fonda made a handsome icon of youth rebellion, and one with undertones of Oedipal defiance. His father, **Henry Fonda**, had embodied American heroes Abraham Lincoln, Wyatt Earp and Teddy Roosevelt on the big screen, but Peter clinched his legend by playing a pot-smoking biker with the audacity to call himself "Captain America" in *Easy Rider* (1969), a drug-fuelled road movie clearly derived from the biker flicks produced by AIP and its demi-studio rivals.

Directed by co-star **Dennis Hopper**, *Easy Rider* proved to be so successful that Hollywood scrambled to hitch a ride on the wandering-hippie zeitgeist. Joan Didion, journalist, novelist and occasional Hollywood screenwriter, observed that in 1969, "every studio in town was narcotized by *Easy Rider's* grosses and all that was needed to get a picture off the ground was the suggestion of a $750,000 budget … a non-union crew, and this terrific 22-year-old kid director." Sadly for the studios, however, most of these rip-offs didn't work commercially.

In 1970, Corman left the AIP fold to form his own production company, **New World Pictures**, where he produced women-in-prison flicks and gave an early shot to **Stephanie Rothman**, one of the rare female directors to figure in the exploitation field. Rothman helmed the hugely enjoyable sexploitation films *The Student Nurses* (1970) and *The Working Girls* (1974). Corman's only requirement for *The Student Nurses*, according to Rothman, "was that the nurses be very pretty and that they be naked as often as possible." The faithful result shows Rothman's raw genius for adapting the stringently budgeted exploitation-film model to her own witty, rambunctious brand of sex-positive feminism.

Though other graduates of the Corman school used their experiences there as stepping stones to more illustrious mainstream careers, director **Paul Bartel** always felt most at home in B-grade exploitation fare. His speciality was the sex comedy, and after helming several Corman productions – *Private Parts* (1972), *Death Race 2000* (1975), *Cannonball* (1976) – he mounted his own cult classic *Eating Raoul* (1982), which he partly self-financed after his mentor declined to put up the cash.

In 1983, with the drive-in and B-movie markets drying up, Corman founded Concorde-New Horizons, which specialized in oversexed, ultra-violent schlock for the cable and straight-to-video markets. With the occasional exception (such as *One False Move* director **Carl Franklin**), few budding Scorseses or Coppolas have since emerged from the Concorde factory, even if Corman, now in his 1980s, remains one of the hardest-working men in show business.

The Masque Of The Red Death
dir Roger Corman, 1964, 89m

The incomparable Vincent Price plays Edgar Allan Poe's malevolent satanic Prince Prospero, who takes pleasure in manipulating and torturing the noblemen and women who seek refuge from the plague in his creepy castle. One of the more high-minded Corman efforts (he intended an homage to Ingmar Bergman), the film benefited from an unusually generous shooting schedule – five weeks! – as well as rich colour cinematography by future director Nicolas Roeg.

The Wild Angels
dir Roger Corman, 1966, 93m

The Hell's Angels sued Corman for defamation after the release of this ultra-violent exploitation flick, which gives renegade biker Heavenly Blues (Peter Fonda) space to expound on the importance of freedom and pleasure while also reserving much time and energy for beatings, mêlées and general nihilism. The movie grossed some $25 million on a $350,000 budget, despite being largely unwatchable.

The Student Nurses
dir Stephanie Rothman, 1970, 89m

Rothman's diverting sexploitation film tracks the professional and personal fortunes of four attractive young nursing students, who variously fall in love, experiment with drugs, seek an illegal abortion and plunge into radical politics. Goofy, socially conscious and weirdly uplifting, the movie proves Rothman's expertise in shaping a personal vision to Corman's exploitation paradigm.

Eating Raoul
dir Paul Bartel, 1982, 90m

The aptly named Paul and Mary Bland dream of escaping hedonistic Los Angeles and opening their own country kitchen, if only they had the money. But after they accidentally kill a sex-crazed intruder and find a wad of cash in his pockets, they hit on a plan and start luring swingers into their home. The uptight Blands' distaste and fear of sex manifests itself in murder and cannibalism in Bartel's satirical black comedy.

Blood feasts: the genre that ate Hollywood

Few mere mortals could rival Roger Corman for speed, output and economy, but **Herschell Gordon Lewis** could give the emperor of the drive-in a run for his money. Hailed as the "Godfather of Gore" and insanely prolific (he made nine films in 1968 alone), Lewis tried his hand at softcore flicks, nudist-camp movies, hill-billy comedies and even blaxploitation films in search of a quick buck. But he soon carved out his own crimson-stained niche with his horror movies, made on the cheap in Florida for the 1960s drive-in market: *Blood Feast* (1963), *Two Thousand Maniacs!* (1964) and *Color Me Blood Red* (1965) comprised his informal "blood trilogy".

Why did he work in the horror genre? "It was simply a business decision," Lewis once said – and many big-studio executives would make the same calculation in the decades to come. As it turns out, Lewis's "business decision" didn't pay much in the way of artistic dividends: narrative incoherence, inept camerawork and atrocious acting characterize much of his work. Nonetheless, he has a devoted cult of admirers. *Two Thousand Maniacs!* inspired the names of both **John Waters'** *Multiple Maniacs* (1970) and the folk-rock band 10,000 Maniacs, and *Blood Feast* is, if nothing else, one of a kind. As the critic Andrew Grossman wrote, the film's "ridiculous nadirs of execution meld, trancelike, with sublime heights of fearless intent." Inarguably an innovator, Lewis set new limits of onscreen violence with *Blood Feast*, one-upping *Psycho*'s (1960) infamous shower scene in its opening moments.

Fortunately, the scary-movie auteurs who followed in Lewis's wake had a greater command of their craft and, more importantly, intuited the

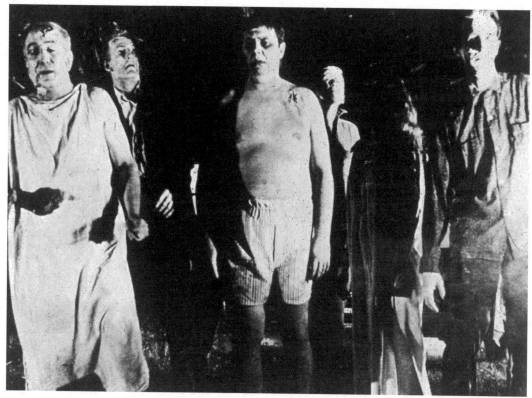

The zombie ensemble in *Night Of The Living Dead*

vast aesthetic and thematic potential of the genre. **George A. Romero** began as a maker of television commercials and industrial films through his company, **The Latent Image** (based in Pittsburgh, hometown of Herschell Gordon Lewis and Andy Warhol), and eventually discovered the many allegorical possibilites of horror. Inspired in part by *Carnival Of Souls* (1962), the no-budget horror benchmark made by fellow industrial filmmaker **Herk Hervey**, Romero mounted his debut feature, *Night Of The Living Dead*.

Premiering in the violent and divisive year 1968, the movie imagined America eating itself alive in its tale of hostile civilians under siege from "ghouls" − flesh-chomping zombies who used to be their families, friends and neighbours. As Romero stated, horror can be "a criticism of the way things are … the genre is meant to bring down reality, or destroy it." Each of the three *Night Of The Living Dead* sequels thus far − *Dawn Of The Dead* (1978), *Day Of The Dead* (1985) and *Land Of The Dead* (2005) − has held up a disturbing mirror to American society and politics.

The *Dead* films also squish, squelch and slosh with unlimited gore, which is integral to their appeal – and that of almost all underground horror movies. We might refer to many of the works in this chapter as "sensation movies", for their ability to produce physical jolts of arousal, fear or disgust, or "emission films", for their liberal flow of blood, sweat and cum, and horror pictures are no different. Pornography and the underground horror flicks of the 1970s share obvious carnal and visceral links. The seemingly endless ordeal of the final female victim in **Tobe Hooper**'s *The Texas Chainsaw Massacre* (1974) – her blood and frenzied screams pouring forth in a torrent, her skintight pants impeding her escape from death – calls to mind a pornographic rape scene.

The genres often overlapped in practical terms, too. Joseph and Louis "Butchie" Peraino of the **Peraino crime family**, who had made some $100 million or more on the back of the hardcore porn flick *Deep Throat*, founded the film company Bryanston in the early 1970s. They distributed the **Andy Warhol** presentations *Flesh For Frankenstein* (1973) and *Blood For Dracula* (1974), both directed by Paul Morrissey, as well as the *ne plus ultra* of slasher flicks, the massively profitable *Texas Chainsaw Massacre*.

Horror director **Wes Craven** began with the softcore free-love testimonial *Together* (aka *Sensual Paradise*) in 1971. His movie brought the young actress **Marilyn Briggs** to the attention of pornographers **Jim** and **Artie Mitchell**, who cast the newly christened Marilyn Chambers in the porn classic *Behind The Green Door*. Craven also cast the prolific porn actor and director **Fred Lincoln** in a nasty role in his shocking second feature – and first horror flick – *Last House On The Left* (1972). Banned for some thirty years in Britain, *Last House* made the family hearth and home

"Dead" reckoning: Romero's ghouls through the years

With the zombie bedlam of *Night Of The Living Dead* (1968), **George A. Romero** crafted a visceral allegory of American society in conflict, and one that proved to be amazingly adaptable over the course of three sequels (so far). He's relocated the desolated farmhouse setting of *Night* to a shopping mall (1978's *Dawn Of The Dead*), an underground bunker (1985's *Day Of The Dead*) and a city torn by civil war and class tensions (2005's *Land Of The Dead*).

His flesh-eating "ghouls" (Romero's original term for the menacing undead) have been staggering stand-ins for mindless consumer consumption (in *Dawn*) and the puppet-victims of a military-industrial complex (in *Day*). By *Land*, they'd become an underclass culture unto themselves – a bogeyman distraction to working-class stiffs, who don't realize that they face just as much of a threat from the super-rich in their gated communities and high-rise towers.

Released the summer after George W. Bush's re-election, *Land Of The Dead* is arguably the most politically charged of the *Dead* films. It critiques Bush's ongoing "War on Terror" and, in one scene, makes a discomfiting prophecy of the refugee catastrophe that would follow in Hurricane Katrina's wake just two months later. The filmmaker's genius is to sneak compelling political and socioeconomic commentary into grossout multiplex entertainment, making shoddy remakes like **Zack Synder**'s 2004 *Dawn Of The Dead* (made for double *Land*'s $15 million budget) seem all the more irrelevant.

Blood-sucking freaks: the Troma trauma ward

Paragons of violence, depravity and extreme bad taste, the brain trust at producer-distributors **Troma Entertainment** – founded in 1974 by **Michael Herz** and **Lloyd Kaufman** – are responsible for some of the most socially irredeemable movies ever committed to celluloid. Troma's specialities include gruesome deaths (unsparing of children, dogs and the elderly), wanton brutality, gratuitous female nudity and rampant radioactivity.

A representative sample of their output could include the titles *Blood Sucking Freaks* (1976), *Girls School Screamers* (1986), *Redneck Zombies* (1987), *Surf Nazis Must Die* (1987) and *Chopper Chicks In Zombietown* (1989). But their signature film is *The Toxic Avenger* (1983), a typically Tromatized spin on the classic superhero plot: the harassed geek – a proverbial 98-pound weakling – falls into a vat of toxic waste and becomes a deformed saviour. A midnight-movie hit in the mid-1980s and infamous for being banned in Ontario, *The Toxic Avenger* spawned several sequels and provided a gamma-radiated template for Troma's other big franchise feature, *The Class of Nuke 'Em High* (1986).

Troma's most forward-thinking release, however accidentally, was *Cannibal! The Musical* (1996), a student film by future *South Park* creators **Trey Parker** and **Matt Stone** that pays melodious tribute to the real-life Colorado flesh-eater Alferd Packer. (*Cannibal!* is also notable for an appearance by legendary experimental filmmaker **Stan Brakhage**, professor of film studies at Parker and Stone's alma mater, the University of Colorado at Boulder.)

the forum for a smackdown between villains and would-be victims (as did **John Carpenter**'s low-budget slasher, *Halloween*, in 1978).

Since making *Last House*, Craven has remained a definitive purveyor of horror filmmaking, cementing trends and usually enjoying great commercial success. As in Romero's films, the visceral mayhem of his 1970s work disregarded the generally accepted boundaries for onscreen violence and gore, while also allegorizing the social and moral disintegration of 1970s America. His second horror film, *The Hills Have Eyes* (1977), pits a vacationing middle-class family against a clan of feral cannibals in a desert showdown, which can be read as an appropriately grisly allegory of the Vietnam War. Released by indie studio **New Line**, *A Nightmare On Elm Street* (1984), perhaps Craven's best-known film, is a potent screamer in which the realization of our worst fears comes from within our own minds, homes and neighbourhoods.

One could make a strong case that Craven is directly responsible for the financial fortunes of two of the biggest indie-turned-majors: New Line and Miramax. *A Nightmare On Elm Street* spawned a television series, *Freddie's Nightmares*, the battle royale *Freddy vs. Jason* (2003) and six increasingly camp sequels, which took their cue from **Sam Raimi**'s low-budget *Evil Dead* trilogy in freely mixing horror and humour. *Nightmare* also enabled New Line to start an art-house division (Fine Line), attracted the corporate buying power of **Ted Turner** and made New Line the envy of their rival, Miramax.

Miramax founders **Bob** and **Harvey Weinstein** then started their own specialty genre wing, Dimension, and recruited Craven for the studio's first franchise movie, *Scream* (1996), which offered an auto-critique of the genre that he had been so instrumental in defining. The whiffs of sexual puritanism evident in *Elm Street* and *Halloween*,

with their virginal heroines and intimations of teen sex as capital offence, came under particularly close scrutiny in the first *Scream* installment.

In the 1990s *Scream* revived both Craven's career and the slasher genre, and it even helped to inspire its own parody franchise, the lamentable *Scary Movie* suite, which actually exceeded the earnings of the *Scream* series for the Weinsteins. Smelling green, other studios hopped on the horror band-wagon. Even a decade on from *Scream*, cheaply made horror films still lure reliable numbers from an apparently insatiable youth market – the same one that would have hit the drive-in for a Roger Corman double feature decades ago.

Lions Gate's *Saw* (2004) made more than $100 million worldwide on roughly a $1 million budget, and its 2005 sequel opened at number one at the US box office, as did Lions Gate's *Hostel* (2005) and Sony's *Silent Hill* (2006) and *The Grudge* (2004), the latter being one of several recent remakes of Japanese horror hits with American actors. Even the execrable *Scary Movie 4*, made under the aegis of the Weinstein Company, set an Easter-weekend box-office record in 2006. Of all the disreputable, degenerate factions in the American underground, it was horror that broke into the mainstream and stayed there, as soon as the studios discovered that screamers print cash.

Two Thousand Maniacs!
dir Herschell Gordon Lewis, 1964, 87m

Lewis aficionados often cite this as his finest hour, a horror riff on *Brigadoon* relocated to Pleasant Valley, a town decimated in the American Civil War. The town only comes to life again once every century, when its

Leatherface out for a jog in *The Texas Chainsaw Massacre*

inhabitants ensnare unsuspecting northerners for ghastly (and inventive) revenge killings. The film is significantly more proficient than *Blood Feast*, but didn't make as much money – perhaps an instructive lesson for the decidedly slapdash director.

Last House On The Left
dir Wes Craven, 1972, 85m

Craven's sleaze-horror revamp of Ingmar Bergman's medieval drama *The Virgin Spring* (1960) depicts the kidnap, torture, rape and murder of two teenage girls by a gang of psycho sadists – and all not far from one of the girls' secluded home in the woods, where the killers coincidentally take shelter with her parents for the night. Setting an almost unwatchable ordeal in an incongruously pastoral setting, *Last House* is an exploitation flick turned surprisingly classical revenge drama.

The Texas Chainsaw Massacre
dir Tobe Hooper, 1974, 83m

A comely gang of dumb kids make all the wrong moves on a road trip, one by one meeting grisly ends in a farmhouse inhabited by the inbred family from hell. Despite his meager budget, Hooper manages some particularly macabre set design chez Leatherface (check out the fine outsider-art collection of skin tapestries and bone-based sculpture), but the prolonged bloody torments become stultifying.

Halloween
dir John Carpenter, 1978, 91m

Jamie Lee Curtis, daughter of original slasher-movie victim Janet Leigh, made her film debut as the teenage prey of evil incarnate, Michael Myers, in Carpenter's hugely successful third feature. With surprisingly little blood or gore, this efficient scare-generator all but invented the American strain of slasher movie as we now know it.

A Nightmare On Elm Street
dir Wes Craven, 1984, 91m

If the viewer can forget Freddy Krueger's later ascension to comedy-mascot icon, this oneirophrenic frightener remains powerful. A group of high-school kids – led by plucky virgin Nancy (Heather Langenkamp) – fight to stay awake in order to elude a serial killer who strikes in his victims' dreams. With its scares hinging heavily on the disorientation and derangement of severe sleep deprivation, this film skillfully blurs the line between dream and reality.

Money Changes Everything:
the Hollywood connection

Criminal mischief: Robert Musgrave, Luke Wilson
and Owen Wilson in Wes Anderson's *Bottle Rocket*

Money Changes Everything:

the Hollywood connection

For better or worse, two entities have significantly shaped American independent film as we now know it: the Sundance Institute and its film festival, founded by Robert Redford; and Miramax Films, founded and formerly run by brothers Bob and Harvey Weinstein. These two powerhouses helped to facilitate an extraordinary blossoming of independent-minded filmmaking in the late 1980s and early 1990s, but – as was the case with the "New Hollywood" era of the 1970s – the bloom began to come off the rose as their power, budgets and profiles grew. Their ascendancy presented a paradox. Begun as alternatives to the big-studio machine, Sundance and Miramax redefined Hollywood. In the process, however, they also became synonymous with Hollywood – and, as we shall see, Hollywood has occasionally outdone the indies in endorsing smart, original filmmaking talent.

Independent vision: beginning to see the light

Now the biggest and most high-profile event of its kind in the United States, the **Sundance Film Festival** began modestly in 1978 as the Utah/US Film Festival, with **Robert Redford** serving as inaugural chairman. Redford's non-profit-making Sundance Institute, founded in 1981 to develop and promote the work of "artists of independent vision", took over the management of the festival in 1985, the year that **Joel** and **Ethan Coen**'s first feature, *Blood Simple*, won the Grand Jury Prize. (The festival was officially renamed Sundance in 1991.)

The Coens' cool, nasty neo-*noir* was an exception to the rule of most Sundance programming, which tended to favour sleepy, homespun "regional" fare. With its abundant soul-searching dialogue and southern local flavour (Baton Rouge, Louisiana, to be exact), **Steven Soderbergh**'s *sex, lies, and videotape* (1989) loosely fit the Sundance profile, and proved to be a breakthrough for the festival, for its young first-time director and for its

The original Sundance kid, Robert Redford, at the opening of his film festival in 1995

distributor, **Miramax**. An independent film studio founded by **Bob** and **Harvey Weinstein** in 1979, Miramax had previously scored art-house successes with **Lizzie Borden**'s sly feminist statement *Working Girls* (1986) and **Errol Morris**'s gripping true-crime documentary *The Thin Blue Line* (1988). The studio's 1989 batting average was especially fine, thanks to the success of *sex, lies, and videotape* and a string of hits imported from the UK.

If 1989 was a watershed year for independent film, it wasn't immediately apparent to some close observers. "Independent Films Get Better but Go Begging" declared the headline to a *New York Times* piece by Aljean Harmetz, reporting from the 1989 US Film Festival. "As little as these pictures cost, the money isn't there," lamented one film rep in the article, but his words were hardly prophetic. *sex, lies, and videotape* was a commercial as well as a critical success, and artists of independent vision such as **Gus Van Sant**, **Spike Lee** and newcomer documentarian **Michael Moore** also enjoyed a terrific year.

Into the early 1990s, a formidable array of independent film talent came to the fore, including **Gregg Araki**, **Carl Franklin**, **Todd Haynes** and – the flashiest of the bunch – **Quentin Tarantino**. And by the end of 1992, the *New York Times* had done an about-face on indie cinema's prospects. An article by Janet Maslin asked, "Is a Cinematic New Wave Cresting?" and named an honour roll of fresh talent, including Araki, Franklin, Tarantino and the Sundance upstarts **Alexandre Rockwell** and **Allison Anders**. Rockwell had won that year's Grand Jury Prize at Sundance for his comedy of errors *In The Soup* – beating Tarantino's ultra-violent *Reservoir Dogs*, which had been developed at one of the Sundance Institute filmmakers' labs.

Quoted in Maslin's article, **Walt Disney Pictures** chairman **Jeffrey Katzenberg** declared, "Commerce has overwhelmed art, which is why

Science/Fiction: the film labs

The **Sundance Institute** is best-known for its flashy annual film-festival extravaganza, but behind the scenes it also cultivates fledgling screen talent through its Screenwriting and Filmmaking Laboratories. There new writers and directors can massage their works-in-progress under the close watch of seasoned film veterans. Though Sundance is often – and rightly – criticized for a preponderance of films about well-heeled suburban angst and twee teenage rites of passage, the labs have nurtured a wide range of styles and subject matters. Alumni include **Paul Thomas Anderson** (1996's *Hard Eight*), **Wes Anderson** (1996's *Bottle Rocket*) **Nicole Holofcener** (1996's *Walking And Talking*), and **Quentin Tarantino** (1992's *Reservoir Dogs*), among many others.

Keeping a somewhat lower profile than Sundance, the **Independent Feature Project** (IFP) runs the "Rough Cuts" lab, where untried directors nearing completion have the opportunity to show their movies to professional mentors. Likewise, at the annual, week-long **IFP Market** in New York City, filmmakers can screen their works-in-progress and show their scripts to potential backers and buyers. Founded in 1979 to promote young filmmaking talent through screenings, workshops, conferences and online library resources, the IFP organization eventually expanded to include chapters in six cities (IFP/LA decided to strike out on its own in 2005). It also gave birth to *Filmmaker* magazine, the Los Angeles Film Festival and the **Independent Spirit Awards**, which in recent years has become a kind of younger, cooler pre-game warm-up to the Oscars.

Hollywood movies aren't as good as they used to be." No doubt Katzenberg had this sentiment in mind the following May, when Disney acquired Miramax for a reported $80 million. The deal appeared to be a match made in heaven for both companies. Family-oriented Disney bought cool cachet and prizewinning prestige at a discount – Miramax had distributed the Academy Award recipients *My Left Foot* (1989) and *Cinema Paradiso* (1989) – and Harvey Weinstein went on to prove himself an unrivalled master of the scorched-earth Oscar campaign. And Miramax, perpetually cash-strapped despite its numerous commercial successes, suddenly had the bank card to a corporate ATM. "People know that if we need to access the big machine, the big machine is there for us," explained Weinstein, who retained creative autonomy on films with budgets of $12 million or less.

A cut-throat competitor who keeps a baseball bat in his office, Weinstein cranked up that big machine to power a buying frenzy. "Releasing more films than all the other indie distributors combined enabled Miramax to shut the competition out of theaters," **Peter Biskind** writes in his delicious history of the Sundance-Miramax era, *Down And Dirty Pictures: Miramax, Sundance And The Rise Of Independent Film* (2004). "…The whole point was to eliminate the opportunity of the competitors to gain access to screens, so they couldn't do business." Weinstein became so grabby he'd sometimes buy a film before he actually got around to watching it. Attracted by the auteur draw of **Jim Jarmusch** and the star power of **Johnny Depp**, he bought the minimalist Western *Dead Man* (1995) sight unseen, but after its chilly reception at the **Cannes Film Festival**, hardly bothered to promote it.

Also in 1993, year of the Disney purchase, Miramax further flooded the market by starting a genre division, **Dimension**. Headed up by Bob Weinstein, Dimension focused on developing inexpensive horror and fantasy fare and aimed to attract the younger demographic that was mostly missing from the audiences of Miramax's high-brow material. Dimension spawned the hugely profitable *Scream*, *Scary Movie* and *Spy Kids* franchises, echoing the success of another independent-turned-subsidiary, **New Line**.

Bob Shaye started New Line in 1968, distributing **Jean-Luc Godard**'s film with the Rolling Stones, *Sympathy For The Devil*, that same year. He also handled **John Waters**' gross-out *Pink Flamingos* (1972), which was a hit on the midnight-movie circuit, and the 1936 anti-marijuana propaganda film *Reefer Madness*, which Shaye repackaged as a campy cult curio for the undergraduate market.

In the 1980s, New Line began carving a supremely lucrative genre niche: they rode high on the success of the *Nightmare On Elm Street* series, starring the pizza-faced serial killer Freddy Krueger, and later scored big with the goofy, low-budget superhero lark *Teenage Mutant Ninja Turtles* (1990). Flush with Freddy Krueger cash in 1990, New Line started its own art-house subdivision, **Fine Line**, which first made its mark with Gus Van Sant's *My Own Private Idaho* (1991) and later released **David O. Russell**'s *Spanking The Monkey* and **Steve James**'s documentary *Hoop Dreams* (both 1994). By this point, Ted Turner of **Turner Broadcasting System** had purchased New Line in a deal that left Shaye – who started the studio out of his Manhattan walk-up apartment with $1,500 in seed money – about $100 million richer.

Thus both New Line/Fine Line and Miramax/Dimension formed a dichotomy of pulp and art: one subsidized by the other, with corporate backup to boot. They could have their

Flight path: a scene from New Line's hit documentary *Hoop Dreams*

cake and turn a profit too, making B-movie earners alongside indie ventures with higher aesthetic ambitions but lower commercial prospects. Rarely could the two go hand in hand, but Miramax struck gold in 1994 with Quentin Tarantino's *Pulp Fiction* – a rare instance of an art film made for a mass audience (and one that several major studios passed up). Although it was produced and distributed by a subsidiary of the Disney corporation, *Pulp Fiction* was perceived as the first independent film to gross more than $100 million, which permanently raised the bar for indie filmmakers. Suddenly, the financial stakes hit the roof for American independent cinema.

Don't believe the hype: Sundance bidding wars

Blame the high altitude at Park City, sleep deprivation or the echo-chamber effects of a whirlwind film festival, but Sundance has a reputation for inciting buyers' panic in even the canniest executives. The most infamous example remains the bidding war that erupted over Lee David Zlotoff's *The Spitfire Grill* (1996), which **Castle Rock** won for an alleged $10 million – a staggering sum for an eventual flop.

Perhaps unsurprisingly, big bruiser **Harvey Weinstein** has been the last man standing in many of these skirmishes. **Miramax** acquired *Next Stop Wonderland* in 1998 for $6 million (six times the film's budget), *Happy, Texas* in 1999 for more than $10 million and the no-budget digital-video comedy *Tadpole* in 2002 for the rather grotesquely inflated sum of $5 million. Needless to say, none of these films made positive returns on their investments, though the precedent didn't stop **Fox Searchlight** from shelling out $10 million in 2006 for the beauty-pageant road movie *Little Miss Sunshine*.

The Sundance Festival also went Hollywood – and Hollywood went to Sundance in droves. For years a sleepy mountain retreat for outdoorsy cinephiles, the festival reached a more frenzied pitch of scene-setting and deal-making with every passing year. The event perhaps attained fully fledged circus proportions in 1994, the year of the incest comedy *Spanking The Monkey*, **Kevin Smith**'s no-budget slacker farce *Clerks* and **Rose Troche**'s lesbian romance *Go Fish*. *Clerks* proved to be a massively profitable acquisition for Miramax, but it was the black-and-white, amiably amateurish *Go Fish* that sparked a bidding war – the first of its kind at Sundance, and a harbinger of things to come. Troche's movie went to Samuel Goldwyn for $450,000, which was mere loose change compared to the millions proffered in subsequent skirmishes.

Reporting from the 1995 Sundance Festival for the *Los Angeles Times*, Kenneth Turan caught the winds of change: "For the Cassandras who worry about the commercialization and Hollywoodization of this shrine to American independent film, there was a lot to point to, starting with an ever-increasing number of visiting 'L.A.-liens' (as they are called locally), and a growing list of corporate sponsors – including Bank of America, AT&T and the Gap." Partly in response to Sundance's "Hollywoodization", the **Slamdance Festival** launched in 1995 to showcase features by first-time directors and ran concurrently with Sundance, although Robert Redford dismissed the upstart event as "parasitical".

Meanwhile, the Grand Jury Prize went to *The Brothers McMullen* (1995), written and directed by 26-year-old **Edward Burns**, who typified the encroaching business realpolitik of Sundance. Burns freely admitted during a festival Q&A

that he made his film "as a calling card, so people would say, 'Hey, this kid made this nice little film, let's see what he can do with a little money.'" *The Brothers McMullen* and many of its Sundance cousins, therefore, weren't just labours of love but a means to an end – a Hollywood screen test for their ambitious young directors.

Working Girls
dir Lizzie Borden, 1986, 93m

This wryly observant, often very funny *kammerspiel* is a long night's journey for an Ivy League-educated photographer, Molly (Louise Smith), who slogs through a punishing double shift at a Manhattan brothel until she arrives at a hard-won epiphany. With a forensic focus on workaday detail (purchase and placement of condoms, logging appointments, answering the phone), Borden refuses to eroticize what she depicts as essentially menial work.

In The Soup
dir Alexandre Rockwell, 1992, 93m, b/w

Flat-broke aspiring director Aldolfo Rollo (Steve Buscemi) puts his 500-page script *Unconditional Surrender* up for sale, attracting the attentions of would-be producer Joe (Seymour Cassel), a tactile, Mob-connected con man whose enthusiasm for making and spending money keeps pushing Aldolfo's ambitions to the sidelines. Rockwell's comedy of errors is charming and loose-limbed, and he fosters a brilliant rapport between Buscemi's put-upon straight man and Cassel's charming, fleet-footed swindler.

Reservoir Dogs
dir Quentin Tarantino, 1992, 99m

Novice filmmaker Tarantino rips off every B-heist picture, blaxploitation flick and John Woo movie he's ever seen and adoringly recombines them in his shocking and hilarious debut feature, in which a group of besuited, colour-coded crims suspect there's a rat in their ranks after a bank job goes wrong. In addition to redefining the 1970s hit "Stuck In The Middle With You" as mood music for psychotics, Tarantino earns terrific performances from Harvey Keitel, Steve Buscemi and Tim Roth (whose character spends much of the film lying in a pool of his own blood).

Hoop Dreams
dir Steve James, 1994, 171m

Shot over five years and nearly three hours long, James's riveting documentary follows two basketball-loving African-American teenagers, William Gates and Arthur Agee, who might have a shot at the NBA. Despite critical and popular adoration, this emotional powerhouse of a movie wasn't nominated for an Oscar – a baffling omission cited as a crucial factor in the Academy's eventual rehaul of their documentary voting procedures.

Dead Man
dir Jim Jarmusch, 1995, 121m, b/w

"Jeem, it's sheet," an audience member infamously called out after the Cannes premiere of Jarmusch's mystical, minimalist Western. At the time, critics, audiences and even the movie's distributor (Miramax) tended to agree, but time has been kind to one of the director's deepest, most ambitious films. Neil Young's mantra-like guitar score tracks every step of the Wild West odd couple William Blake (Johnny Depp), an accountant who falls foul of the law, and Nobody (Gary Farmer), his blunt-spoken Indian guide.

Adventures in Indiewood and the "New New Wave"

At the midpoint of the 1990s, Miramax and New Line were considered part of a quintet of "mini-majors" – or what *Clerks* director Kevin Smith once dubbed the "five families", a tongue-in-cheek reference to the Mafia clans in *The Godfather*. The other three studios were **Sony Pictures Classics** (distributor of Hal Hartley's *Amateur*, Terry Zwigoff's *Crumb* and a wealth of UK and foreign-language gems), **Samuel Goldwyn** (Charles Burnett's *To Sleep With Anger*, Rose Troche's *Go Fish* and Scott McGehee and David Siegel's *Suture*) and **October Films** (Victor

Indie godheads Steve Buscemi and Harvey Keitel in the iconic standoff from Quentin Tarantino's *Reservoir Dogs*

Nunez's *Ruby In Paradise*, John Dahl's *The Last Seduction* and Abel Ferrara's *The Addiction*).

The triumph of *Pulp Fiction* and other quasi-indie hits ensured that all of the major studios would, sooner or later, either acquire or establish a speciality films unit – their own private Miramax, making award-calibre movies on a tight budget.

As corporations co-opted independent cinema for prestige and profit, industry observers coined disparaging terms like "Indiewood" and "dependies" for this new business model.

Sony had been ahead of the curve, forming Sony Pictures Classics in 1992, and Twentieth Century Fox set up **Fox Searchlight** in 1994, right on *Pulp Fiction*'s heels. In 1996, **Time Warner** acquired Turner Broadcasting System, making Fine Line a sub-subsidiary of the biggest media company in the world (and one that grew even bigger after the merger with America Online in 2000). After a flurry of corporate mergers and sell-offs in the late 1990s, October and another small company, **Gramercy**, joined together to become USA Films, which by 2002 had shape-shifted once again into **Focus Features**, the speciality arm of Universal. **Paramount Classics** launched in 1998, and the latecomer of the bunch, **Warner Independent Pictures**, released its first film in 2004.

It was Miramax, however, that remained the sole superstar among demi-studios. With his foul mouth, outsized personality and outrageous temper, Harvey Weinstein had all the bearings of an old-school studio mogul, and his stable of well-known talent (Quentin Tarantino, **Gwyneth Paltrow** and the *Good Will Hunting* team of **Matt Damon** and **Ben Affleck**) also harkened back to Hollywood's golden-age studio system. *Entertainment Weekly* later hailed the studio for "the reinvention of the idea of a movie company as an entity whose very name meant something to moviegoers." For much of the 1990s, Miramax could do no wrong, sweeping up armfuls of cash, Oscars and blanket media coverage for *The English Patient, Sling Blade, Swingers* (all 1996), *Good Will Hunting* (1997), *Shakespeare In Love* and *The Cider House Rules* (both 1999).

Studio ownership of a self-styled maverick film company did not come without its sticking points, of course. **Larry Clark**'s *Kids* (1995), about New York teenagers wandering through a hazy summer day's worth of sex, drugs and violence, contravened Disney's rule against releasing films rated NC-17. The Weinsteins were forced to set up a one-off company, called

Shining Excalibur, to release the movie. (In a less publicized incident, Miramax gave up the raunchy comedy-concert film *You So Crazy* to Samuel Goldwyn in 1994 for much the same reason.)

In 1998, October Films similarly ran afoul of its new owner, Universal, with *Happiness* (1998). **Todd Solondz**'s suburban dystopia featured a semi-sympathetic depiction of a child molester, much to the horror of Universal's CEO Ron Meyer. Two of the film's producers, **Ted Hope** and **James Schamus** of Good Machine, bought *Happiness* back and distributed it themselves, and the contretemps translated into free publicity for the hot-potato movie. "At the end of the day," Schamus later concluded, "we had a film that benefitted in the marketplace by being both suppressed and promoted by one and the same system." October co-founder **Bingham Ray**, however, was far less sanguine about the *Happiness* imbroglio. "This is where we bottomed out," Ray said in Peter Biskind's *Down And Dirty Pictures*, "where the ideal was corrupted, the dream of being able to work within the studio system as some maverick, autonomous independent – it was just total horseshit."

And yet maverick, autonomous independents *did* work within the studio system in the 1990s, and often, they flourished. In many ways, **Spike Lee** led the way, making divisive, deeply personal films on modest budgets for big companies. For about $6.5 million, he made the racially charged *Do The Right Thing* (1989) for Universal, and the studio's promotional muscle pumped the movie into the controversial must-see of the summer. Lee doubled his Universal budget for the less accomplished *Jungle Fever* (1991), which made the cover of *Newsweek* before it was released.

In *That's My Story And I'm Sticking To It* (2005), an authorized biography of Lee by Kaleem Aftab,

Dylan Baker as a suburban paedophile in *Happiness*

producer's rep **John Pierson** praises Lee's early arrangement with Universal as "a model for how an independent-minded person could work with studio money." (Pierson famously wrote a $10,000 check made out to Lee for completion of his first feature, *She's Gotta Have It*.) However, Lee chafed at the restrictions set by Warner Bros for the making of *Malcolm X* (1992). The studio capped the budget at $20 million for Lee's epic biopic of the black nationalist leader, so the writer-director forfeited much of his $3 million fee and asked African-American celebrities including

Bill Cosby, Janet Jackson, Michael Jordan and **Oprah Winfrey** to kick in post-production costs after he overran his budget.

Despite his anti-blockbuster sensibilities, **Wes Anderson** also became the beneficiary of studio largesse. Made when Anderson was in his early twenties, the 16mm short *Bottle Rocket* caught the attention of powerful producer-director **James L. Brooks**, who helped pave the way for its expansion into a feature for Columbia Pictures in 1996, with novice actors **Luke** and **Owen Wilson** remaining in the lead roles. *Bottle Rocket* made

The disposition of excess desire: pitching *Happiness*

To the layman's eye, **Todd Solondz**'s controversial film *Happiness* is a black comedy about the misfits, malcontents and banal monsters of the director's native New Jersey. However, in an essay written for *The Nation* in 1999, producer **James Schamus** suggests that the film is actually a primer on the economics of material cravings.

According to Schamus the US spends around a third of its gross national product on advertising in order to maintain the desire to buy all the rubbish produced by the industrial world. The need to stimulate all that desire means that traditional values can no longer contain it. "The average American has too much desire to know what to do with, and it is in the disposition of this excess desire, in the inability of the social structure to absorb it properly, that trouble starts in suburbia. And that's what *Happiness* is about."

feeble returns at the box office, but then-Disney honcho **Joe Roth** was such a fan of the movie that he ensured Anderson's follow-up, the wistful, loopy love triangle *Rushmore* (1998), was born under the sign of Mickey Mouse.

Disney also backed Anderson's *The Royal Tenenbaums* (2001), starring **Gene Hackman** and **Anjelica Huston** as the divorced parents of a dysfunctional family (the dream cast also includes **Ben Stiller**, Gwyneth Paltrow, **Bill Murray** and the Wilson brothers), and *The Life Aquatic With Steve Zissou* (2004), a Cousteau-style sea adventure with Murray, Huston, Owen Wilson and **Cate Blanchett**. Despite his use of all-star personnel and exquisite production design, Anderson managed to keep his budgets for these films beneath $25 million, and he remains a heartening rarity:

a young, idiosyncratic auteur endorsed by the studio system. "I have the final cut of the movie and I control the casting," Anderson told this writer in 2001. "It's the same way it would be if I was raising the money myself. And with this cast of people [in *The Royal Tenenbaums*], what are they going to say? We got this cast for nothing."

As Anderson's fortuitous experiences with James L. Brooks and Joe Roth make clear, sometimes all a young, hungry filmmaker needs are fans in high places. **Lorenzo di Bonaventura**, an executive at Warner Bros, pressed the case for the Wachowski brothers' philosophical action smash *The Matrix* (1999) and David O. Russell's *Three Kings* (1999), a rollicking action-comedy that condemned the US government's conduct in the first Gulf War – a strong political statement funded by a major studio well-known for playing it safe.

New Line president **Mike De Luca** acted as patron to wunderkind director **Paul Thomas Anderson**, backing the porn chronicle *Boogie Nights* (1997), the **Robert Altman**-style ensemble melodrama *Magnolia* (1999) and the marvellous goof *Punch-Drunk Love* (2002). New Line spent a whopping $42 million on the three-hour-plus *Magnolia* (although one-quarter of the sum went to co-star **Tom Cruise**, who alone among the superlative cast received an Oscar nomination). "I would do *Berlin Alexanderplatz* with Paul," De Luca once said, referring to Rainer Werner Fassbinder's 900-minute opus. "He's Orson Welles. I'm the blank check guy."

At Fox, entertainment chief **Bill Mechanic** advocated **David Fincher**'s anarchic *Fight Club* (1999), about a secret society of brawlers who mutate into a fascist guerrilla group. Ordinarily a hands-off businessman, **Rupert Murdoch** fumed that Fincher's violent, arguably nihilist vision had been bankrolled at his studio, and in an infamous review for the *Evening Standard*, the late critic Alexander Walker wrote, "The movie is not only anti-capitalist but anti-society and, indeed, anti-God." (Fincher was pleased, as he later reported: "I read that and I was like, 'I'd go see that movie in a *heartbeat!*'") Mechanic lost his job following *Fight Club*'s mediocre box-office performance, but the film later became a cult classic via its handsome, jam-packed two-disc DVD release.

Other improbably original efforts simply slipped through the radar. Sharon Waxman's instructive book *Rebels On The Backlot* (2005) which profiles six of the studio-backed "mavericks", makes the case that *Being John Malkovich* (1999), directed by **Spike Jonze** and written by **Charlie Kaufman**, entered the world with all its wondrous strangeness intact largely because it escaped close attention amid a battery of studio mergers and staff reshuffles. Once *Being John Malkovich* had become an Oscar-nominated cult classic in the making, perhaps it was a no-brainer for Sony to take on Jonze and Kaufman's equally bizarre and brilliant next effort, *Adaptation* (2002). USA Films, the short-lived entity behind *Being John Malkovich*, also produced and distributed *Traffic* (2000), the multi-threaded "War on Drugs" drama for which indie axiom **Steven Soderbergh** won an Oscar for best directing.

At the close of 1999, many an article hailed the arrival of a new vanguard of audacious young filmmakers, all of them backed by major studios: Fincher, Jonze, Russell, Wes Anderson, Paul Thomas Anderson and **Alexander Payne**, who made his acrid high-school farce *Election* (1999) for MTV Films in partnership with Paramount. These directors comprised the "New New Wave", the "Class of 99" or, as New Line's De Luca dubbed them, "all the young dudes" – although a few ladies figured into the mix, including first-timers **Kimberly Peirce** (*Boys Don't Cry*) and daughter of the film aristocracy **Sofia Coppola** (*The Virgin Suicides*, which premiered at Cannes that year).

Intriguingly, none of these filmmakers were working with Miramax. Once the first port of call for hot young movie talent, Miramax now evinced more conservative tastes, with the occasional exception such as **Todd Field**'s *In The Bedroom* (2001), a superb exploration of bereavement and revenge. The studio passed up *Boogie Nights*, and in the year of the New New Wave, they dropped Kevin Smith's irreverent religious satire *Dogma* (1999), under pressure from the Catholic League and other religious groups. During the 2000-2001 Oscar campaign, the studio previously identified with the full-frontal gender-bending of 1992's *The Crying Game* and the violent virtuosity of *Pulp Fiction* was now putting all its weight behind *Chocolat*, a bland homily to tolerance, as its Best Picture hopeful.

Miramax's cautiousness translated into opportunity for other studios. Sony Pictures Classics prospered with films that one could easily imagine finding a home with Miramax, including **Neil LaBute**'s Darwinian three-hander *In The Company Of Men* (1997), **Don Roos**' sarcastic domestic comedy *The Opposite Of Sex* (1998) and **Ed Harris**'s underrated portrait of the artist, *Pollock* (2000). Among the other studio boutiques, Paramount Classics' early slate was far more checkered, although they did champion the affecting brother-sister drama *You Can Count On Me* (2000), while Fox Searchlight scored with *Boys Don't Cry*.

Lions Gate, which formed out of the Canadian company **Cinepix**, eagerly snatched up the discarded *Dogma* and made hay out of the controversy. Taking a page from Miramax's handbook, Lions Gate placed a premium on daring, even sensational work, distributing **Henry Bean**'s *The Believer* (2001), based on the true story of a Jewish neo-Nazi youth, and **Steven Shainberg**'s *Secretary* (2002), about the sado-masochistic relationship between a white-collar boss and his assistant.

Perhaps the gold standard among speciality divisions has been set by Universal's Focus Features. Founded in 2002 and headed up by James Schamus, in a few short years Focus gave audiences Todd Haynes's *Far From Heaven* (2002), **Michel Gondry**'s *Eternal Sunshine Of The Spotless Mind* (2004) (from a script by Charlie Kaufman), the impassioned polemical thriller *The Constant Gardener* (2005) by Brazilian director **Fernando Meirelles**, Jim Jarmusch's first foray into studio financing, *Broken Flowers* (2005), and **Ang Lee**'s wrenching cowboy love story, *Brokeback Mountain* (2005).

Wild Wild Wes: Anderson's cracked crooks in *Bottle Rocket*

Ruby In Paradise
dir Victor Nunez, 1993, 114m

Ruby (Ashley Judd) escapes small-town life in Tennessee and runs away to Florida, where she draws a few quiet but revelatory conclusions about herself and her world through adventures in romance and retail. Judd is luminous in the title role of this acutely observed, character-driven coming-of-age tale.

Bottle Rocket
dir Wes Anderson, 1996, 92m

Dignan (Owen Wilson) is an overgrown boy obsessed with planning the perfect heist, and his similarly arrested pals Anthony (Luke Wilson) and the strikingly named Bob Mapplethorpe (Robert Musgrave) are helplessly loyal to their cracked but enthusiastic buddy's dreams. An embellishment on a 16mm short made in 1992, Anderson's first feature (co-written with star Owen Wilson) is a rigorously understated caper that's also a droll, surprisingly melancholic comedy about the vicissitudes of friendship.

In The Company Of Men
dir Neil LaBute, 1997, 97m

As symbolic payback to all the women who've ever let them down, a white-collar shark (Aaron Eckhart) and his sidekick (Matt Malloy) decide to woo and then betray a sweet, gullible deaf woman (Stacy Edwards). There's a certain astringency to this nasty, brutish world that LaBute captures in Stanley Kubrick-style master shots, but it's unconvincing as a parable on the battle of the sexes.

Fight Club
dir David Fincher, 1999, 139m

Made in a superlative year for studio pictures, Fincher's audacious adaptation of Chuck Palahniuk's novel divided most critics into love-it or hate-it camps. A dangerously alienated insomniac (Edward Norton) encounters the anarchic ironist Tyler Durden (Brad Pitt), who preaches an anti-consumerist gospel of self-destruction and world annihilation. Norton's somnolent voiceover is a perfectly judged counterpoint to the symphony of digitally enhanced chaos that Fincher conducts onscreen; the movie is as propulsive, even concussive, as its title suggests.

Pollock
dir Ed Harris, 2000, 122m

Director-star Ed Harris spent a decade shepherding a Jackson Pollock project through the production mill, before deciding to direct it himself and eventually contributing a portion of the budget. His canvas of the mercurial, alcoholic Abstract Expressionist is remarkably attuned and respectful to the agony, ecstasy and mundanity of Pollock's epoch-defining labours and the rhythms of his day-to-day life with steadfast partner Lee Krasner (Marcia Gay Harden, who deservedly won an Oscar). This is an exceedingly rare example of the biopic done right, and one of the best movies about art and artistry in recent memory.

You Can Count On Me
dir Kenneth Lonergan, 2000, 111m

After losing their parents at a young age, siblings Sammy (Laura Linney) and Terry (Mark Ruffalo) sped off in opposite directions. Now she's a frazzled, small-town single mother who's ambivalent towards her beau and sleeping with her boss, and he's a drifter and occasional prison inmate who wanders back to Sammy's for some room and board. Though it's visually drab and awkwardly edited, the film-directing debut of playwright Lonergan is a moving study of the ties that bind, with faultless dialogue and performances.

The Believer
dir Henry Bean, 2001, 98m

Based on the true story of a neo-Nazi who committed suicide in 1965 after a *New York Times* article revealed him to be Jewish, this incendiary study of an anti-Semitic Jew won the top prize at Sundance in 2001. Languishing for a year and a half without a distributor, the film eventually premiered on the Showtime cable network before its small theatrical release. Ryan Gosling is ferociously convincing as Danny, the yeshiva student turned neo-Nazi, and writer-director Bean digs deep into this bright, passionate, terrifying young man's tangled psyche. *The Believer* is genuinely startling and thought-provoking, not least for proposing bigotry as an internalized intellectual pursuit.

In The Bedroom
Todd Field, 2001, 130m

Based on the short story "Killings" by the late Andre Dubus (to whom the film is dedicated), Field's astonishingly assured debut feature, set in coastal Maine, observes a husband and wife (Sissy Spacek and Tom Wilkinson, both extraordinary) mourning the violent death of their only child (Nick Stahl). With exquisite patience, grace and attention to detail, Field dissects the couple's implacable sorrow and anger, until the rage they've bottled up behind closed doors and projected upon each other is finally turned outwards.

Secretary
dir Steven Shainberg, 2002, 104m

Though it considerably softens and mollifies the Mary Gaitskill short story on which it's based, this S&M romance is a superb vehicle for James Spader and Maggie Gyllenhaal (in her breakthrough performance). He is an iron-fisted boss who brandishes a marker pen like a dagger, and she is the shy, troubled young woman who finds personal liberation in becoming her employer's faithful slave.

The age of the "indie blockbuster"

Just a few years into the new century, Miramax Films found itself at the centre of a *succès de scandale* worthy of a Weinstein, when Disney chief **Michael Eisner** refused to release Michael Moore's *Fahrenheit 9/11* (2004). (Reportedly, Eisner's refusal stemmed in part from concerns that the Bush-bashing film could jeopardize tax breaks that the Disney corporation enjoys in Florida, the state governed by President Bush's brother, Jeb.) The Weinstein brothers then formed an ad-hoc group with Lions Gate (always eager to adopt Miramax/Disney orphans) and **IFC Films** to release the movie, while Moore brayed to any journalist who would listen about corporate censorship. By the time the dust had

Hate accompli: outstanding achievements in trash-talk

"Why don't you defend her so I can beat the shit out of you?"

Harvey Weinstein to Julie Taymor's husband after a test screening of her film, *Frida*

"He is a pushcart peddlar who is more than happy to put his thumb on the scale when the old woman is buying meat."

Saul Zaentz, producer of *The English Patient*, on Harvey Weinstein

"They treat you like used Kleenex."

David O. Russell on the Weinstein brothers

"If he comes near me, I'll sock him right in the fuck-ing mouth."

George Clooney on his *Three Kings* director David O. Russell

"Well, she played an actress who was so bad that the director committed suicide ... So yeah, I thought she was a perfect choice. No. C'mon. She can't act her way out of a paper bag."

Abel Ferrara on his *Dangerous Game* leading lady, Madonna

"I would openly celebrate Quentin Tarantino's death."

Natural Born Killers producer Don Murphy; Tarantino later punched Murphy in a restaurant, in view of Harvey Weinstein

"Slime, just barely passing for humans."

Steven Soderbergh on producers Don Simpson and Jerry Bruckheimer

"You wanna play me?": Tina Majorino and Jon Heder in *Napoleon Dynamite*

that the director had known for a year before the film's opening that distribution through Disney channels was not an option. Furthermore, the controversy symbolized Miramax's increasingly fraught relations with its corporate parent. Disney did not renew the Weinsteins' contract when it expired in September 2005, and an era came to a wistful close as Bob and Harvey parted ways with the organization that still bears their parents' name; they moved on to found the **Weinstein Company** later that same year.

Meanwhile, over at the hectic corporate marketplace known as Sundance, synergy was the watchword. At the 2004 festival, Fox Searchlight acquired the Sundance hits *Garden State* and *Napoleon Dynamite*. For the latter, the studio joined forces with MTV in an increasingly common stroke of cross-medium marketing – and one that helped *Napoleon*, which was shot for just $400,000, to earn a $44 million domestic box-office take and a loyal cult following. Fox wasn't the only company to see the benefits of corporate cooperation: Warner Independent (who lost out in the bidding war for *Napoleon Dynamite*) went into partnership with **National Geographic** to present the nature documentary *March Of The Penguins* (2005); Lions Gate teamed up with the **Discovery Channel** for **Werner Herzog**'s *Grizzly Man*

settled, *Fahrenheit 9/11* had won the 2004 Palme d'Or (from a jury headed by Quentin Tarantino), and earned $120 million at the box office.

Moore's public blow-up with Disney was something of a contrived publicity stunt, given

(2005); and Paramount Classics secured blanket promotion on partner channels MTV and BET for **Craig Brewer**'s *Hustle & Flow* (2005), the rags-to-riches tale of a Memphis pimp who dreams of hip-hop stardom.

Writing in *Slate* magazine, critic Christopher Kelly cited *Hustle & Flow* as a case study in a new phenomenon known as the "indie blockbuster": an independently financed film (in this case, by established director **John Singleton** and his partner **Stephanie Allain**) with minor or unknown actors that arrives essentially pre-sold to its youthful demographic.

Terrence Howard earned a Best Actor nomination for his lead role in *Hustle & Flow* in 2005, the year of the "indie Oscars", which was so named because most of the top contenders were Indiewood productions, including four of the five Best Picture hopefuls: *Brokeback Mountain* (Focus Features), *Capote* (Sony Pictures Classics), *Good Night, And Good Luck* (Warner Independent Pictures) and the eventual winner, *Crash* (Lions Gate). All had budgets under $10 million, except for *Brokeback Mountain* at a mere $14 million, and all approached literary, historical or politically charged subjects with well-known stars working for a fraction of their usual rates. Thus the boutique studios had landed on a fruitful division of labour: prestigious Oscar bait on the one hand, and youth-oriented sleeper hits on the other, both procured inexpensively.

These developments don't bode well, however, for films lacking the benefit of a high concept, a big-name star, a corporate bankroll or an all-media marketing plan. This dilemma was further highlighted in early 2006, after the Weinstein Company bought a seventy percent stake in the parent company of **Wellspring Media** (formerly Winstar), which had lately released **Jonathan Caouette**'s *Tarnation* (2003), **Vincent Gallo**'s *The Brown Bunny* (2003) and Todd Solondz's *Palindromes* (2004), as well as a host of fine foreign-language films. The ensuing corporate realignment strategy effectively sealed the small company's doom, and seemed to put one more nail in the coffin of "true" indie films and studios.

Writing in 2005, *LA Weekly* film editor Scott Foundas alerted readers to the dire straits of "independent American films – by which I mean the real thing and not the pseudo-independents produced by the studio-owned subsidiary divisions." Foundas cited the pitiable grosses of several fine, genuinely independent efforts (including **Debra Granik**'s *Down To The Bone*, 2005, **Lodge Kerrigan**'s *Keane*, 2004, and **Michael Almereyda**'s *Happy Here And Now*, 2002). "If a movie opens in a cinema and no one is around to hear it," Foundas asked, "does it make a sound?"

"We're now in a situation where independent films have the pressure to be Oscar-worthy," director **Jim McKay** told a reporter at the 2004 Sundance Film Festival. McKay, who has never worked with a major studio or with established stars in familiar genres, continued, "What I'd always learned from independent film was the Oscars have nothing to do with us … I've got to feel like independent film as we know it from its original definition is dead."

 Fahrenheit 9/11
dir Michael Moore, 2004, 122m

Relying less on personality-driven schtick than in the past, Moore reviews the Bush II administration to date, from Dubya's highly contested ascent to power in the 2000 election, to his less-than-presidential initial reaction to the September 11 attacks, to America's deadly rodeos in Afghanistan and Iraq. Moore's Palme d'Or winner attempted nothing less than the unseating of the US commander-in-chief, and though it wasn't to be, the documentary still stands as an exemplary piece of political propaganda, and Moore's most mature work to date.

Fact-check this! Michael Moore's research flubs

Michael Moore's first documentary, *Roger & Me* (1989), came under fire when a few critics pointed out that he'd conveniently rearranged the chronology of events to bolster the film's polemic against the corporate downsizing of his hometown of Flint, Michigan. With the release thirteen years later of *Bowling For Columbine* (2002), some observers concluded that the agitprop maestro hadn't learned from his past mistakes. Moore apparently staged the scene in which he waltzes into a bank and gets a free gun for opening an account, and viewers also deduced that he'd altered a photo caption over a Bush-Quayle campaign commercial, took a **Charlton Heston** speech out of context and wrongly implied that Lockheed Martin manufac-

tures weapons in Littleton, Colorado, site of the 1999 Columbine High School massacre. (In fact, they make weather and communications satellites there.)

Infuriated by the attacks on his credibility, Moore announced that he was hiring fact-checkers from *The New Yorker*, considered the gold standard for accuracy, to vet *Fahrenheit 9/11* (2004), but the critics pounced again. They poked holes in Moore's conspiracy theories about the **Bush** family's links to the **Bin Ladens** and chastised the film for fabricating a newspaper headline. What's especially curious about Moore's fact-fudging is that the distortions in question are so trivial – fix or remove any of them and little or no damage is done to his case.

Napoleon Dynamite
dir Jared Hess, 2004, 86m

The debut feature by the 24-year-old Hess became the subject of a Sundance bidding war and the quotable sleeper hit of 2004. The plot is minimal – frizzy-haired high-school nerd Napoleon (Jon Heder) seeks a date to the prom, deals with his creepy Uncle Rico (Jon Gries) and helps his pal Pedro (Efren Ramirez) run for class president – but the loopy charm of the film lies in its comic acumen and non sequitur gags, with Hess drawing on the deadpan influences of Jim Jarmusch and Wes Anderson.

Keane
dir Lodge Kerrigan, 2004, 90m

The ghost of a missing child haunts Kerrigan's extraordinary third completed feature, shot on location in the concrete outskirts and transport inter-zones of New York City. The

attentive camera sticks as close as possible to its mentally disturbed protagonist, William Keane (Damian Lewis), who forges a fraught bond with a little girl (Abigail Breslin) and her financially strapped mother while he searches desperately for his own daughter.

Hustle & Flow
dir Craig Brewer, 2005, 116m

It's hard out there for Memphis pimp DJ (Terrence Howard), who slouches towards a midlife crisis and dreams of rap stardom while trying to keep all his "bitches" in line. Writer-director Brewer's *Rocky*-style crowd-pleaser sold for a spectacular $9 million at Sundance 2005. The film boasts a convincingly sultry, grimy ambience and a fine performance from Howard, but it fails to transcend its rags-to-riches clichés, and its female characters are little more than shrill caricatures.

The Information: the wider picture

Hardy festivalgoers brave the cold outside the
Egyptian Theater at Sundance 2006

The Information:
the wider picture

Just as American independent film can be defined in many ways, the sources and resources related to the movement take many forms on page, screen and elsewhere. Happy hunting and surfing!

Audiovisual

Amerindies on TV

Independent Film Channel
www.ifctv.com

Launched in the autumn of 1994, IFC was the first television network to screen indie movies all day, every day, and they started producing and distributing their own theatrical releases a few years later. On the IFC's cluttered website, you can access IFC Uncut on Demand, a broadband video channel featuring original documentary content and clips from featured movies, and the IFC Media Lab, where you can upload your own films and vote on your favourites.

Sundance Channel
www.sundancechannel.com

The Sundance Institute's television network (which also has a home-entertainment wing) mixes Amerindie fare with original documentaries, world cinema (including the "Asia Extreme" series of Far East shockers), themed programming ("Hangover Theater" screens undemanding chestnuts to enjoy from your couch at weekends) and television hits from around the globe.

HDNet
www.hd.net

High-definition television (HDTV) is a particular boon to picky viewers because movies can be presented in their original widescreen formats, without letterboxing. The first national network to broadcast all content in high-definition, HDNet broadcasts original series as well as licensed programming and sports events. Its sister channel, HDNet Movies, screens feature films without commercials, as well as original productions that premiere simultaneously in theatres, on DVD and on HDNet – the first of these "day-and-date" productions was Steven Soderbergh's *Bubble* in 2005.

Soundtracks

Easy Rider
Hip-O

This album of late-1960s rock is generally considered to be the first mainstream film soundtrack composed entirely of pop music. As well as Steppenwolf's classic heavy-metal biker anthem "Born To Be Wild", it includes tracks by The Byrds, Smith and Jimi Hendrix. The 2004 deluxe edition includes a second disc of eighteen classic songs from the 1960s not in the movie, but "inspired" by it.

Pimps, Players & Private Eyes
Sire/London/Rhino

Blaxploitation soundtracks often outshone the movies they accompanied, and this ten-track compilation of the genre's greatest hits is an excellent beginners' manual. It includes essentials such as Curtis Mayfield's "Pusherman" (from *Superfly*) and Isaac Hayes's unforgettable "Theme From Shaft", as well as the themes from *Foxy Brown* and *Across 110th Street*. For an alternate starting point, try *Baadasssss Cinema* (TVT), which includes tracks by soul legends James Brown, War, Roy Ayers and Earth Wind & Fire.

Double Feature: Soundtracks from the Quentin Tarantino Films Reservoir Dogs & Pulp Fiction
MCA

Nobody makes a mix tape like Quentin Tarantino, and here the infectious mix of funk, R&B and 1970s rock (from "Stuck In The Middle With You" to "Son Of A Preacher Man") that propelled his first two features shares air time with choice tasters of the writer-director's rat-a-tat-tat dialogue (including Mr. Brown's "Like A Virgin" exegesis in *Reservoir Dogs* and the catchphrase-spawning "Royale with Cheese" conversation from *Pulp Fiction*).

O Brother, Where Art Thou?
Lost Highway

The Coen brothers' Depression-era fugitive comedy *O Brother, Where Art Thou?* starring George Clooney and loosely based on Homer's *The Odyssey*, facilitated one of the biggest soundtrack hits of recent years. This Grammy

MUSIC FROM THE MOTION PICTURE
O BROTHER, WHERE ART THOU?

award-winning album features contemporary musicians performing traditional arrangements of classic folk, country, bluegrass and gospel records. The album's great success also inspired the live album *Down From The Mountain* and the women's bluegrass companion piece *O Sister!*

Dazed And Confused
Giant/WEA

For his first studio picture, 1993's *Dazed And Confused*, Richard Linklater could afford the rights to a classic roster of longhair 1970s hits by the likes of Alice Cooper, Lynyrd Skynyrd and Foghat (not to mention colour-coded bastions of rock such as Deep Purple, Black Sabbath and Black Oak Arkansas). The popularity of this nostalgic blast of catchy arena rock led to a second volume, *Even More Dazed And Confused*, being released in 1994.

The Thin Blue Line
Nonesuch

Errol Morris has enlisted composer Philip Glass to provide the music for most of his documentaries, and on this album the anxiety and foreboding of Glass's undulating compositions is the perfect complement to Morris's jaw-dropping murder mystery. Unlike most soundtracks, this one doesn't isolate the score from the movie's dialogue and sound effects.

Recordings Of Music For Film
Warp

Vincent Gallo's matter-of-factly titled album collects the music he composed for his feature debut, *Buffalo '66*, and three movies by other directors. Achieving a quiet, keening mood familiar from his earlier solo recording, *When*, the tracks are all bolstered by evocative titles ("Her Smell Theme", "A Brown Lung Hollering", "Goodbye Sadness, Hello Death").

Crumb
Rykodisc

Ghost World
Shanachie

Robert Crumb's beloved old 78 rpm recordings of 1920s and 30s blues, jazz and string-band music are the stuff of the soundtrack to Terry Zwigoff's *Crumb* as well as his next film, *Ghost World*, which also includes the hip-shaking Bollywood treasure "Jaan Pehechaan Ho" by Mohammed Rafi and an excerpt from David Kitay's orchestral score.

Festivals and events

Sundance Film Festival
www.sundance.org

Born in 1978 as the sleepy, modest Utah/U.S. Film Festival, Sundance took the name of Robert Redford's Sundance Film Institute in 1991 and soon grew into the behemoth of Indiewood schmoozing, dealmaking, partygoing and, oh yes, moviegoing that it is today. Sundance is an industry zoo, but it still makes room for the average moviegoer – same-day rush tickets are available throughout the festival for those brave and hardy souls willing to endure the long lines in the January chill.

Slamdance Film Festival
www.slamdance.com

Now in its second decade, Slamdance began as a self-styled David to Sundance's Goliath, and still runs concurrently with the bigger, older festival as a more independent alternative. Unlike Sundance, Slamdance limits its main competition to works by first-time directors, and only screens films that don't already have distribution deals lined up. Slamdance also sponsors screenplay and teleplay competitions and the "$99 Special" series of short films (directors get $99 and 99 days to make a movie). You can also submit your own film to the website's online short film competion, Anarchy, or watch and vote on other people's entries.

New York Underground Film Festival
www.nyuff.com

Housed each March in that famous temple of under-ground film, downtown's Anthology Film Archives, the NYUFF began with a bang in 1994 with its controversial opening-night selection, the disturbing paedophile docu-mentary *Chicken Hawk: Men Who Love Boys*. Since then, the festival has continued to cook up a heady mix of experimental films, psycho-tronic curiosities and pen-etrating non-fiction works.

Independent Feature Project
www.ifp.org

The IFP runs year-round screenings, workshops and seminars in its four chapter locations (New York City, Chicago, Minnesota and Seattle) and also organizes the annual IFP Market in New York, a week-long networking opportunity for screenwriters, producers and directors with works in progress.

Tribeca Film Festival
www.tribecafilmfestival.org

Founded in 2002 to rejuvenate lower Manhattan and showcase its film culture after the shock of the September 11 attacks, the Tribeca Film Festival uses blockbusters as the flashy gift-wrapping for a less marketable art-house film bonanza. It typically boasts an impressive documentary line-up and a speciality line in shorts and features by promising New York filmmakers.

South By Southwest Film Conference & Festival
www.sxsw.com/film

Cooler and more laid-back than some of its festival fellows, this event in Austin, Texas is an offshoot of the long-running SxSW Music Conference. It blends informational panels with premiere screenings, concerts and excellent parties. Alongside the usual awards for shorts, features and audience favourites, the festival also reserves a prize for promising Texas high school students.

Books

General

American independent cinema has spawned dozens of general critical overviews and essay collections. Although there are too many to gloss here, a solid shortlist of recommendations would include *The New American Cinema* edited by Jon Lewis (Duke University Press, 1998), *American Independent Cinema* by Geoff King (I.B. Tauris, 2005) and *Contemporary American Independent Film: From The Margins To The Mainstream* edited by Chris Holmlund and Justin Wyatt (Routledge, 2005).

BFI Publishing
www.bfi.org.uk/booksvideo/books/

The British Film Institute's publishing division issues the fantastic BFI "Film Classics" and "Modern Classics" series of monographs, which includes *Shadows* by Ray Carney, *Dead Man* by Jonathan Rosenbaum, *Do The Right Thing* by Ed Guerrero and *Pulp Fiction* by Dana Polan. Jason Wood's *100 American Independent Films* (2004), a pocket-sized compendium of erudite essays on Amerindie landmarks, is a joy to read, and *American Independent Cinema: A Sight & Sound Reader* edited by Jim Hillier (2001) collects relevant articles and interviews from the BFI's esteemed monthly magazine.

Cinema Of Outsiders: The Rise Of American Independent Film
Emanuel Levy (New York University Press, 2001)

A professor of film and sociology and a critic for *Variety*, Emanuel Levy sets out to define indie films against Hollywood products, drawing on analysis of hundreds of films made between 1977 and 1999. Cleanly written and smartly arranged, this lengthy book (565 pages in paperback) has both breadth and depth in impressive measures, and devotes significant space to discussion of individual films and directors as well as larger trends.

Easy Riders, Raging Bulls: How The Sex 'N' Drugs 'N' Rock 'N' Roll Generation Saved Hollywood
Peter Biskind (Simon & Schuster, 1998)

Down And Dirty Pictures: Miramax, Sundance, And The Rise Of Independent Film
Peter Biskind (Simon & Schuster, 2004)

Perfectly described by one reviewer as "highbrow gossip", Peter Biskind's dishy, delectable histories of the American independent scene's movers and shakers – or rather its egomaniacs, Machiavellians, coke fiends and tantrum-throwers – deserve the hoariest cliché in the book reviewer's word bank: they cannot be put down. A few quibbles: both books (but especially *Down And Dirty*) are riddled with spelling and grammatical errors, and Biskind gives short shrift to some true-blue independents.

Midnight Movies
J. Hoberman and Jonathan Rosenbaum (Harper & Row, 1983)

Still the best book on the outré, often shocking cult films that won large urban followings in late-night theatres, Hoberman and Rosenbaum's *Midnight Movies* weaves comprehensive narratives about the production history and reception of midnight hits such as *Night Of The Living Dead*, *Pink Flamingos* and *Eraserhead*, and provides colourful scene descriptions and analysis. Most importantly, the writers provide a cultural, social and political context for films too often dismissed as degenerate trash at the time of their release. (The authors also appear in Stuart Samuels' 2005 documentary *Midnight Movies: From The Margins To The Mainstream*.)

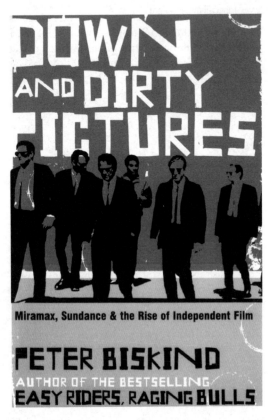

DOWN AND DIRTY PICTURES

Miramax, Sundance & the Rise of Independent Film

PETER BISKIND

AUTHOR OF THE BESTSELLING EASY RIDERS, RAGING BULLS

The Other Hollywood: The Uncensored Oral History Of The Porn Film Industry
Legs McNeil & Jennifer Osborne (HarperCollins, 2005)

This addictive read is a fittingly voyeuristic peek into an industry rife with pathology. Through wildly entertaining interviews with hundreds of porn personnel, their associates and a nemesis or two, it traces the history of porn flicks from the more innocent days of the "nudie-cutie" to the modern silicon-enhanced video age. Teeming with homicide, derangement, sleazy machinations and the ravages of drugs and AIDS, this book also gives a particularly gripping run-down of the courtroom censorship battles and Mafia intrigues linked to *Deep Throat*, the first mainstream hardcore porn film.

Rebels On The Backlot: Six Maverick Directors And How They Conquered The Hollywood Studio System
Sharon Waxman (HarperEntertainment, 2005)

Focusing on business and personality rather than movies and moviemaking, *New York Times* Sharon Waxman profiles six directors who have managed to hold onto their daring and originality while working for a studio paycheck: Paul Thomas Anderson, David Fincher, Spike Jonze, David O. Russell, Steven Soderbergh and Quentin Tarantino. None of the filmmakers comes across particularly well – they seem at turns disloyal, insecure, ill-tempered, egomaniacal or, in Russell's case, a little bit crazy – which only enhances the satisfactions of Waxman's book.

Biography and autobiography

Faber & Faber
www.faber.co.uk

Faber & Faber's "Directors on Directing" series, now comprising more than twenty titles, gives filmmakers the floor to discuss their lives and works in their own words, and the results are invariably illuminating. (Subjects thus far include Robert Altman, John Cassavetes and David Lynch.) Faber has also published the screenplays of many of the films featured in this book. Other notable titles on the publisher's roster include James Mottram's *The Sundance Kids* (2006), which covers similar ground to Sharon Waxman's *Rebels On The Backlot*, and Kaleem Aftab's authorized biography *Spike Lee: That's My Story And I'm Sticking To It* (2005). Aftab's account of Lee's life and work isn't exactly warts-and-all, but it certainly captures the director's irreverent voice and provides some valuable insight into Lee's sometimes fractious dealings with his financial backers.

Spike Mike Slackers & Dykes: A Guided Tour Across A Decade Of Independent American Cinema
John Pierson (Hyperion/Miramax, 1995)

Producer's representative John Pierson has been the point man on several landmark Amerindie movies, including *She's Gotta Have It*, *Roger & Me*, *Slacker* and *Go Fish*. Pierson is a fun writer and a straight shooter. He is also self-deprecating enough that his miserable experience handling Rob Weiss's lamentable gangster flick *Amongst Friends* provides some of his best material, while his dialogues with *Clerks'* director Kevin Smith give this book a conversational through-line.

How I Made A Hundred Movies In Hollywood And Never Lost A Dime
Roger Corman with Jim Jerome (Random House, 1990)

"King of the Bs" Roger Corman comes across as a self-effacing charmer here, and makes no claims for his films except as economic models. Somewhat spicier are the essays and reminiscences by his many illustrious collaborators, including Martin Scorsese, Francis Ford Coppola and Jack Nicholson.

Shooting To Kill: How An Independent Producer Blasts Through The Barriers To Make Movies That Matter
Christine Vachon with David Edelstein (Harper, 1998)

"Low-budget filmmaking is like childbirth. You have to repress the horror or you'll never do it again," says veteran independent producer Christine Vachon, whose enjoyable, no-nonsense memoir also doubles as a handbook for the aspiring indie film maven. Sample advice: "NEVER compare your film to *Mean Streets*. If I get another pitch that invokes *Mean Streets*, I might have to stop accepting unsolicited scripts." (A follow-up, *A Killer Life: How An Independent Film*

Producer Survives Deals And Disasters In Hollywood And Beyond, co-written with Austin Bunn, was published in 2006.)

Big Bosoms And Square Jaws: The Biography Of Russ Meyer
Jimmy McDonough (Random House, 2005)

Jimmy McDonough's enthusiastic but hardly hagiographic biography brims with unpretentious wit and energy. With typical brio, the writer hails Russ Meyer as "a pioneer who represents what's most seductive *and* most repulsive about the USA. Think Henry Ford, Howard Hughes, Elvis Presley. Meyer: a man who made an empire out of female flesh."

John Cassavetes: Lifeworks
Tom Charity (Omnibus, 2001)

Accidental Genius: How John Cassavetes Invented The American Independent Film
Marshall Fine (Miramax, 2006)

Tom Charity and Marshall Fine's books both strike a superb balance between scholarly depth and lively accessibility. Offering meticulous analysis of John Cassavetes' methods and themes alongside interviews with many of his key collaborators (although neither could snag his widow, Gena Rowlands), both authors give ample proof of Cassavetes' influence on filmmakers in America and the world over.

Sexploitation godfather Russ Meyer ponders where he can go from here...

Magazines

Filmmaker Magazine
www.filmmakermagazine.com

The official publication of the IFP is a quarterly that mixes industry news, festival reports and director profiles from the indie and Indiewood worlds. The magazine also has an impressive Internet presence that includes a voluminous online database of resources for the novice filmmaker, searchable by category ("Post-Production", "Equipment", "Agents and Reps", etc.).

Cineaste
www.cineaste.com

This quarterly with an academic bent declares itself to be "America's leading magazine on the art and politics of the cinema". It's a rare haven for long, academic but generally accessible essays on film, and an Amerindie movie often graces its cover.

Film Comment
www.filmlinc.com/fcm/fcm.htm

The handsomely illustrated magazine produced by the Film Society of Lincoln Center has a worldwide remit, but its coverage of American independents is generally robust; its "Distributor Wanted" section often showcases as-yet homeless American gems.

Cinema Scope
www.cinema-scope.com

Like *Film Comment*, this Canadian magazine has a global sweep in terms of coverage, but also an especially keen eye for festival films that are just too daring, subtle or original – you might say too independent – to attain a distributor or much publicity.

Sight & Sound
www.bfi.org.uk/sightandsound

With its elegant design, ample illustrations and highly regarded mix of journalists and academics contributing to its pages, the BFI's monthly publication is arguably the definitive film magazine of the English-speaking world. The completist approach to film reviews means that each and every Amerindie film to secure a theatrical release on British shores will receive close attention.

Premiere Magazine
www.premiere.com

This glossy general-interest monthly is always a witty, informed read, and as "independent" film has become a Hollywood genre unto itself, the magazine has provided a broader context for small indie gems making their way in the marketplace.

Websites

General

Recent years have seen a proliferation of online daily-digest blogs, which run through the day's film-related stories, provide links to trailers and supply original content in the form of reviews, interviews, commentary and rants. Just a few of the sites that fall into this loose category include: the GreenCine blog, housed by the DVD rental service of the same name (daily.greencine.com), Movie City News, which hosts the Movie City Indie blog (www.moviecity.com), Cinematical (www.cinematical.com) and the Independent Film Channel's blog (blog.ifctv.com).

The Internet Movie Database
www.imdb.com

Arguably the biggest and best film reference database available on the web, the IMDB has an "Independent Film" page with news, links, trailers and a weekly "Ask a Filmmaker" feature.

The Greatest Films
www.filmsite.org

An invaluable resource since 1996, this website by the tireless Tim Dirks is devoted to American and other English-language films, and consists of thousands of pages of film history, genre study, detailed reviews and much more. It's also the best source for film-related lists, whether of greatest films, scenes, quotes, directors, death scenes, Oscar winners or box-office hits.

indieWIRE
www.indiewire.com

Founded in 1996, indieWIRE provides comprehensive coverage of all things indie, with breaking news, interviews, on-the-scene reports from festivals and premieres, industry and box-office analysis and "First Person" essays by film-world insiders. indieWIRE is also home to a number of blogs (including the passionate, frequently updated group effort Reverse Shot), and users can log on and socialize at indieLOOP, the "independent media social network".

Bright Lights Film Journal
www.brightlightsfilm.com

Based in Portland, Oregon, this online quarterly brings sharp wit and indepth knowledge to its politically attuned coverage of independent, exploitation and international film, a sphere of activity that pays plenty of attention to Amerindie movies.

Senses Of Cinema
www.sensesofcinema.com

Like *Bright Lights*, this Australian publication is a serious and worldly online journal with lots of Amerindie-related material. The site is ambitious and ever-expanding, and it has a large "Great Directors" database of essays and filmographies and an excellent archive of interviews, features, festival reports and book reviews.

The Criterion Collection
www.criterionco.com

Virtually unrivalled as a producer of beautifully packaged special-edition DVDs, Criterion also offers an online repository for excellent film writing. Their website reproduces the text of the liner notes that accompany each DVD release, including Gary Giddins on *Shadows*, John Pierson on *Slacker* and Luc Sante on *Down By Law*.

Slant Magazine
www.slantmagazine.com

This self-titled "non-commercial entertainment website" has smart, pointed coverage of film, television and music and a notable archive of movie reviews. Co-creator and film editor Ed Gonzalez is one of the most incisive and knowledgeable young film critics in America.

Strictly Film School
www.filmref.com

This so-called "evolving personal homage journal" is written by a NASA design engineer with the nom de plume Acquarello. His useful, well-written website is deftly organized (categories include Films & Directors, Genres, Themes and Imagery) and obviously a labour of love and informed passion.

The films and filmmakers

The John Cassavetes Pages
people.bu.edu/rcarney/

Ray Carney, the contentious professor of film and American studies at Boston University and author of *Cassavetes On Cassavetes* (Faber & Faber, 2001), is so territorial about his status as the world's foremost Cassavetes scholar that he's even co-opted the filmmaker's name for his own homepage (see www.cassavetes.com). There can be little doubt about Carney's expertise on all things Cassavetes, but his website is as fascinating for its insights into Carney's unique personality as it is for its informative take on American independent film history.

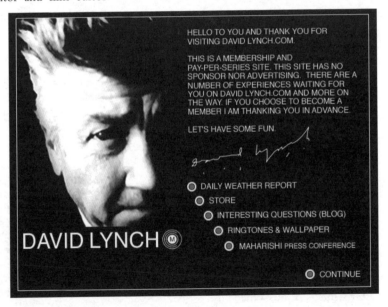

Coenesque: The Films Of The Coen Brothers
www.coenbrothers.net/

A straightforward, rather elegant tribute to Joel and Ethan Coen featuring biographies, bibliographies, a discussion forum, latest news links and sections devoted to each of the Coens' films.

The Jim Jarmusch Resource Page
jimjarmusch.tripod.com

This unofficial Jim Jarmusch site has the director's biography, lots of web links, a far-reaching bibliography, and a stills gallery, as well as "Jim's Picks" – the director's favourite movies, books, guilty pleasures and more.

David Lynch
www.davidlynch.com

Distinguished by its spooky white-on-black design, David Lynch's official website eschews sponsorship or advertising in favour of paid membership. Enticements include the "Interesting Questions" blog ("Is there gold in Fort Knox?" "Is there any new information about 9-11?"), a daily weather report, film trailers and downloadable episodes of Lynch's animated series *Dumbland* (which the filmmaker describes as "a crude, stupid, violent, absurd series. If it is funny, it is funny because we see the absurdity of it all.").

Michael Moore
www.michaelmoore.com

Michael Moore's jam-packed site is as much a news blog and political-action site as it is a filmmaker's resource. Along with the expected data on the muckraker's movies and books, links to the "Newsroom" section are updated daily and, in the midst of the war in Iraq, the "How Can I Help the Soldiers" section provides information on how to aid injured veterans, send books to soldiers and contact your local representative to express your views on the occupation.

Errol Morris
www.errolmorris.com

Errol Morris's pleasurable site is a treasure trove of his work in adverts and short films, all ready to download. It is also home to his minimalist blog, "The Grump", where he posts pessimistic aphorisms and observations under titles such as "Misanthrope's Creed" and "Anti-Humanist".

Deadites Online: The Fan's Official Source For Evil Dead
www.deadites.net

That the most recent entry in Sam Raimi's cult horror series appeared in 1993 makes it all the more endearing that this site is updated so frequently. As well as all the usual links, interviews, news items and fan forums, it also features contests, "fan tattoos" and downloadable scenes from the *Evil Dead* films.

Movie Poop Shoot
www.moviepoopshoot.com

Pitched somewhere between being a homepage, a fansite and a film blog, Kevin Smith's forum takes as its maxim "All the news that's shit to print", and posts regular columns, comics, movie news stories and even reviews of action figures (see Michael Crawford's meticulous "Toybox" features).

The Quentin Tarantino Archives
www.tarantino.info

QT's legions of obsessive fans give you plenty of sites to choose from, but interested parties would do well to start here. The Archives have regular news updates, neatly categorized forums and a wiki, and devotees can opt for a subscription to the newsletter.

Dreamland
www.dreamlandnews.com

Laid out in sweet pastels, John Waters' site offers monthly updates on Waters-related news and appearances, as well as informative links to the director's disparate influences, a filmography, and bibliography and a tribute to his late star Divine.

Dreamland is the ultimate online guide to John Waters. It's our tenth anniversary!

News   History   Filmography   In Print   On the Net   Fans   Divine

Picture credits

The Publishers have made every effort to identify correctly the rights holders and/or production companies in respect of film stills featured in this book. If despite these efforts any attribution is inco rrect, the Publishers will correct this error once it has been brought to their attention on a subsequent reprint.

Cover Credits

Steve Buscemi in *Ghost World* (2001), courtesy Capitol Films and Granada Film

Illustrations

Corbis: Independent Pictures Miramax Films Buena Vista Home Video (50) Taplin Perry Scorsese Productions Warner Bros Pictures Warner Home Video (78) R. Michelson/Corbis Sygma (228) Sam Mirocovich/Reuters/Corbis (245) Kobal Collection: Bronze Eye Productions Poison L.P. Zeitgeist Films WinStar Home Entertainment (95) Navaron Films Image Entertainment (151) Pandora Cinema Flower Films Adam Fields Productions Gaylord Films Newmarket Films 20th Century Fox (156) This Is That Productions Sony Pictures Classics (161) Warner Independent Pictures 2929 Productions Participant Productions Davis-Films Redbus Pictures Tohokushinsha Film Corp Section Eight Metropolitan Warner Bros (189) 20th Century Fox Columbia TriStar Warner Home Video (204) Factory Films Andy Warhol Films Sherpix Inc Image Entertainment (210) Moviestore: Producers Releasing Corporation (PRC) Image Entertainment Alpha Video Distributors (7) Michael Laughlin Productions Universal Pictures Anchor Bay Entertainment (12) Foxton Entertainment River Road Productions Circle Films USA Films Columbia Tristar (17) A Band Apart Jersey Films Miramax Films Miramax Home

Entertainment (22) Bad Lt. Productions Aries Films Lions Gate Films Artisan Entertainment (34) Castle Rock Entertainment Detour Filmproduction Filmhaus Wien Universa Filmpro Sunrise Production Columbia Pictures Corporation Columbia Pictures Columbia Tristar (36) Haxan Films Artisan Entertainment Lions Gate Films (41) Hart-Sharp Entertainment Independent Film Channel Killer Films Fox Searchlight Pictures 20th Century Fox Home Entertainment (45) Cinépix Film Properties Lions Gate Films Muse Productions Universal (47) 40 Acres & A Mule Filmworks MCA/Universal Pictures The Criterion Collection (54) Renaissance Pictures New Line Cinema Anchor Bay Entertainment (63) Excalibur Films Guys Upstairs Independent Pictures Kids NY Limited Miramax Films Shining Excalibur Films Lions Gate Films Trimark Video (71) Columbia Pictures Corporation Los Hooligans Productions (75) F/M Near Dark Joint Venture Anchor Bay Entertainment (87) IRS Media Columbia Pictures (91) American Playhouse Theatrical Films Chemical Film Good Machine Kardana Productions Channel Four Film Arnold Semler Kardana Films Sony Pictures Classics Columbia Tristar (105) Outlaw Production Virgin Miramax Films The Criterion Collection Columbia Tristar (109) Buckeye Films Swelter Films Fine Line Features New Line Home Video (120) SVS Films Samuel Goldwyn Films (131) JDI Productions Lemon Sky Productions Sony Pictures Classics Columbia Tristar (145) Polygram Filmed Entertainment Working Title Films Gramercy Pictures Universal Studios (149) Fox Searchlight Pictures Michael London Productions Sideways Productions 20th Century Fox (154) Infinity Features Entertainment United Artists A-Line Pictures Cooper's Town Productions Eagle Vision Sony Pictures Classics (159) Alliance Atlantis Dog Eat Dog Films Iconolatry Productions Salter Street Films Time Film- und TV-Produktions

PICTURE CREDITS

GmbH United Broadcasting Vif Babelsberger Filmproduktion GmbH & Co. Zweite KG MGM Home Entertainment (172) Cinépix Film Properties Lions Gate Films Muse Productions Universal (176) Addis Wechsler Pictures Live Entertainment Muse Productions Orion Classics Artisan Entertainment (182) Jerry Weintraub Productions NPV Entertainment Section Eight Village Roadshow Pictures WV Films Warner Bros (185) Arena British Broadcasting Corporation (BBC) Goldwyn Pictures Corporation Playhouse International Pictures Samuel Goldwyn Company Evergreen Entertainment MGM Home Entertainment (191) Dreamland Saliva Films New Line Home Video (195) Imagine Entertainment HBO Documentary Films World of Wonder Home Box Office (HBO) Universal Pictures (207) Image Ten Laurel Group Market Square Productions Off Color Films Walter Reade Organization Continental Distributing New Line Cinema Elite Entertainment 20th Century Fox Madacy Entertainment Alpha Video Distributors Republic Pictures (219) KTCA Minneapolis Kartemquin Films Fine Line Features New Line Home Video Criterion Collection (231) Live Entertainment Dog Eat Dog Productions Miramax Films Artisan Entertainment (234) Good Machine Killer Films Lions Gate Trimark (236) Moviestore (255) Rex Features: American Empirical Pictures Peter Newman/ Interal Productions Original Media Seven Hills Pictures Andrew Lauren Productions (ALP) Ambush Entertainment Destination Films InterAL Squid and Whale Samuel Goldwyn Films Sony Pictures (27) E. Charbonneau/BEI/Rex Features (198) Ronald Grant: Independent Production Company (IPC) International Union of Mine, Mill & Smelter Workers Independent Productions Alpha Video Distributor (5) Little Fugitive Production Company Joseph Burstyn Kino Video (8) Ronald Grant (10) IRS Media Sony Pictures (24) The Con Roadside Attractions Samuel Goldwyn Films (28) Columbia Pictures Pando Company Raybert Productions RCA/Columbia Pictures Home Video (59) Eve Productions RM Films (66) Desperate Pictures Academy Strand Releasing (73) I Remember Productions Newmarket Capital Group Summit Entertainment Team Todd Newmarket Films Columbia Tristar (82) Salsipuedes Productions Anarchist's Convention Films UCLA Film and Television Archive IFC Films MGM Home Entertainment (101) Allied Artists Pictures Corporation F & F Productions The Criterion Collection (115) Cinesthesia Productions Grokenberger Film Produktion Zweites Deutsches Fernsehen (ZDF) Samuel Goldwyn Films MGM Home Entertainment (122) Suburban Pictures Sony Pictures Classics Columbia Tristar (134) Faces International Films Touchstone Home Video Criterion Collection (137) Ghoulardi Film Company Lawrence Gordon Productions New Line Cinema New Line Home Video (142) Beverly Detroit Clinica Estetico Good Machine Intermedia Magnet Productions Propaganda Films Sony Pictures (165) Castle Rock Entertainment Detour Film Production Sony Pictures Classics (170) Bandeira Entertainment Miramax Films Buena Vista Home Entertainment (175) Taplin Perry Scorsese Productions Warner Bros (180) American Playhouse Fine Line Strand Home Video (193) Metro-Goldwyn-Mayer (MGM) Shaft Productions Turner Entertainment Warner Home Video (212) American International Pictures (AIP) MGM Home Entertainment (213) American International Pictures (AIP) Embassy Home Entertainment Metro-Goldwyn-Mayer (MGM) Orion Home Video (216) Vortex Bryanston Distributing Company New Line Cinema Dark Sky Films Pioneer Entertainment (222) Columbia Pictures Corporation Gracie Films Columbia/Tristar (239) Access Films Fox Searchlight Pictures MTV Films Paramount Pictures 20th Century Fox (242)

Index

Page references to films discussed in the Canon chapter, people described in the Icons chapter and specific feature boxes are indicated in **bold**.

INDEX

INDEX

INDEX

INDEX

Rough Guides presents...

"Achieves the perfect balance between learned recommendation and needless trivia"
Uncut Magazine reviewing Cult Movies

Other Rough Guide Film & TV titles include:

American Independent Film • British Cult Comedy • Chick Flicks • Comedy Movies
Cult Movies • Gangster Movies • Horror Movies • Kids' Movies • Sci-Fi Movies • Westerns

BROADEN YOUR HORIZONS

Listen Up!

"You may be used to the Rough Guide series being comprehensive, but nothing will prepare you for the exhaustive Rough Guide to World Music . . . one of our books of the year."

Sunday Times, London

ROUGH GUIDE MUSIC TITLES

Bob Dylan • The Beatles • Classical Music • Elvis • Frank Sinatra • Heavy Metal • Hip-Hop
iPods, iTunes & music online • Jazz • Book of Playlists • Opera • Pink Floyd • Punk • Reggae
Rock • The Rolling Stones • Soul and R&B • World Music

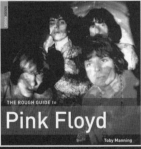

BROADEN YOUR HORIZONS

Get Connected!

"Brilliant! ... the unmatched leader in its field"
Sunday Times, London, reviewing The Rough Guide to the Internet

THE ROUGH GUIDE to

ebaY

Ian Peel

A DIGITAL MUSIC GUIDE FOR MAC & PC

iPod

Music
Photos
Videos
Extras
Settings
Shuffle Songs

THE ROUGH GUIDE to

iPods

iTunes & music online

4TH EDITION:
COVERS IPOD NANO, VIDEO IPOD & IPOD SHUFFLE

HOW TO DO ALMOST ANYTHING WITH AN APPLE

THE ROUGH GUIDE TO

Macs & OS X

Peter Buckley & Duncan Clark

12 Editions • 3 Million Copies Sold • PC & Mac

THE ROUGH GUIDE to
The

Internet

Peter Buckley & Duncan Clark

THE ROUGH GUIDE

Website Directory

Shopping Online & Surfing The Net

2007 edition

ROUGH
GUIDES

Rough Guide Computing Titles
Blogging • eBay • iPods, iTunes & music online
The Internet • Macs & OS X • Book of Playlists
PCs & Windows • Playstation Portable • Website Directory